With abundance and variety

YORKSHIRE GARDENS AND GARDENERS ACROSS FIVE CENTURIES

THE YORKSHIRE GARDENS TRUST

With abundance and variety

YORKSHIRE GARDENS AND GARDENERS ACROSS FIVE CENTURIES

Editor
SUSAN KELLERMAN

Associate Editor
KAREN LYNCH

PUBLISHED BY
THE YORKSHIRE GARDENS TRUST

This publication is supported by the Calmcott Trust and the Leeds Philosophical and Literary Society

ISBN 978 0 9564347 0 8

COVER ILLUSTRATION
Studley Park, Norway Firs near the Bathing House, drawn and engraved by W. Westall, ARA, published by J. Rodwell, London, 1847 (detail). *By kind permission of Bill Barber*

DESIGNED AND PRODUCED BY OBLONG CREATIVE LTD
WETHERBY LS23 7FG, UK

Contents

THE YORKSHIRE GARDENS TRUST

The Yorkshire Gardens Trust, formed in 1996, works to conserve and foster the county's garden heritage for the benefit of present and future generations, aiming to improve awareness and appreciation of the value of parks, gardens and designed landscapes as part of our local and national inheritance.

Registered charity No. 1060697
Company registration No. 3256311

Contributors

DR PATRICK EYRES is editor-publisher of the *New Arcadian Journal*, which engages with the cultural politics of designed landscapes and specialises in Georgian Britain. He represents the Georgian Group on the Wentworth Castle Heritage Trust and, as a member of the Little Sparta Trust, helps to conserve the garden of Ian Hamilton Finlay.

SUSAN KELLERMAN followed a 30-year career in applied linguistics as a teacher, researcher, and teacher trainer, with much of that time spent overseas. Eventually, her interest in garden history (particularly garden architecture) supplanted that in language, and led to research into eighteenth-century bath houses.

KAREN LYNCH is a writer and researcher. She was formerly the Researcher to the Harewood House Trust and continues to write on the Lascelles family and their estates, and on any other subject that takes her fancy. Her current projects include an eccentric nineteenth-century vicar and an eighteenth-century domestic goddess.

SALLY O'HALLORAN is a PhD student in the Department of Landscape at the University of Sheffield. She is currently researching the forgotten role of the gardener in England from 1600 to 1730. This interest stems from her Master's dissertation when she looked at gardening in Yorkshire, in particular at Thrybergh estate, Rotherham, during the seventeenth century.

LINDA POLLEY is a senior lecturer at the University of Teesside, with research interests in the local and regional built environment. That research has always included the landscapes of municipal parks, and more recently the relationships between Middlesbrough's elites and their domestic relocation into the surrounding countryside.

DR GEORGE SHEERAN works in the School of Lifelong Education and Development at the University of Bradford, where he is a senior lecturer and Head of Academic Programmes. His areas of research and teaching are in urban history, architectural history, and eighteenth-century landscape.

DR FIONA STIRLING is a landscape architect with particular expertise in cemetery design, management and conservation. The paper in this volume is based on findings from Fiona's recent doctoral research. The ESRC-funded research, completed in the Department of Landscape at the University of Sheffield, has focused on the potential to implement grave re-use at a detailed site-specific level and is the first study of its kind.

Martin Wainwright tries to garden but has not inherited his father and grandfather's skill. He is Northern Editor of *The Guardian* and a regular broadcaster. His most recent books are *Morris Minor: The Biography* (Aurum Press) and *Leeds: Shaping the City* (RIBA Publications). He was the first chair of the National Lottery Charities Board in Yorkshire & the Humber and was awarded the MBE for reforms to the grant-making process in the region.

Dr Jan Woudstra is a landscape architect and historian, who holds an MA in Conservation Studies from the University of York and a PhD from the University of London. He worked in private practice before starting to teach at the Department of Landscape at the University of Sheffield in 1995, and has published widely on history and theory topics relating to garden design and landscape architecture.

Preface

Yorkshire is Britain's largest historical county, with a wide variety of geology, topography, soils and vegetation, and a corresponding diversity of designed landscapes. It is appropriate, therefore, that a collection of papers focusing on the county's gardens and parks, and their creators and custodians, should exemplify this diversity – indeed, the quotation in our title, 'with abundance and variety', taken from Yorkshire gardener William Lawson (*A New Orchard and Garden*, 1618), reflects the range of material.

The designed landscapes featured here span hundreds of years; some are grand, others unpretentious. Some of their creators enjoyed great wealth, others were of more modest means; some were fortunate enough to enjoy their garden and the acclaim it brought – although such an opportunity was sadly denied to one keen gardener, Sir John Reresby at Thrybergh, by the upheaval of civil war and his premature death.

What motivated the creation of these gardens and parks, determined their particular characteristics, and influenced their subsequent development or demise, also varies enormously from one to the other. Some were originally intended for private and personal enjoyment, while others became public statements of status and achievements. In contrast, the cemetery landscapes at Burngreave and Crookes in Sheffield have always been, and continue to be, for public use. Change of circumstances has sometimes resulted in the loss or reduction of a garden or landscape, sometimes in its blossoming. That at Kirkleatham has decayed and almost disappeared, and the future of Stewart Park in Middlesbrough is still somewhat uncertain. Delphiniums standing to attention in serried ranks, the *sine qua non* of The Heath, have fallen from grace; and the bath house as garden building was condemned as long ago as the early nineteenth century, when cold bathing fell out of fashion. But Wentworth Castle is a fine example of survival and renaissance, achieved through greater understanding of the landscape's significance, and by widening public access and involvement.

For several of the individual gardens featured here, politics played a role in their planning and use. At Wentworth Castle and Kirkleatham, the garden became a political statement in itself, expressing ideologies, allegiances, and the achievements of high office. The Wainwright family's delphiniums may have been blue, but the garden at The Heath occasionally took on a yellow, even reddish, hue when it hosted political events. But more usually, the garden is the antithesis of politics, bringing physical, mental and spiritual well-being to its creator and those who enter it. For the Lascelles family, Plumpton Rocks became a distraction and sanctuary from the stresses and strains of business and public life; for the bereaved, a cemetery should provide respite, succour, and solace.

When not out in their garden enjoying the benefits to body, mind and spirit, gardeners – both hands-on and armchair – may find inspiration, diversion, and food for thought in this collection of papers. The editors are grateful to the referees who have assessed the papers and advised on their content, and to all those who have assisted in a variety of ways in the preparation of this volume.

In particular, the Yorkshire Gardens Trust acknowledges the very generous financial support of the Calmcott Trust; and of the Leeds Philosophical and Literary Society.

Susan Kellerman and Karen Lynch

Foreword

THE EARL OF HAREWOOD
President of the Yorkshire Gardens Trust

I have always thought of gardens as an integral part of the Yorkshire landscape – occurring whenever a house of some distinction was apparent. If I am right, as I am sure I am, it is fairly obvious that there are many gardens of distinction in our part of the world and of course it is the purpose of the Yorkshire Gardens Trust to celebrate what we have got and to add to the achievement.

My parents were keen gardeners and a walk round the gardens was a regular part of every Sunday morning after Church. As a result, small bits of knowledge came the way of my brother and myself and stuck with us, and I can often come up with the names of plants in a quite unexpected set of circumstances. I rather enjoy this apparent (though quite bogus) wisdom though anyone connected with Yorkshire Gardens Trust would be able to outdo me without any difficulty. Nonetheless, gardens remain a major source of pleasure and I am always sorry for people who don't appreciate them. The Trust does its best to reduce the number of people who belong in this category and I applaud its endeavours. This is our first publication and these essays will add to the knowledge of anyone who reads them and are a source of genuine pleasure in themselves. To pull one plum out of the pudding, Plumpton Rocks was a source of delight for my brother and me from the many visits we used to pay with our parents. This is a delightful part of the world and we enjoyed almost everything about it, not least the echoes which we found were abundant. On one occasion when we went there with Benjamin Britten other visitors would have been astounded at the merry cries of 'Henry James!' with which we tested the echoes of which we were so proud. But this is a serious publication and readers will find much useful and delightful information, much of it previously outside their knowledge. I hope we shall produce others!

A Hundred Shades of Blue: The Heath, Adel

MARTIN WAINWRIGHT

Visitors to the Leeds suburb of Roundhay in the late 1920s would have been distracted by two things if they had turned into The Drive, an avenue of comfortable houses with generous gardens and large street trees sheltering the pavements. One was a rockery of brightly coloured flowers, tiered back from the road but completely open to it (Figure 1). The other was a series of printed boards in front of this vivid display, staked in the same way as sponsorship notices on modern roundabouts.

Like them, it was an advertisement but not a commercial one. It asked in bold type: 'Why opt for privet hedges, so time-consuming and dull, especially when duplicated in front of house after house? Try something like this instead, to make your neighbourhood as well as your own home more attractive! Enquire within to learn more.'

Not many enquired, but few complained either. In a street of doctors from Leeds General Infirmary and university academics, the creator of both rockery and signs, Henry Scurrah Wainwright, was well known and generally held to be a good neighbour. If Scurrah, as he was always called, had a thing about plants, then so be it. He was generous with cuttings, Methodist chapel flowers and help with the annual flower show at Roundhay Park. His wife Emily was sweet in looks and nature and their small son Richard was a pretty if serious-minded child, often seen in the garden 'helping' with bamboo stakes and twine. Less overtly, as he confided to his grandchildren many years later, he also speared slugs with his mother's hatpins.

Scurrah, a family name taken from forebears who left Well near Ripon (where Scurrahs still abound) in the 1830s to start a butcher's shop in Leeds, was a chartered accountant with a flair for investing in new business ideas. He inherited a little capital but a lot of imagination from his father Richard Wainwright, whose many business projects included a gadget to reduce chimney smoke which earned him, briefly, the title of 'Leeds' Smoke King' from the *Yorkshire Post*. More funds accrued through Scurrah's marriage to Emily, whose father Frederick White ran a successful herbalist's and pharmacy and featured in the 1902 social directory *West Riding Contemporary Biographies*. The solid bourgeois status of the family is evident from photographs of Scurrah and Emily's wedding reception: morning coats, imposing hats and a marquee in the garden of Pendleton House in Spencer Place, Chapeltown, which survives intact, albeit in an interesting role as part of Leeds Central Mosque.

Scurrah was also financial director of the medical supply company Thackray's of Leeds which he founded with Charles Thackray, a young pharmacist, also in 1902.

FIGURE 1 One of the rockeries at Sandhurst in The Drive, Roundhay, which Scurrah Wainwright promoted as an alternative to privet hedging. *Wainwright Archives*

Between 1914 and 1930 this business trebled in size and its workforce rose from 14 to 100. Scurrah's business acumen was partly responsible but he found time to use his canniness elsewhere. Among inventors to whom he acted as a merchant banker was a young engineer called Hardy whose system for transferring the driving power of car engines became famous, and lucrative, as the Hardy-Spicer universal joint, eventually sold extremely profitably to the industrial giant GKN.

Business success was demanding, however, and it took its toll on Scurrah's health. Professionally, he felt that he had to accept office in the Leeds Society of Chartered Accountants, of which he in due course became President. Brought up as a Methodist, he had a strong sense of social obligation, and this meant further commitments: to the Leeds Central Methodist Mission at Lady Lane chapel and its social work in the slums of Quarry Hill, to the management board of the Leeds Dispensary and to the Leeds Traders' Benevolent Association.

His work in medical supply exempted him from military service in the First World War, but he would also have been rejected on health grounds according to his doctor, who became increasingly concerned in 1919 about his general well-being. Ironically, in a household whose outbuildings had a distinctly medical tang from the tin boxes of herbs and spices which the Whites often stored there (the firm's big seller, Kompo for Colds, was a banjaxing mixture of chemicals and spice), the GP prescribed something simpler: taking up gardening.

So began a collection of plants which was to become a glory of Leeds and Yorkshire for more than 60 years and in its heyday the finest collection of delphiniums – the monarch of the mixed herbaceous border – in the country. It was not in The Drive because Scurrah's ambitions far outran the limited space available in a suburban street; but it had its origins and seedbed there. Roundhay was the testing ground for Scurrah's longer-term plans. Their culmination was in Adel and their legacy blooms today in many gardens in Yorkshire and beyond, notably at Temple Newsam, where the national collection of delphiniums was started in the 1980s with invaluable help from Scurrah's garden.

He was a man of firm ideas who gave short shrift to things he disliked; hence the propaganda rockery and a lifelong aversion to privet and its successor Leyland cypress. He took the opportunity to buy a vacant plot on the other side of The Drive and began to experiment there with different plants. The challenge of protecting roses against their many pests and diseases energised him; he would recall in later life how much harder this became after the 1956 Clean Air Act which removed the plant's sooty defences against bacteria and bugs. He developed an interest in genetics and plant-breeding through a fondness for lupins, whose colours had recently been revolutionised by George Russell in nearby York.

But although his health improved, and he and Emily were given lasting happiness by Richard's unexpected birth 16 years after their marriage when they had given up hope of children, Scurrah was not entirely satisfied. The mind that raced in business needed challenging in the garden too. The moment arrived one spring day in 1922 when, as Richard remembered all his life, 'a cardboard box came in the post containing Millicent Blackmore.' This was a particularly lovely example of one of the 'flowers of the day', the grand family of delphiniums, whose hybridisation had become fashionable and vigorous. Richard was there when the box was opened and remembered Millicent's reverential reception and the moment when she flowered in July: 'The spikes were long and wide and the florets were a lovely combination of mauve and sky blue with a large brown eye.' Scurrah had met his mission.

He made inquiries about delphiniums and sought out local growers, discovering that a group of them had recently set up a northern delphinium association. He was soon a member of its committee. When the national Delphinium Society was formed in 1928, he promptly joined and six years later became a member of the committee of that too. He ordered more plants and became particularly interested in experiments by specialist growers, notably Blackmore & Langdon of Bath, to breed stouter-stemmed, taller and more vigorous varieties. He was no geneticist, but he rightly reasoned that keen and sensible amateur growers had a vital role to play in plant trials. Especially if they had the orderly approach to record-keeping of a chartered accountant.

The surge of interest in which Scurrah took part was new, but delphinium cultivation had a long history. The name is classical Greek for dolphin, describing the shape of the florets which, as John Gerard noted in his *Herbal* of 1597, 'have a certaine shew and likeness of those Dolphins which old pictures and armes of certain antient families have expressed with a crooked or bending finger'. In his day, the plant was grown mostly for medicine and known as lousewort because of the effectiveness of its poisonous seeds in potions for infestation. Italian herbalists also used the larkspur *Delphinium consolida* in the catch-all way of pre-Enlightenment doctors: for purgatives, wound antiseptic, minor eye complaints and toothache.

The bee larkspur, *Delphinium elatum*, was imported for similar reasons from Russia to Elizabeth I's London and it appears in Parkinson's *Paradisi in sole, paradisus terrestris* of 1629. But it was not until the 1850s that the magnificent, towering blue spikes with which we are familiar today made their debut. The first really dramatic hybrids appeared from the nursery of Victor Lemoine at Nancy in France. Descended from a long line of nurserymen, Lemoine was the first foreigner to receive the Victoria Medal of the Royal Horticultural Society and his work soon inspired British imitators. First in the field was James Kelway of Langport in Somerset but the really heroic work was done by James Blackmore and Charles Langdon, two delphinium enthusiasts who set up a nursery in Bath in 1901.

Along with Lemoine, who died in 1911, they introduced stunning new hybrids every year: 'Statuaire Rude' from Nancy entranced gardeners in 1907 with its unusually large florets coloured pale sky blue and lavender. It was then eclipsed at Holland House, where the RHS committee sat in judgement, by Bath's offering: the dark purple-blue and white-eyed spikes of 'Rev. E. Lascelles'. Charles Langdon had been an apprentice gardener to the real-life Revd Lascelles, a distant relative of the Harewood family who lived at Newton St Loe near Bath. He repaid his employer handsomely by naming this wonderful cultivar after him. It won an Award of Merit in 1907, again in 1925 and for a third time in 1933.

These excitements in the world of gardening, comparable to the launch of 'celebrity' roses today, reached their height just as Scurrah Wainwright was taking up his trowel in Leeds. 'Millicent Blackmore' began a procession of grand delphiniums, coloured a hundred shades of blue, which arrived at The Drive from professional growers. Wainwright experimented with different colour arrangements, sometimes growing the delphiniums in massed clumps, sometimes placing them at intervals in his herbaceous borders. The results were so spectacular in late June, July and early August that people began to come from all over Leeds to look. They appreciated the absence of hedges or fences to stop them from seeing the garden from the road and this was grist to Scurrah's anti-privet mill. He supplemented his notices with a letter to the *Yorkshire Evening Post* in February 1927 which suggested that he was winning converts:

> There are districts in the Leeds suburbs where the morning and evening walk to and from the tram is made full of interest and pleasure by a succession of open gardens with differing colour schemes and well-cultivated flowers. The owners of these gardens emulate, and vie with one another, discuss and exchange until the whole neighbourhood becomes 'garden proud.' Some of the Englishman's reserve is thereby broken down and a new general interest created. Compare this with the dreary avenues of unbroken privet hedges, hiding comparatively barren gardens, which one walks through in other parts of Leeds.

Wainwright was by nature a do-er and campaigner, and while his experiments at The Drive matured, he started promoting gardening, which had done so much for his own health, as a remedy for some of the notorious ills of Leeds. A lifelong Liberal, he tended towards the radical wing of the party, taking young Richard to hear Communist street orators outside Leeds Town Hall, and pointing out barefoot children in the street when the family went to chapel in Lady Lane. He strongly supported the controversial slum clearance programme driven through by the socialist vicar and Labour city councillor Revd Charles Jenkinson in the early and mid-1930s. As the filthy yards round Quarry Hill came down, 'garden estates' such as Belle Isle and Gipton went up to replace them, with gardening officers to help tenants as well as local rent and maintenance managers. As a chapel trustee, Wainwright was instrumental in Lady Lane's decision to move to the Gipton estate and build a new chapel there for its rehoused congregation. He was also an enthusiastic promoter of an annual competition for the city's best council house gardens.

Family 16 mm cine reels, now in the Yorkshire Film Archive at York, show him accompanying parties of civic dignitaries around Gipton, Middleton and other estates, admiring flowerbeds and window boxes. Vegetables too: Scurrah was an advocate of growing-your-own and most of the Green shibboleths rediscovered in modern times, although he did not warm to gardens or allotments that entirely banished flowers. In those pioneering days, his enthusiasm met with a welcome from those who disagreed with him politically. This was not so much the case in later years, when Wainwright maintained his interest but encountered less warmth from entrenched post-war politicians. In the 1950s heyday of Alderman Albert King, Labour's 'King of Leeds', he had several run-ins with Alderman Mary Pearce, Lord Mayor in 1958, who gave him the impression that anything to do with council houses was her business, not his. Scurrah felt that he had profited in Leeds and had a civic duty to do something in return; he was reminded of his father's example every time he walked through City Square, where the statue of James Watt paid for by Richard Wainwright the Smoke King still stands.

In 1936 Scurrah was made king of his own castle when the National Assistance Board appointed him chairman of its Leeds and District advisory committee. This involved interviewing every unemployed man aged under thirty in the city in an attempt to find them jobs. Inevitably the exercise was criticised by some as soft to the workshy, but Wainwright robustly countered this through interviews with local newspapers. He also brought his gardening experience to bear, both in promoting the virtues of outdoor work and in specific cases such as that of a Theodore Fawcett of Morley, who was suspected of claiming assistance for his six sons aged between two and twelve while running a secret market gardening business on the side. A surviving report from the Board's staff notes of Fawcett:

It is thought he is endeavouring to disguise the full nature of his transaction; he has been asked to produce particulars of recent takings from the sale of fruit and flowers. When visited, it was found that flowers were exhibited for sale and a large greenhouse contained a quantity of green tomatoes which would probably ripen and be saleable.

A note in Wainwright's handwriting confirms the assistance payments.

Personal papers meanwhile bear out the importance of his own garden as a relief from public work, and in particular the responsibilities of accountancy and directorships at the Leeds printing firm of Jowett & Sowry and the Metropole Hotel, as well as Thackray's which was continuing to expand. At a dinner of Yorkshire chartered accountants he spoke with feeling of returning in the tram every evening to

Mother Earth, my companion recreation, my garden where one forgets balance sheets and after-dinner speeches. A place whose dividend warrants are things of beauty, with nothing about them of the Proper Officer for the Receipt of Taxes and with a Reserve Fund built up by last year's sunshine, showers and fresh air.

It was now time for Scurrah to realise his long-term plan. In 1936 he noted that a large Victorian villa called The Heath in Adel was up for sale, with very large grounds sloping gently over three acres, screened by trees and facing south. The soil was promising for delphiniums – deep, heavy loam above a barrier of clay. The housing market was falling and demand for such big properties, which in The Heath's case included two entrance lodges, was torpid. Wainwright was prepared to wait. Twelve months later, when the price had fallen even further than he had expected, he put in an offer which was accepted.

His family was initially dubious. Emily now had to govern a considerable household, with a chauffeur/handyman in the North Lodge and a gardener in the South one. Richard came home from Cambridge University to 'a wilderness of weeds' and wondered if his father's dreams had outweighed commonsense. The Heath's previous owner, a Mrs Nicholson, had a morbid fear that home-grown vegetables were contaminated by the soil and had ordered the vegetable garden to be abandoned. Large parts of the estate were reverting to dense, bramble-entwined scrub.

But the property had the overriding advantage of lots of space. The Heath was the last of a prematurely-aborted line of 'gentlemen's villas' which a speculative company began in the 1870s from The Hollies, where the Leeds ring road now swoops down into the Meanwood valley, and up Long Causeway to Moortown. The development was scuppered when United States trade tariffs sent the British economy into a slump. The company went into receivership and the fifth plot in the line, laid out but undeveloped, was bought by The Heath's first owner – and designer and builder – William Hill, a local architect who had prospered in the good times. He got twice as much land as everyone else (Figure 2).

Hill still surveys the front garden at The Heath from beneath a bedroom window, where he had the gargoyle heads of his wife, daughter and himself carved into the now blackened millstone grit. If there were fewer trees to the west of the house, and the ground sloped more gently towards Headingley and Cookridge, he would be able to see some of his other local monuments in Leeds: the fine terrace of Oakfield in Grove Lane, or Yeadon Town Hall.

Scurrah Wainwright was appreciative of the house's history, and Hill's silent presence above a fine pair of stone moustaches, but the garden was what really mattered to him. Emily sorted out the decoration of the house, whose interior was a barn-like piece of Victoriana twice the size of The Drive, while Scurrah set to work outdoors. He knew exactly what he wanted. On three sides of the house, pleasant but conventional planting was revived and enhanced by specimen trees and a more varied range of shrubs than Mrs Nicholson's dominating rhododendrons and laurels. A tennis court surrounded by heather, which gave the house its name, was discovered beneath more brambles on the site of Hill's kitchen garden and brought back into use. The courtyard of outbuildings, a spacious square of stables, carriage house, wash house and potting sheds behind a large conservatory, was converted into Garden HQ.

From here, Scurrah and his gardener Ernest Rae, a quiet Ulsterman who had previously worked at McReady's famous rose nursery in Portadown, advanced into the fifth plot with its mass of weeds. The chauffeur/handyman Ron Clark helped too, as did Richard Wainwright in his university vacations. The plan was to lay out two herbaceous borders of truly heroic dimensions, with a hinterland of cold frames, nursery beds, vegetable and fruit rows and a herb garden – the horticultural equivalent of an army's supply lines.

One flower, naturally, was to dominate. When *Country Life* magazine came to look at the completed garden, it put the strategy like this: 'Other people had rose or lime walks, or paths of thyme, but when he settled at The Heath, Adel, in the leafy outskirts of Leeds, Scurrah Wainwright decided that he would have a delphinium walk.' More than 100 cultivars were on his wish-list, three of each to be planted beside two gravel paths, both wide and fringed with narrow strips of mown grass across which nasturtiums, pinks and other groundcover could creep. Each path ran east–west for 70 yards (some 63 m) and the slope of the land allowed the delphiniums to give the appearance of rising even higher than was actually the case, while avoiding excessive shade.

On paper the design resembled a purple, white and blue – above all blue – floral version of Manhattan. The spikes were additionally dense between the two borders, where three delphinium trial beds measuring some 25 yards square, added an extra mass of plants behind the walls of colour alongside the paths. These beds were serious horticultural laboratories where Scurrah tested the latest arrivals from Blackmore & Langdon. Protected by the main borders, with belts of trees to the north and east of the garden and the long, high wall of The Heath's outbuildings to the west, the beds were sheltered but with enough wind getting through to give the plants a genuine test. Wainwright was also determined to propagate his own stock, to achieve the strong, distinctive and truly perennial plants that the Delphinium Society and the specialist growers wanted to promote. He made it a rule to buy only one of each cultivar and then grow the other two, for his groups of three, from cuttings taken in March.

The delphiniums were not to stand alone, however. The sobriquet 'King of the Border' (or 'Queen', according to taste) had not yet come into common use to describe the plant, but it was central to Wainwright's opinion of how his 'delphs' should be displayed. He surrounded them with scores of other herbaceous perennials, working on a grand scale which he had tried in miniature at The Drive and then tested on a temporary basis at the Leeds Flower Show in Roundhay Park which he chaired from 1930 to 1959. His Gold Medal Displays at the show covered 300 square yards at their zenith (Figure 3). When he decided to finish off The Heath garden with a further border, just of roses, he arranged for them to arrive in one delivery from Harkness in Hertfordshire, 300 bushes, standards and climbers. The entire household worked from first light until after nightfall to plant them out straight away.

Cultivation of the new garden also proceeded according to a long-deliberated and now precisely executed plan. Rich soil and plenty of water were crucial to success. Mains were

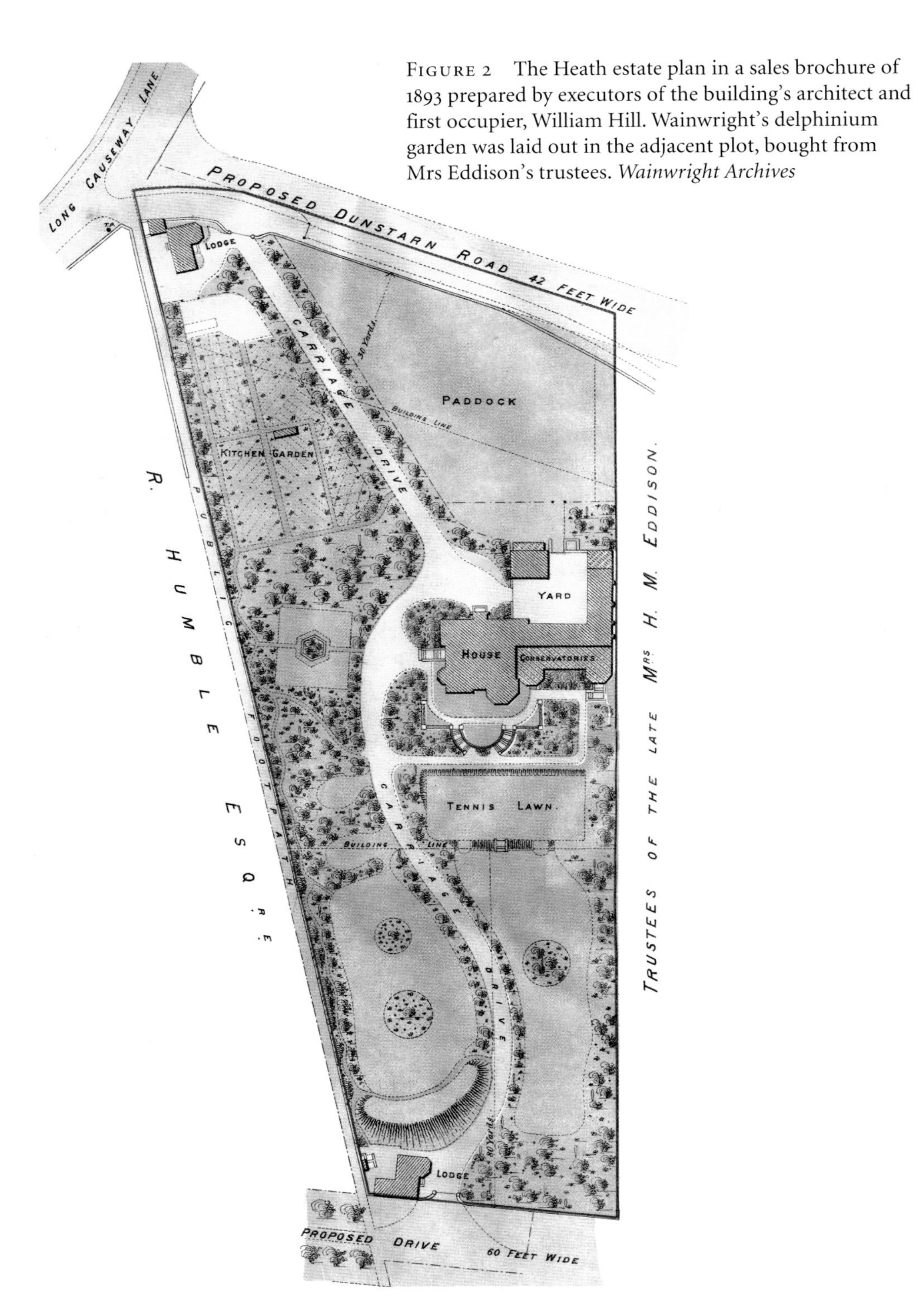

FIGURE 2 The Heath estate plan in a sales brochure of 1893 prepared by executors of the building's architect and first occupier, William Hill. Wainwright's delphinium garden was laid out in the adjacent plot, bought from Mrs Eddison's trustees. *Wainwright Archives*

FIGURE 3 Wainwright in his element – inspecting his Gold Medal exhibit at the 1954 Leeds Flower Show in Roundhay Park. *Wainwright Archives*

laid to the top of the garden where a sunken storage tank was surrounded by hooks for hessian bags of gunky manure and compost which Scurrah immersed in the pool. A fascinating pale green scum developed on the dark surface of the water, dark because it was sheltered by shrubs and camouflaged by a bristling pernettya hedge. Although of enormous interest to fellow-gardeners, this Jungle Juice was not to be seen by the main audience sauntering along the borders. Like the cold frames, with their three neat courses of old bricks and massive wood and glass covers, it was part of the garden's backstage.

So too were the technical necessities for growing prize delphiniums. Hidden hoses snaked from mains taps to the top of the borders and their water sank to the layer of impermeable clay, shaped like a shallow pie dish, which ensured that within an hour water bubbled back up to the surface just beyond the rose bed. The delphiniums relished this, as they did the loamy soil above the clay, which was fortified by manure, spent hops from Tetley's Leeds brewery, and the contents of the Jungle Juice tank – which for all its vile appearance had an unforgettably wholesome, earthy smell. Bamboo canes were deployed as concealed staking in their hundreds (stacked in forests in the potting sheds over winter, graded according to length). They were also used – a Wainwright speciality – to repair wind-damaged spikes by insertion through a small hole cut in the stem to provide a splint. This device had been tested in the show blooms for Roundhay which Richard used to accompany on the back of a flatbed truck. Later it was used for even more hair-raising trips to the Royal Horticultural Society's halls in London.

The behind-the-scenes world also included Scurrah's contribution to the Great Slug Question. The Heath was far too big for Richard to dart about with a hatpin (and anyway, he was now a dignified young man approaching his twenties). Instead, a large zinc collar was placed on the soil around each plant. This kept the slugs at bay, while more conventional methods of poison, half-orange traps and size 12 boots were also deployed.

Stocking the garden occupied Scurrah for all of 1938 and much of 1939, with the new delphiniums joining the ones brought carefully in cardboard boxes from The Drive. Along with the Harkness roses, phlox, lupins, dahlias and many other plants were ordered and installed, most designed to provide the yellows, reds and oranges which were absolutely banned from the delphinium palette. Wainwright's firmly-held views were usually rational, but he was emotionally traditionalist on the subject of delphinium colour. When a noted Dutch breeder called Legro announced his intention of breeding a red delphinium, the reaction at The Heath was a loud snort. Scurrah's grandchildren had recently been read *Uncle Tom's Cabin* with its sadistic cotton planter character, Legree, and the two names became a malevolent composite in their minds.

In 1938, Scurrah also made a rare appearance in fiction, as one of the real-life models for a central character in Lettice Cooper's best-known novel *National Provincial* which is set in Leeds. Cooper was brought up in the city, although she made her literary name in London where bookshops in Hampstead, where she settled, used to offer special displays of her books entitled 'Try our local Lettice'.The Liberal textile manufacturer in *National Provincial*, William Marsden, is a composite of assorted Leeds worthies, including the Luptons and Kitsons, but there is no doubt whom Cooper had in mind when Marsden hosts a performance of *A Midsummer Night's Dream* in his beautiful garden, and says to an old friend: 'Before you go, you must have a look at my new delphinium.'

Gardening had restored Scurrah's health and relieved his mind between business and National Assistance Board work, for which he received an OBE in 1939. His ambitious plans for The Heath and a lasting contribution to delphinium cultivation were under way. But he was well aware of the desperate state of political affairs, and foresaw the outbreak of the Second World War in September 1939. Preparations had been set in hand months earlier for the garden to be scaled back if necessary. The delphiniums were concentrated in one large bed and much of the rest of the newly cleared land was turned over to fruit and vegetables.

This was a pleasure as well as a national duty. Delphiniums were never to be toppled from their throne in Wainwright's mind, but he greatly enjoyed growing food to eat, as did Ron Clark and Ernest Rae who also got their share to take home. Visitors were often sidetracked away from the remaining flowers to the enticing rows of gooseberry bushes, raspberries, redcurrants, blackcurrants, runner beans, broad beans and peas which sank their roots into the 'delphinium soil' and fruited in profusion. For small children, there was just room for a tricycle to negotiate the soil between the rows, which had been hardened by pickers' boots. Overhung by pendulous trusses of berries or beans like sabres, the experience was unforgettable; a licensed free-for-all in an outdoor greengrocery.

Once the Battle of the Atlantic was over, however, the need to Dig for Victory was less pressing and the flowers took charge once more. Scurrah resumed his original garden plan, fortified by a national post-war mood of relief and optimism in spite of the sacrifices demanded by the Austerity period which saw rationing in force until 1954. His missionary approach to gardening was also rekindled and along with the revival of the council house gardens competition, which had been suspended during the war, he began opening The Heath's borders on a regular basis. The first receipt from the National Gardens Scheme is dated 21 July 1946, recording takings of a guinea followed by another three days later for £12. 6*s*. This began a record of 60 years of opening in aid of the scheme.

In between public openings, Scurrah and Emily invited hundreds of other people to enjoy the borders, through visits by groups such as the Delphinium Society or local horticultural societies, and at informal parties on summer evenings. Richard was courting now, and his future wife Joyce Hollis turned the corner by The Heath's old stables which led to a 'hole-in-the-hedge' approach to the garden, and exclaimed in amazement as she saw the sea of blue for the first time. She remembers her grandmother Emmeline, a strictly teetotal Methodist, being (wrongly) convinced that Scurrah's cheese and wine parties could be no such thing, because of his connection with the Lady Lane and Gipton chapels. The elderly lady was reassured that Joyce would come to no harm.

The almost concealed entrances to the garden were the nearest Scurrah came to the subtler side of design that dominates gardens today. Visitors either progressed round the front of the house, along a raised path with neatly clipped strips of lawn and borders of tobacco plants backed by tumbling clematis, or by taking a lower gravel path between a mixture of shrubs, rockeries and two curving flights of stone steps, and the large main lawn which sloped to rhododendrons, azaleas and a spinney of trees which sheltered Ernest Rae's small but fine garden at South Lodge. The two routes continued past a small rose garden and another rockery below the conservatory and then, suddenly, dog-legged past the southern gable of The Heath's outbuildings and – in one glorious and immediate moment – came on the borders. The alternative and less formal route, the one taken by Joyce, wound in a similar way round the back of the house, through the outbuildings' yard and up a paved slope to an orchard where hens clucked; then dog-legged like the other path but round the outbuildings' northern gable to a similar sudden view.

But the borders themselves had no such subtlety, apart from the concealed techniques for growing and Scurrah's skilful use of the slope to add to his delphiniums' already imposing height. They were a full-on, uninhibited mass of blazing colour, orchestrated to develop from something which looked like a dormant allotment for most of the winter months. There was no attempt at all-the-year-round interest, beyond the rotation of the vegetable garden's crops. Flowers were for summer, although the range of them from irises to roses, meant that summer – and colour – began in late April and lasted until the end of October. Scurrah was also determined that visitors should know what they were seeing and he labelled every plant with all his old enthusiasm for notices. When John Neave came round for *The Delphinium* magazine in 1984, long after Scurrah's death, he was pleased to find Richard continuing the policy. 'The plant labels are the size of a T-square but nevertheless blend unobtrusively with all the border foliage,' he wrote.

FIGURE 4 The Heath never had the subtlety of a landscape garden; but in the 1980s, a reduction in delphiniums allowed greater variety and room for small lawns. *Courtesy Derek St Romaine*

'What a boon this is to old-age pensioners with fading sight and what an education to those of us who find difficulty in christening our seedlings until the next season.'

The fact that not everyone agreed was acknowledged by Richard Wainwright, who said in several newspaper and magazine interviews that he could imagine the garden designer Gertrude Jekyll making acid comments about the crude northern simplicity of the approach. As strong-minded and opinionated as his father (and equally fond of notices), he added that he would have relished debating the point with her. But it was not surprising that the smaller but much more subtle garden created by Sybil and Frederick Spencer and their son Robin just up the road at York Gate in Adel, has always been more popular since its opening in 1968 (Figure 4).

Scurrah was now deputy chairman of the national Delphinium Society and he enthusiastically applauded when the chairman, E. R. James, told members at the 1948 AGM: 'Some day we shall see beautiful delphiniums flourishing across the land. We shall have planted new beauty in countless gardens – if we have dug steadfastly.' The steadfast digging, and manuring and watering, at The Heath was winning compliments for exactly that. Arthur Hellyer, editor of *Amateur Gardening*, visited in 1958 and declared The Heath to be 'one of the loveliest gardens in the North of England' (Figure 5). A photograph of the borders formed the cover of an *AG* book, *The Beginner's Garden* (Figure 6), which echoed a tiny booklet made by Richard Wainwright in 1928, when he was ten, recording the doings of his 'Roundhay Beginners' Horticultural Society' including a child's version of Leeds flower show held on the lawn of the house in The Drive (Figure 7).

By the mid-fifties, The Heath garden was hardly a beginner's operation, but Scurrah was pleased that it was chosen to promote the book. The title chimed with his lifelong hope that others would come to gardening as he had and learn to love it in the same way. Meanwhile, his fellow experts were also treated to photographs of The Heath's borders in their full splendour, on the souvenir menu of the Delphinium Society's annual dinner in 1957 at Peter Jones in Sloane Square, where everyone tucked into asparagus, poulet à l'américaine and profiteroles, and Vita Sackville-West proposed the loyal toast.

FIGURE 11 Geoffrey Smith in The Heath's borders, filming for his 1984 TV programme *Geoffrey Smith's World of Flowers*. From *Geoffrey Smith's World of Flowers* (Part 2). *Courtesy BBC*

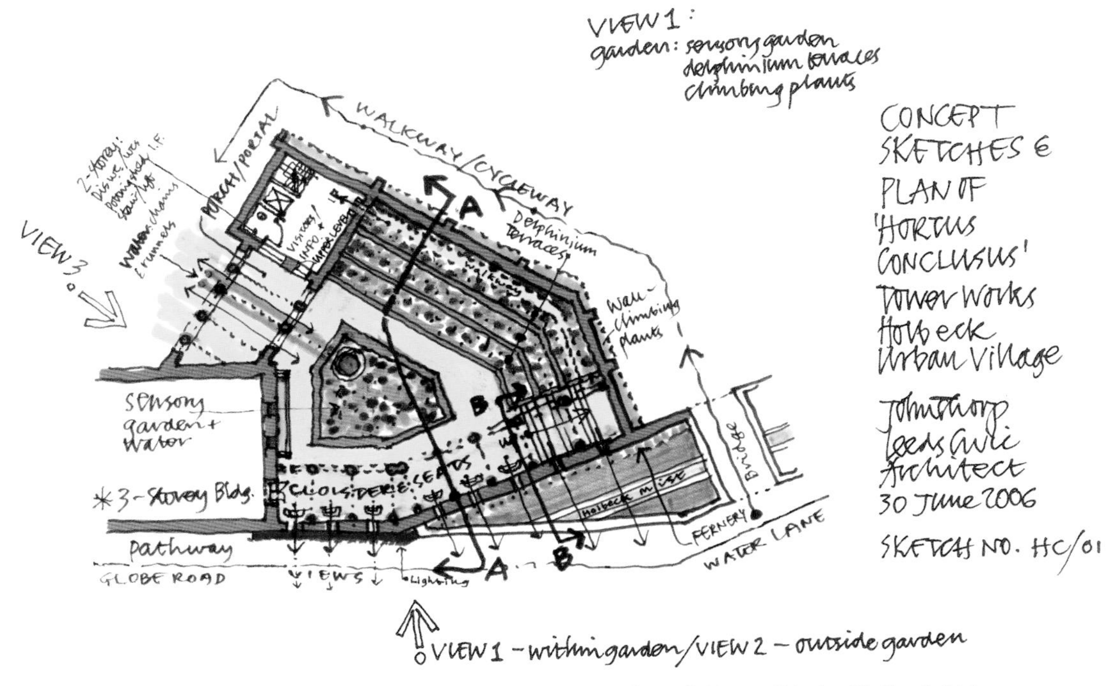

FIGURE 12 'Concept sketches & plan of "Hortus conclusus", Tower Works, Holbeck Urban Village'. A 'table napkin' sketch in 2006 by Leeds civic architect John Thorp of a possible transplant of part of The Heath garden to the centre of Leeds. *Wainwright Archives*

to London by train. Recalling the episode many years later, when he was president of the Delphinium Society, Richard couldn't resist telling the AGM at Wisley: 'Of course they always last much longer in flower in Yorkshire than they do in Surrey.'

The long and successful policy of taking cuttings and thus maintaining famous old names in the delphinium borders brought the late Geoffrey Smith of Harlow Carr and the BBC to the garden, where he used the borders to illustrate his 1984 TV series *The World of Flowers* as well as the book which accompanied the programmes (Figure 11). The same year, John Neave of the Delphinium Society came and recorded his astonishment in the Society's yearbook at the number of historic cultivars thriving in Leeds. Old faithfuls such as 'Faust', 'Fanfare', 'Blue Nile' and 'Chelsea Star' were everywhere, he said, 'but I turned quite pale when I read the following labels: Reverend E. Lascelles, Lady Eleanor and Mrs T. Carlile – all in robust health and holding their heads proudly aloft.' Lascelles we have met, but Mrs T. Carlile's pale blue and mauve florets with their white eyes go back to 1930, when the spike won an RHS Award of Merit, while 'Lady Eleanor', a stately semi-double spike also coloured pale blue and mauve, took a first-class certificate on her debut a year later, along with another delphinium, 'Alice Artindale', which Neave also found at The Heath.

Conscious of an uncertain future, because of the cost of maintaining the garden and a lack of expertise among their own four children, Richard and Joyce, together with Raymond, made sure that these treasures had a future. They systemised their regular exchanges with Temple Newsam and in 1986, after consulting with Leeds City Council's experts there, sent 61 cultivars to the national collection, from 'Betty Baseley' to 'Watkin Samuel'. Other plants went to Alan Bloom's nursery at Bressingham and Ken Harbutt's at Rougham Hall, as well as to scores of individual enthusiasts who were given free cuttings every spring. Peter Goodchild of the Centre for the Conservation of Historic Parks and Gardens at York University took a plant of 'Rev. E. Lascelles', writing in terms reminiscent of the arrival of 'Millicent Blackmore' in her box in 1922: 'I have found a good home for him with some friends who would be very happy to pick him up, if you can confirm that he is still available.'

The final stage of what might be called Scurrah's legacy is currently in discussion: a plan put forward by his grandchildren and Leeds civic architect John Thorp to create a garden in the city centre, using The Heath's remaining stock and cuttings from Temple Newsam (Figure 12). It would delight Scurrah, who died peacefully in his bedroom at The Heath in 1968, overlooking the borders which he so loved. His garden survived him until 2007, three years after the death of Richard and seventeen after that of Raymond Lister, who sadly lived for only two years after retiring. Raymond lives on in a beautiful sky-blue and mauve delphinium named after him following eight years of patient breeding by Joyce Bott of County Durham, from the cultivar 'Kathleen Cooke' and an unnamed but striking seedling. Work is in hand on a second plant to be named after Richard and there may be a third in due course; yet another shade of blue to honour the man who began it all.

'Rather extravagant than curious': The Ornamental Plant Collection of Sir John Reresby at Thrybergh, Yorkshire, from 1633 to 1646

SALLY O'HALLORAN AND JAN WOUDSTRA

INTRODUCTION

The Thrybergh estate is located in South Yorkshire, three miles east of Rotherham with the towns of Doncaster and Barnsley to the north east and north west respectively. Today it is managed as a golf course by Rotherham Golf Club Ltd with the club house located in Thrybergh Hall, built 1813–14 for the Fullerton family following designs by the architect and landscape gardener John Webb (*c.* 1754–1828).[1] The size and layout of the estate and the location of Thrybergh Hall have been altered by various owners, with the history of the estate dating back to the eleventh century; it is recorded in the 'Domesday Book' (1086) as Triberga.[2] Information on the history of the development of the estate is scarce and it is not until 1740 with the surviving survey by Joseph Colbeck that a clear insight into the earlier layout of the estate can be established.

The 1740 Colbeck survey records the estate and its surroundings and reveals the location of the original hall, north of St Leonard's church, with associated gardens to east and west. It also includes a deer park with a series of fish ponds, and Old Park to the east (Figure 1).[3] In addition to this, the personal memoirs of Sir John Reresby (1634–1689, son of the subject of this paper), published first in 1734, document the early history of the estate including the origin of the first gardens in Thrybergh.[4] Two contemporary illustrations of the house by Nathaniel Johnson (*c.* 1673) portray the only known images of the original manor house that was finally demolished in the early nineteenth century (Figure 2).[5] This documentation enables contextual interpretation of the recently discovered garden notebook of Sir John Reresby (1611–1646), which recorded details of the

[1] Howard Colvin, *A Biographical Dictionary of British Architects 1600–1840*, 3rd edn (New Haven and London: Yale University Press for the Paul Mellon Centre for Studies in British Art, 1995), p. 1031.

[2] Ann Williams and G. H. Martin, *Domesday Book: A Complete Translation* (London: Penguin, 2002), p. 833.

[3] Sheffield Archives (SA), MD 5885, Colbeck Survey, 1740.

[4] *The Memoirs of Sir John Reresby of Thrybergh, Bart., M.P. for York, &c., 1634–1689*, ed. by James J. Cartwright (London: Longmans, Green and Co., 1875). To avoid confusion between father and son, the younger Sir John will be referred to as Sir John Reresby Jr.

[5] Rev. Canon H. Leigh Bennett, 'The Old Hall at Thrybergh', *Ivanhoe Review*, 1.10 (1898), 120–121 (p. 121).

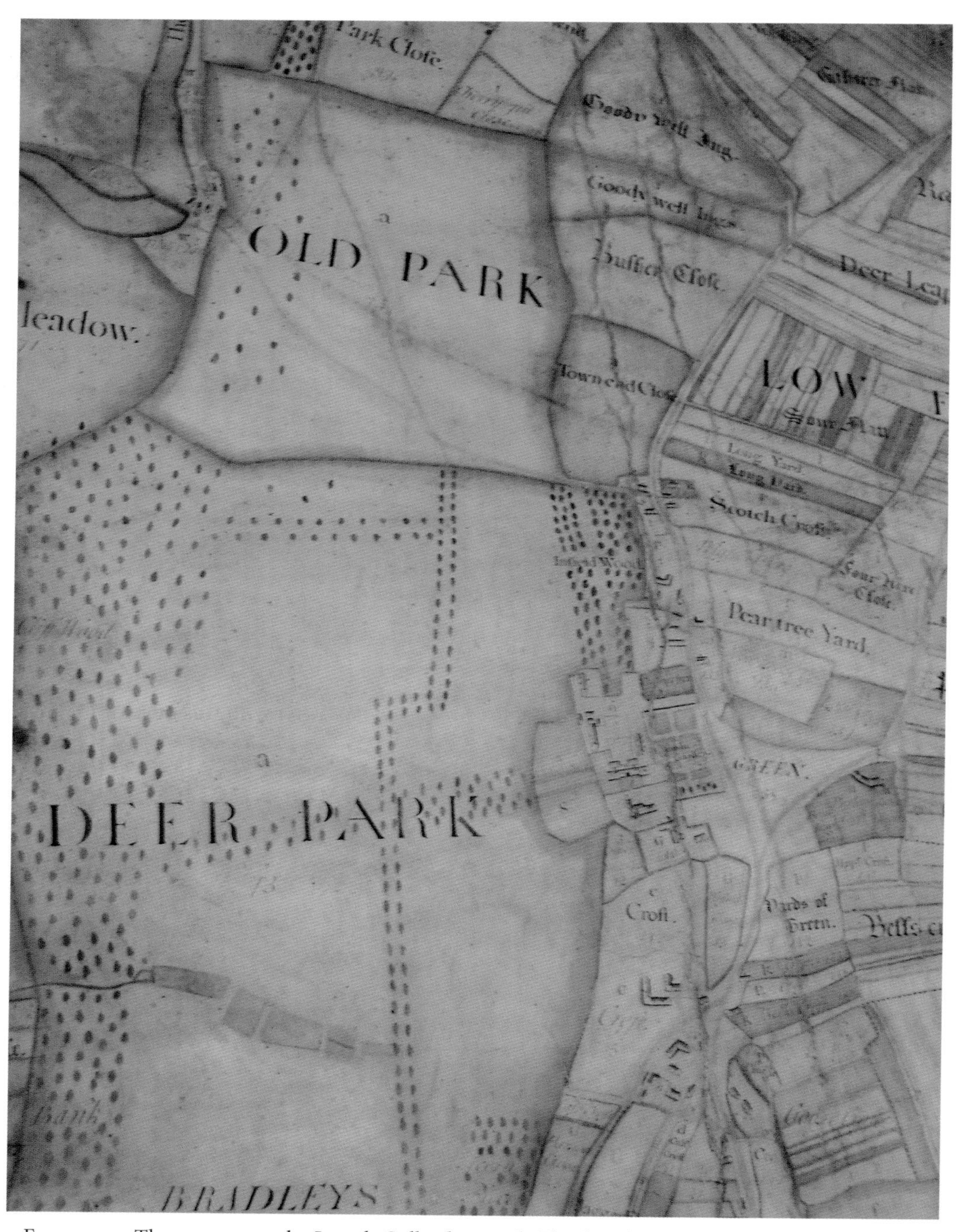

FIGURE 1 The 1740 survey by Joseph Colbeck records Thrybergh estate and its surroundings, and reveals the location of the original hall, north of St Leonard's church, with associated gardens to east and west. *Courtesy Sheffield Archives, MD 5885 (detail)*

FIGURE 2 Redrawing of a sketch by Nathaniel Johnson (*c.* 1673) of the north façade of Thrybergh Hall (original in Sheffield Archives, BFMS, Book 1). This illustrates the arrangement of walls as shown on the 1740 Joseph Colbeck survey, and explains the approach to the house. *Ivanhoe Review*, 1 (1898), p. 132

plant and fruit collections growing in Thrybergh between 1633 and 1644.[6] Extensive lists provide an insight into the diversity of the fruit trees and the ornamental plant collection, which Sir John carefully planned and managed over an eleven-year period. Recorded names of plants received from other estates highlight an active network of plant exchange between the local gentry and fellow Royalists within a fifty-mile radius from Thrybergh, including Revd Walter Stonehouse (1597–1655) who was developing his garden in nearby Darfield at the same time. Following an exploration of the context of the collection of fruit trees published in *Garden History*, the status of Sir John's fruit collection has been established as being on a par with that of other collections, including most remarkably that of John Tradescant in South Lambeth.[7]

This paper concentrates on the ornamental plant collection and highlights the range and availability of plants in Yorkshire during the first half of the seventeenth century. This information adds further context to the Stonehouse garden notes (1640–44) and confirms a pivotal position of Yorkshire gardeners at the time.

SIR JOHN RERESBY (1611–1646)

Sir John Reresby was born in Thrybergh in April 1611 as the eldest son of Sir George Reresby and Elizabeth Tamworth. On the death of his father in 1628, he was forced to end his formal education at Jesus College, Cambridge, and return home to manage the family estate and affairs. Although his university education ended abruptly it appears that he

[6] West Yorkshire Archive Service, Leeds, WYL 156–473. All following WYL references are from the Leeds archive.

[7] Jan Woudstra and Sally O'Halloran, ' "The exactness and nicety of those things": Sir John Reresby's Garden Notebook and Garden (1633–1644) at Thrybergh, Yorkshire', *Garden History*, 36.1 (2008), 135–193.

was highly educated for the period; his son stated in his memoirs that he was 'learned both in Greek and Latin tongues, read and wrote much as may appear by several things of his composure and written by his own hand'.[8]

Sir George had led a lavish lifestyle and his son inherited a 'narrow' fortune. In 1633 Sir John married Francis, the daughter of Edmond Yarburgh, of Snaith Hall, in Yorkshire, who brought with her 'between three and four thousand pounds'.[9] However this did not increase his fortune greatly as his mother made him repay two thousand pounds from the dowry for money which she claimed she had paid to buy off his wardship in 1628.[10] Sir John therefore began his management of the Thrybergh estate on limited means. Taking his financial status into account, and the fact that there are no existing records of any works being undertaken to Thrybergh Hall at that time, the indication is that all his available resources were used to improve the grounds and estate.

From his son's memoirs we know that Sir John's passion for gardening did not come about until he had been managing the estate for five years after his father's death. Other interests included being 'a lover of hawks for some time, but he left that off soon after and kept beagles, and was weary of them after a short trial but was ever constant to his garden'.[11] In 1633, at 22 years of age, Sir John began work on the development of the gardens and orchards at Thrybergh, which he recorded in a notebook over an eleven-year period. The first entry in his garden notebook details how Sir John began by establishing a fruit collection. He lists an extensive assortment of fruit, including numerous varieties of peaches, pears, plums, apples, apricots, cherries, and quince, which he planted in the 'Orchards & Gardens at Thrybergh'.[12] Sir John began to increase his fruit stock as the orchards matured and by 1638 he was proficient in propagation, recording the quantities of various plants grafted, inarched and grown from seed.[13] It appears his fruit collection was well known, as in 1640 Revd Walter Stonehouse, the botanist-parson of Darfield, six miles north of Thrybergh, obtained several varieties of apples and pears from Reresby's new orchards. Stonehouse was respected and well connected within the circles of the gardening elite of the time; one of his close friends was John Parkinson (the well-known herbalist at Long Acre).[14] Stonehouse had taken part in a botany expedition to north Wales with the apothecary Thomas Johnson, and he had many plants from overseas in his garden, probably from the plant collector John Tradescant.[15] Although only ever referred to as a 'neighbour' in any of the literature on Stonehouse, he obviously considered Sir John to be a proficient gardener of the highest standards as he obtained several plants from Sir John's collection, which he recorded in his notes:

[8] Cartwright, p. 17.
[9] Ibid., p. 18.
[10] Ibid., p. 4.
[11] Ibid., p. 14.
[12] WYL 156-473, fol. 2.
[13] Ibid., fol. 10.
[14] Prudence Leith-Ross, *The John Tradescants: Gardeners to the Rose and Lily Queen* (London: Peter Owen, 1984), p. 121.
[15] Ibid.

9. Apple from Sr. Jo: Reresby
A. Cowick Peare Sr. Jo: Reresby
19. An Apple from Sr. Jo: Reresby
C. Twenty marke Peare, Sr. Jo: Reresby
D. An Apple from Sr. Jo: Reresby
28. Apple from Sr. John Reresby[16]

As Sir John developed the gardens at Thrybergh there appears to have been ongoing contact between the two men with many similarities in the management of both their gardens. In his garden notebook Sir John records his 'best Tulipas 1641', listing twenty-seven named varieties with colour descriptions.[17] Stonehouse listed twenty-three of the same varieties in 1640.[18] In 1643 and again in 1644 Sir John recorded the names of several plants received from 'Mr. Stonehouse'.[19] There is no evidence that Sir John received any formal instruction in gardening, but it appears that both he and Stonehouse were learning from each other, with Sir John using John Parkinson's *Paradisi in sole, paradisus terrestris* (1629) as a basis, relying upon this for both practical advice and botanical information. By 1642 he had compiled a plant list entitled 'Omnium stirpium que in horto neo continentur Thribergh', being a record of all plants grown in the gardens of the estate. Included are some 402 plant species and cultivars of some 187 genera and, unlike the previous lists, these names have been written in Latin and consistently refer to the page numbers in Parkinson's herbal. Sir John was continuously expanding this collection; the following year he recorded 'what new sortes is grafted & (G W) shall bee 1643',[20] containing names of both fruit and ornamental plants which had been propagated and were awaiting propagation.

However, it all came to an abrupt end, due to the turbulent political atmosphere in England in the mid-1600s. Sir John was a Royalist, and during his life in Thrybergh was unable to ever increase his fortune, not due to 'ill-husbandry, but by reason of the war'.[21] He supported King Charles I in two wars. In 1639 he was a 'major in the militia regiment' and marched to York in the Bishop's War, supporting King Charles I in his attempt to reform the Scottish church.[22] In 1642 he had no command but surveyed under the Duke of Newcastle, supporting King Charles I against the Parliament in the Civil War. In recognition of his support to the King he was created Baronet on the 16 May 1642.

As a result of the Civil War he suffered considerable financial loss and was obliged to sell a sizeable acreage of woodland, which changed the layout of the estate. To raise sufficient funds he was forced to sell 'the wood in a park called the old parke & separate it from the rest'. The location of the 'old park' can be seen on the north side of Thrybergh

[16] R. T. Gunther, 'The Garden of the Rev. Walter Stonehouse at Darfield Rectory, in Yorkshire, 1640', *Gardeners' Chronicle*, 67, 3rd series (12 June 1920), 296–97 (p. 296).
[17] WYL 156-473, fol. 14.
[18] R. T. Gunther, 'The Garden of the Rev. Walter Stonehouse at Darfield Rectory, in Yorkshire, 1640', *The Gardeners' Chronicle*, 67, 3rd series (29 May 1920), 268–69 (p. 268).
[19] WYL 156-473, fols 58–59.
[20] Ibid, fol. 60.
[21] Cartwright, p. 21.
[22] Ibid., p. 14.

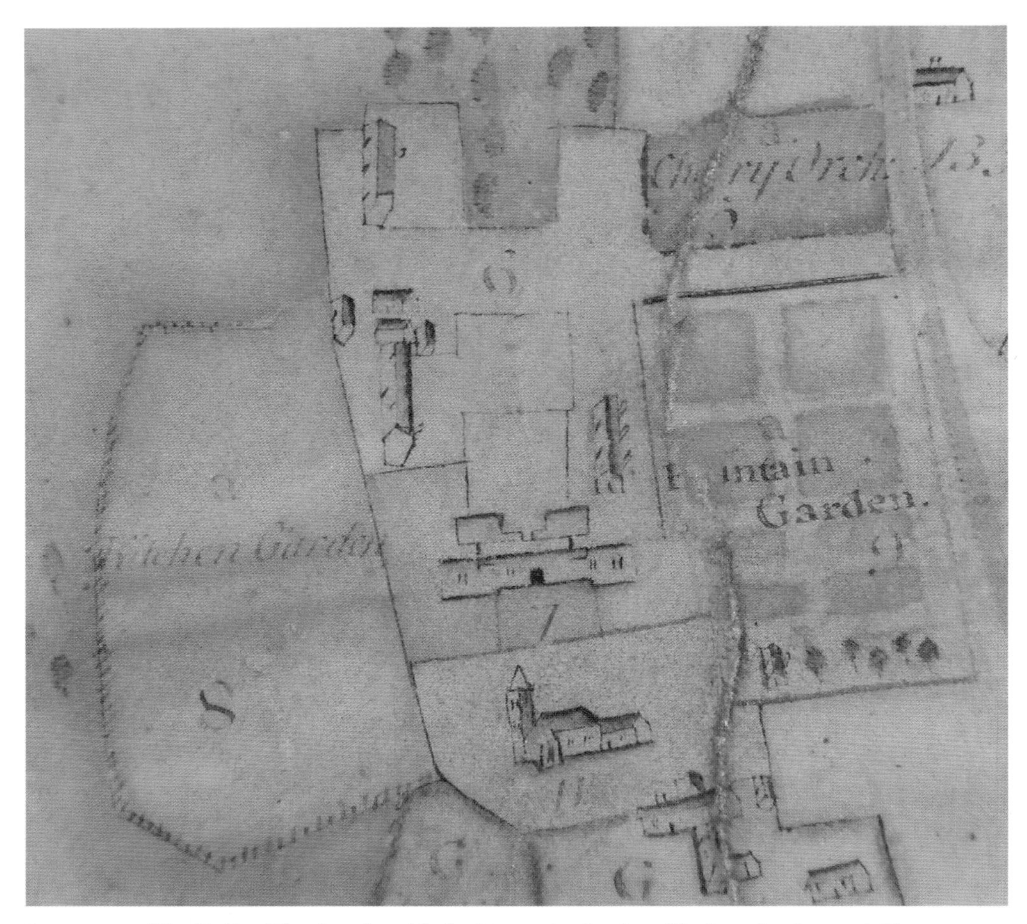

FIGURE 3 The Hall at Thrybergh, with the Fountain Garden, Kitchen Garden and Cherry Orchard. Sir John Reresby Jr (1634–1689) rebuilt the garden walls, replacing a lower dry stone wall which his father had previously built, a situation that remained well into the eighteenth century when Joseph Colbeck made his survey. *Courtesy Sheffield Archives, MD 5885 (detail)*

Hall on the 1740 map (Figure 1). In 1644 Sir John Reresby was taken prisoner by the Parliamentary party and kept in strict confinement in Thrybergh until March 1646. The whole estate was confiscated by Parliament as a result of his Royalist affiliation and when released from imprisonment he went to London to reclaim his estate. On his return he caught a fever and died a month later in April 1646 at the age of 35. According to his son, 'great lamentation was made for him at his death, by the country foreseeing how much he must be wanted in several respects.'[23]

[23] Ibid., pp. 16–17.

LAYOUT OF THE GARDENS

The general asymmetric layout of the gardens and courtyards reflected a range of alterations over a long time, but during Sir John's time this has been described as having

> the main house located immediately north of St Leonard's Church, with a narrow rear court providing access to the churchyard. A series of walled gardens lay on flat land between the forecourts and the main road, while a kitchen garden lay to the west. The forecourts were approached between the walled garden and separately walled cherry orchard, providing an awkward relationship with the road, whereby it was necessary to turn a ninety-degree angle on approaching the house. This was entered through two succeeding courtyards flanked by estate buildings.[24]

The kitchen garden, located on a west-facing slope, was rectangular in plan, with rounded corners towards the deer park. It appears to have been surrounded by a timber fence of upright stakes at the time of the 1740 Colbeck survey.[25] Dictated by limited resources and influenced perhaps by prudent management, the chosen enclosure was not unusual for the period: it was also used for the western boundary of the garden of John Tradescant (*c.* 1570–1638), which was at the time described as 'an old pale'.[26] Sir John was intensively propagating his fruit collection. By 1640 he had successfully grown '936 stock' of pear[27] which were most probably planted in a separate area north of Thrybergh Hall marked on the 1740 survey as 'Pear tree Yard' (Figure 1). Sir John grew twenty-eight cultivars of cherries at Thrybergh; these are most likely to have been cultivated in another area identified on the 1740 survey as the 'Cherry Orchard'.[28]

Sir John surrounded the Hall 'with a low dry wall', the location of which can be interpolated from two sketches of the estate by Nathaniel Johnson, *c.* 1673 (Figure 2)[29] and the Colbeck survey (Figure 3). However, the height of the walls as they appear in the drawing is presumably higher than the 'low' walls erected by Sir John and indeed his son, Sir John Reresby Jr, recorded he had rebuilt them 'in lime and sand' and raised them to a greater height. However, he recorded that he 'encompassed the same ground' as his father had before him[30] and indeed a note by Johnson suggests that Thrybergh Hall was 'surrounded on the east, south, [and] west with gardens or Orchards',[31] which appears to confirm that there were no major changes in the general layout.

The gardens lying to the east of the house can be clearly seen with four square and four rectangular-shaped beds (Figure 3). While Sir John would have determined the general organisation and arrangement, the design as recorded in the Colbeck survey reflected that of Sir John Reresby Jr, changing the content in 1668 to add 'the *jet d'eau* or

24 Woudstra and O'Halloran, p. 139.
25 SA, MD 5885 (1740 survey).
26 David Sturdy, 'The Tradescants at Lambeth', *Journal of Garden History*, 2.1 (1982), 1–16 (p. 8).
27 WYL 156-473, fol. 11.
28 SA, MD 5885 (1740 survey).
29 SA, BFMS 8, Book 1.
30 Cartwright, p. 78.
31 SA, BFMS 8, Book 1.

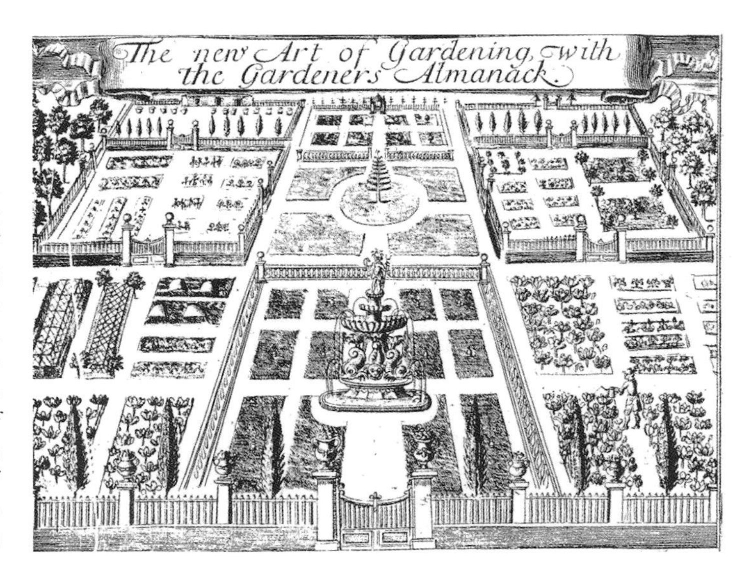

FIGURE 4 Sir John Reresby Jr adapted the gardens to the latest fashion by removing flowerbeds in favour of grass plats and installing a fountain in the southernmost walled garden. This frontispiece from Leonard Meager's *The New Art of Gardening* (1697) is revealing of the type of gardening that became fashionable in the 1670s

the fountain in the middle of the parterre'.[32] This change in design was not unique to Thrybergh as according to Sir John Jr 'the form of gardening was so different' than that practised during his father's time (Figure 4).[33]

There is no surviving plan of the orchards or gardens from the seventeenth century in existence, thus the location or arrangement of individual plants is unknown, but the general arrangement is likely to have reflected what was popular at that time, as seen in the gardens of Stonehouse or Tradescant.

ORNAMENTAL WOODY PLANT COLLECTION

The initial impression from the garden notebook is that Sir John was primarily focused on establishing a collection of fruit trees at Thrybergh; the first five pages contain lists of the numerous cultivars of apricots, plums, peaches, nectarines, apples, pears and cherries, which he planted in 1633.[34] It is not until Folio 7 that an interest in ornamental plants is revealed. This priority is in line with the advice of Parkinson in his *Paradisi in sole*, in that, having planted the orchards, the next step was to supplement the collection with woody plants that did not bear edible fruit but provided 'ornament'.[35] In the chapter entitled 'The Corollarie to this Orchard', Parkinson listed twenty-two types of trees and shrubs, which he saw as an essential complement to a collection of fruit trees (Figure 5).[36]

Sir John distinguished these plants in his notebook under the heading 'Trees w*it*hin this ground of severall sortes besides Aples, Peares, Plombs, Cherries, Nectorins and

32 SA, MD 5885 (1740 survey).

33 Cartwright, p. 78. See also Leonard Meager, *The New Art of Gardening* (1697), frontispiece, in *Early English Books Online* ‹http://eebo.chadwyck.com› [accessed 13 December 2008].

34 WYL 156-473, fols 2–6.

35 John Parkinson, *Paradisi in sole, paradisus terrestris* (1629; repr. London: Methuen, 1904), p. 598.

36 Ibid., p. 601.

The Corollarie to this Orchard. 601

1 *Pinus.* The Pine tree. 2 *Abies.* The Firre tree. 3 *Ilex.* The euer greene Oake. 4 *Cupreſſus.* The Cipreſſe tree. 5 *Arbutus.* The Strawberry tree. 6 *Alaternus.* The euer greene Priuet.

G 4

FIGURE 5 As an amateur gardener, Sir John Reresby used John Parkinson's *Paradisi in sole* (1629) as a guide for his collections. In a chapter 'The Corollarie to this Orchard', Parkinson provided a range of ornamental shrubs that might be included in orchards, including strawberry tree, Alaternus and evergreen oak, all grown at Thrybergh. John Parkinson, *Paradisi in sole, paradisus terrestris* (1629; repr. London: Methuen, 1904), p. 601

Peaches etc', and had planted eleven of the twenty-two recommended trees in his first years of gardening at Thrybergh.[37] Within this list some of the plants were indexed with page references to Parkinson's volume, showing the extent to which, from the onset, Sir John relied upon this book for practical advice. Unfortunately, his notes do not provide an indication as to the location of plants in the gardens, and some may not have been planted solely in the orchards at Thrybergh, as Parkinson provided guidance on other locations. Cupressus (*Cupressus sempervirens* L.) could be planted 'in rowes on both sides of some spatious walks'.[38] Taxus (*Taxus baccata* L.) could be placed 'both in the corners of Orchards and against the windowes of Houses, to be both a shadow and an ornament'.[39] Sabina (*Juniperus sabina* L.) could be 'planted in out-yards, backsides or voide places of Orchards as well as to cast clothes thereon to dry'.[40]

These same woody plants retained their popularity and were listed in *The English Gardener* (1670) by Leonard Meager as ideal because of their hardiness and ease of propagation: 'the most of them are increased by cutting and laying, some of seed.'[41] Sir John, who had quickly become a proficient propagator of fruit, would have been able to use the same skills to enlarge his stock of ornamental woody plants. The range of plants would also have been increased through active exchanges amongst local gentry, acquiring some of the varieties as 'impes', i.e. as saplings, suckers, slips or scions, growing them on himself.[42] 'Mr Childers' sent Arbutus (*Arbutus unedo* L.) and Alaternus (*Rhamnus alaternus* L.);[43] this referred to Hugh Childers who owned extensive property around Doncaster, with the family home at Carr House, but also owning Cantley Hall, nine miles north east of Thrybergh.[44] 'Fran Baker', whose background is not currently known, sent the 'euer greene Hawthorne or prickly Corrall' (*Pyracantha coccinea* 'M. J. Roemer') and the 'euer greene Oake' (*Quercus ilex* L.).[45]

Sir John followed the advice of Parkinson diligently, and by 1642 recorded his various recommendations in his garden notebook. However, within this list he also included several plants not suggested by Parkinson; most surprisingly amongst them are the numerous varieties of roses. In 1629 Parkinson thought the rose 'better fit a Garden then an Orchard',[46] yet it would appear Sir John did not follow this advice, listing them initially with woody ornamental plants and later with the 'winter Greenes'.[47] Sir John could have also been taking advice from the earlier writers: William Lawson (1553–1635), one of the first Yorkshire gardeners to make a name for himself with his book *A New*

37 WYL 156-473, fol. 7. Note that where Sir John uses abbreviations, and these contractions have been expanded in transcription, these are indicated by use of italics, as in 'w*it*hin'.

38 Parkinson, p. 602.

39 Ibid., p. 606.

40 Ibid., p. 607.

41 Leonard Meager, *The English Gardener* (London, 1670), p. 248.

42 *Impe*, *impa*, or *imp* is defined as 'a young shoot of a plant or tree; a sapling: a sucker, slip, scion'; the word dated from medieval times, and remained current till the end of the seventeenth century. It derives from the same source as the Dutch *ent*, which is still in current use. See *OED* (1989), VII, 693–94.

43 WYL 156-473, fol. 20.

44 SA, CWM/397 and WWM/E Donc/164.

45 WYL 156-473, fols 18–20.

46 Parkinson, p. 546.

47 WYL 156-473, fol. 56.

Orchard & Garden (1618), encouraged the use of roses as part of the plantings in an orchard. He considered the pleasure of an orchard adorned with flowers, herbs and a number of garden features: 'what can your eye desire to see, your eares to heare, your mouth to taste, or your nose to smell, that is not to be had in an Orchard, with abundance and variety?'[48]

In his chapter titled 'Ornaments', Lawson recommended 'the Rose red, damske, veluet, and double prouince Rose, the sweet muske Rose double and single, the double and single white Rose', the majority of which were grown by Sir John at Thrybergh. Sir John did not include the rose collection with his list of 'choyce flowers',[49] which were primarily the bulbs and other spring flowering plants, yet he managed and maintained his roses with the same care as his other plants. In 1643 he planned to propagate six 'new [sorts]'[50] and by 1644, when Stonehouse gave him the 'Cristall Rose', he grew twenty-one varieties.[51] This was a considerable size collection for an amateur gardener, the significance of which is clear when it is compared with that of John Tradescant the elder, who produced a catalogue of his plant collection in 1634, and Stonehouse's catalogue of 1640 (Table 1).[52] With thirty-one varieties Tradescant had the largest collection on a par with Parkinson, who in 1629 grew 'thirty sorts at the least, every one notably differing from the other' (Figure 6).[53] However, of these Parkinson only recommended twenty-four in his *Paradisi in sole*. Sir John grew nineteen of these and would presumably have further expanded his collection had he been given more time. As it was, this collection was notable as the availability of roses at that time was very limited; even over a decade later Sir Thomas Hanmer, who had a renowned garden in Bettisfield, Flintshire, only recorded twenty-one kinds in his garden book.[54]

Other plants within this list included a series of tender plants, such as olive tree, lemon, and orange, which would not normally survive the winters in the outdoors. Without the availability of protection from a greenhouse (there is no evidence of there having been one at Thrybergh at this stage), one of the methods used at that time was to re-position tender plants in flowerpots in September before the arrival of the severe weather, enabling them to get established so that they could be 'housed', either in a spare room or shed, during winter. This shows a considerable level of horticultural knowledge, with practice on a par with other contemporaries in the country.

GARDEN DESIGN

As Sir John was already using Parkinson's *Paradisi in sole* as guidance for horticultural practice and as a standard for his plant collecting, he is also likely to have used this source for the layout of the gardens. Parkinson suggested that the usual design was to divide the

[48] William Lawson, *A New Orchard and Garden* (1618), Chapter 17, p. 56, in *Early English Books Online* ‹http://eebo.chadwyck.com› [accessed 12 December 2008].
[49] WYL 156-473, fols 16–17.
[50] Ibid., fols 60–61.
[51] Ibid., fol. 57.
[52] Leith-Ross, pp. 221–24; Gunther (12 June 1920), p. 296.
[53] Parkinson, pp. 412 and 415.
[54] Miles Hadfield, *A History of British Gardening* (Middlesex: Hamlyn Publishing Group, 1969), p. 98.

FIGURE 6 By 1644 Sir John Reresby grew twenty-one varieties of roses, a substantial number, considering that even Tradescant's collection contained only ten more. Sir John's collection included Rosa Damascena, Rosa lutea multiplex, and Rosa rubra humilis, illustrated here. John Parkinson, *Paradisi in sole, paradisus terrestris* (1629; repr. London: Methuen, 1904), p. 415

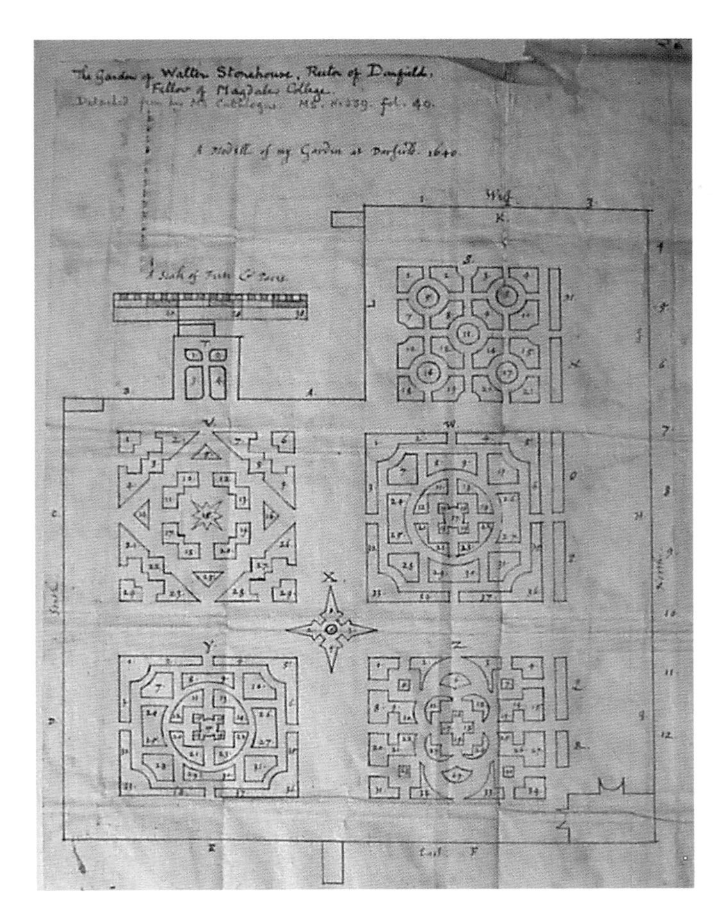

FIGURE 7 'A Modell of my Garden at Darfield 1640.' Revd Walter Stonehouse (1597–1655) of nearby Darfield was a friend of Sir John Reresby and exchanged plants with him. His garden consisted of knots and beds arranged in geometric patterns, and the walled gardens at Thrybergh would have been similarly disposed. *Courtesy the President and Fellows of Magdalen College, Oxford*

garden into four squares with 'walks, cross the middle both [ways], and round about it also with hedges, squares, knots and [trails]'.[55] He provided a range of patterns as to how this might be done. The implementation of such a scheme at Thrybergh can be qualified with a description by Johnson which confirms the existence of 'a delightful garden & maze or labyrinth of close walls'.[56] Patterns such as those suggested by Parkinson for flower gardens were often compared with labyrinths. A surviving plan shows that such a design was also implemented in Stonehouse's garden (Figure 7)[57] and Sir John would presumably have selected a variation of these patterns for the beds in his garden at Thrybergh.

To border the beds and knots, Parkinson discussed suitable plants, listing numerous herbs but advising that these were all short-lived and high in maintenance, recommending the use of the more long-lived 'boxe' (*Buxus sempervirens* L.).[58] Sir John recorded

[55] Parkinson, p. 5.
[56] SA, BFMS 8, Book 1.
[57] Magdalen College Archives (MCA), Oxford, MS 239, fol. 40.
[58] Parkinson, p. 6.

growing two types of box, the common and the gilded, and it is possible that the former was used to border the beds and knots. Within the borders Parkinson recommended the 'fine flowers' to be planted, selecting what he described as the 'out-landish' flowers first, namely 'Daffodils, Fritillarias, Iacinthes, Saffron-flowers [*Crocus* sp., referring to both spring- and autumn-flowering forms], Lillies, Flowerdeuces [*Iris* sp.], Tulipas, Anemones, French Cowslips, or Beares eares [*Primula auricula* L.]'.[59] In contrast to these were the 'English flowers', referring not necessarily to native plants, as the name suggests, but to flowers traditionally grown in gardens, such as *Dianthus*.[60] Parkinson also included the months in which plants flowered,[61] a method which Sir John adopted in his notebook under the heading 'My choyce flowers & plantes wth a mem^{rl} what month they beare'.[62]

The variety of 'out-landish' plants grown by Sir John was noteworthy in that it provided interest throughout the seasons. The year started with the first flowering crocus in January, followed by an array of colour in the summer from the various forms of fraxinella (*Dictamnus albus* L.), with the display continuing into the autumn from the 'siclamen' (*Cyclamen hederifolium* L.) right through to the hellebores (*Helleborus niger* L.) in December.

The white & Blew Cro:	Jan.24	
The Small purple Cro:	14 feb	
Parkinsons Daffodill	Mar 30	
Chroune Emperiall	15th Aprill	
The Calsedon Anemone	May 16	
The Fraxinella	Midsomer	
Siclamen vel sow breade	Aug 25	
The Black Ellebor	vel ~~Christmas flower~~	26x: Cris[63]

By 1642 Sir John recorded nine varieties of crocus, which was a small collection when compared to the twenty-seven recorded by Parkinson (1629),[64] but was on a par when compared to Stonehouse's collection of twelve and Tradescant's of eleven (Table 2). Similarly, when comparing the numbers of lilies grown in these three gardens, Sir John only recorded four species, Stonehouse six, and Tradescant ten (Table 3). The low numbers of these plants probably reflects the speed at which they might be propagated, for example crocus may have taken up to three years to flower when grown from seed and lilies even longer taking up to five.

Sir John managed his 'choyce flowers' with similar care as his fruit collection, constantly increasing the quantities either through propagation or acquiring them through exchange. When comparing the number of iris varieties grown, Sir John in 1642 only recorded five compared to Tradescant's thirteen and Stonehouse's twenty-one (Table 4),

[59] Ibid., p. 8.
[60] Ibid., p. 11.
[61] Ibid., p. 16.
[62] WYL 156-473, fol. 16.
[63] WYL 156-473, fols 16–17. 'Sow bread' is the common name for cyclamen.
[64] Parkinson, pp. 160–67.

but included in the 'gotten 1644' list he had 'Irises wth Tuberous roots, Iris Dalmatica, Iris Germanica, Camerarii, Alba florentinii = lutea variegata minor Calcedonica clusii flore cimplice et flore pleno alba variegate Camdiris variegata'.[65] Since Sir John appears to have used Parkinson's advice in building his collection he was keen to select what he considered the best varieties. Thus it is not surprising that, when Parkinson lists the 'Crowne Imperiall' (*Fritillaria imperialis* L.) as deserving 'the first place in this our Garden of delight',[66] Sir John included it within his 'choyce flowers', recording its flowering date as the '15th Aprill'.[67] All these plants were informally listed within his garden notebook, randomly mixing common and botanical names, but by 1642 Sir John considered his collections complete enough to compile a catalogue using a markedly more formal and scientific approach.

1642 PLANT CATALOGUE

In 1642, Sir John compiled a list of all his plants which he titled in Latin as 'Omnium stirpium que in horto neo continentur Thribergh'.[68] This broadly translates as 'All the plants which are kept together in the pleasure gardens or enclosure in Thrybergh', and as it is dated (11 April 1642) it provides the most accurate record of what was grown in Thrybergh during that particular year. The plants were given their botanical name, listed in alphabetical groups, with many of the names accompanied by page references to Parkinson's *Paradisi in sole*. This more formal scientific approach reflected the influence of Stonehouse, who in 1640 had devised a recording system which he catalogued in his garden notes under the title 'CATALOGVS, Plantarum Horti mei Darfeldiae, Quibus is instructus est Anno Domini 1640'[69] (a catalogue of the plants in my garden at Darfield, which was prepared in the year of the Lord 1640). Although similar in concept, the style and content of both their catalogues varies, providing an insight into the differences in management of both plant collections.

Stonehouse, having most probably gained hands-on experience of recording on a botanical excursion to North Wales in 1639, wrote his first catalogue a year later, which he titled 'Catalogus planta*rum* in horto Gualt. Stonehouse Darfeldia in agro Eborac*um* 1640' (a catalogue of the plants in the garden of Walter Stonehouse, Darfield, in Yorkshire).[70] Botanical names were listed in strict alphabetical order in a firm clear hand, italic in style, using one-line spacing, apart from a double spacing to divide the alphabetical blocks (Figure 8). In this first draft Stonehouse recorded 422 perennials and 125 annuals, a total of 537 plants, dated 'Aug 26 1640'.[71] It must have become immediately apparent to Stonehouse that with one-line spacing any additions to the collection would be impossible to include and thus a second and final draft was written with the format

65 WYL 156-473, fol. 59.
66 Parkinson, p. 27.
67 WYL 156-473, fol. 16.
68 Ibid., fol. 22.
69 MCA, MS 239, fol. 2.
70 MCA, MS 345, fol. 1. Note that italics indicate an expansion of Stonehouse's abbreviations.
71 Ibid., fols 16–17.

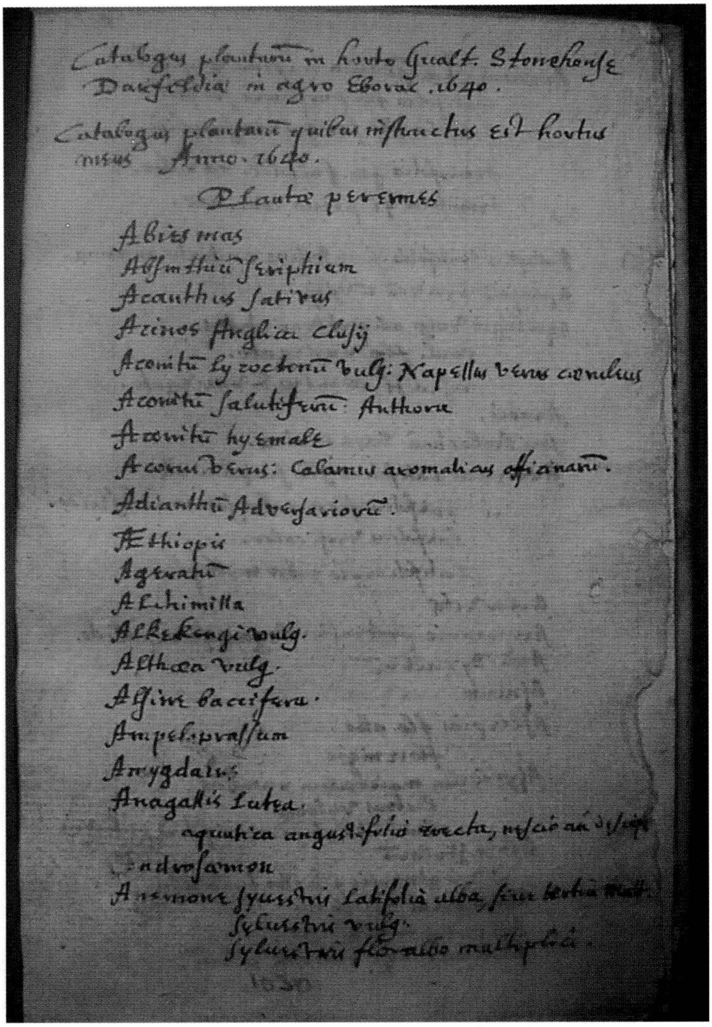

Catalogus plantarū in horto Gualt. Stonehouse
Darfeldia in agro Eborac. 1640.
Catalogus plantarū quibus instructus est hortus meus Anno. 1640.
Plantae perennes
Abies mas
Absinthiū Seriphium
Acanthus sativus
Acinos Anglica Clusij
Aconitū lycoctonū vulg: Napellus verus coeruleus
Aconitū salutiferū: Anthora
Aconitū hyemale
Acorus verus: Calamus aromaticus officinarū.
Adianthū Adversariorū.
Aethiopis
Ageratū
Alchimilla
Alkekengi vulg.
Althaea vulg.
Alsine baccifera.
Ampeloprassum
Amygdalus
Anagallis lutea.
aquatica angustifolia erecta,
Androsamon
Anemone sylvestris latifolia alba,
Sylvestris vulg.
Sylvestris flore albo multiplici.

FIGURE 8 The first draft of Stonehouse's plant catalogue is titled 'Catalogus plantar*um* in horto Gualt. Stonehouse Darfeldia in agro Eborac*um* 1640'. Folio 1 is depicted. *Courtesy the President and Fellows of Magdalen College, Oxford*

changed to double spacing. These later entries are easily distinguishable today with the ink appearing darker in colour. Ruled side margins were used to ensure the writing within the pages appeared justified as seen in a professional publication (Figure 9).[72] By 1644 his collection had increased to hold 651 perennials and 215 annuals, totalling 866 plants, but his catalogue maintained its formal professional appearance.[73] This systematic or methodical arrangement of plant names was in sharp contrast to Sir John's catalogue, which was most probably initially for reference use but over time turned into a 'working list'.

[72] MCA, MS 239, fol. 19.
[73] Ibid., fol. 61.

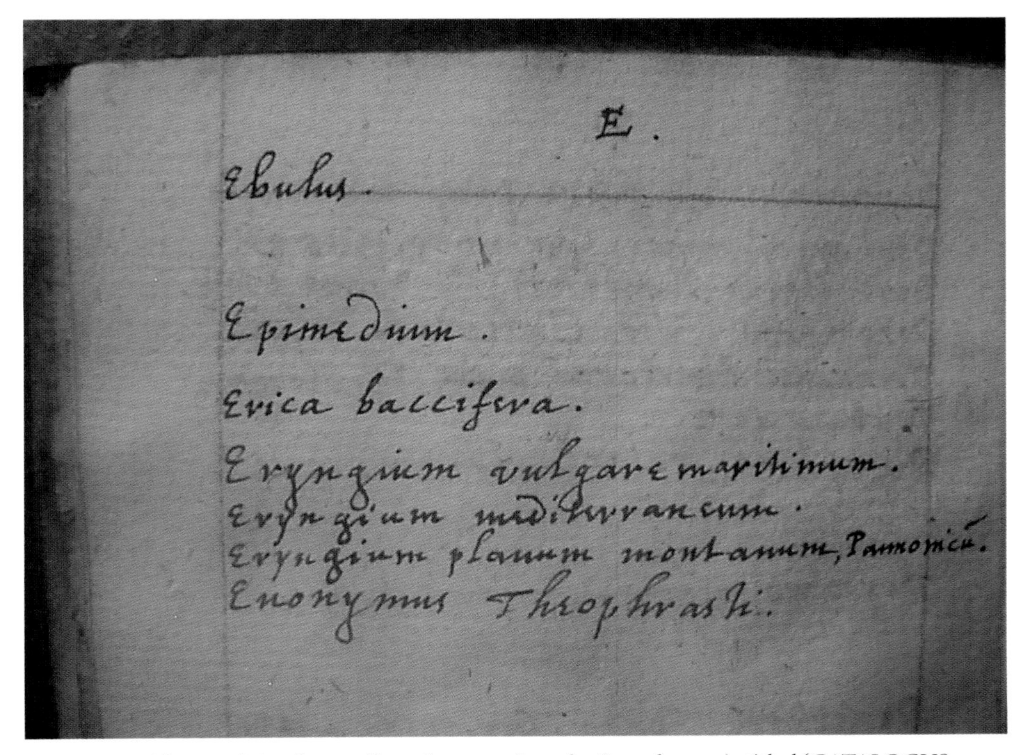

E.

Ebulus.

Epimedium.

Erica baccifera.

Eryngium vulgare maritimum.

Eryngium mediterraneum.

Eryngium planum montanum, Pannonicu.

Euonymus Theophrasti.

FIGURE 9 The surviving 'second' catalogue written by Stonehouse is titled 'CATALOGVS, Plantarum Horti mei Darfeldiae, Quibus is instructus est Anno Domini 1640'. Although not a professional hand, care has been taken to write as evenly as possible using ruled side-margins for straightness of lines. Depicted is Folio 19. *Courtesy the President and Fellows of Magdalen College, Oxford*

Sir John began by dividing the plants into alphabetical blocks, writing with the same style hand as Stonehouse, but with an ever-increasing collection and limited space the orderly appearance was notably lost (Figure 10).[74] Uneven spacing, ink blots and wandering lines reveal a rushed hand, possibly even written while in his gardens. The list shows all the changes that were occurring in his garden with additions and removals all recorded. Sir John's focus was in collecting all the plants recommended by Parkinson and not in the meticulous recording of botanical names like Stonehouse. When comparing their plant lists by alphabetical blocks this contrast is easily seen. Looking at the plants under the section 'B', one hundred percent of Reresby's plants were recommended by Parkinson; Stonehouse, although recording the same genera, had numerous varieties not listed by Parkinson (Table 5).

Although these records suggest that Reresby was more of an enthusiastic amateur rather than a knowledgeable botanist, his collection provides a valuable insight into the

[74] WYL 156-473, fol. 28.

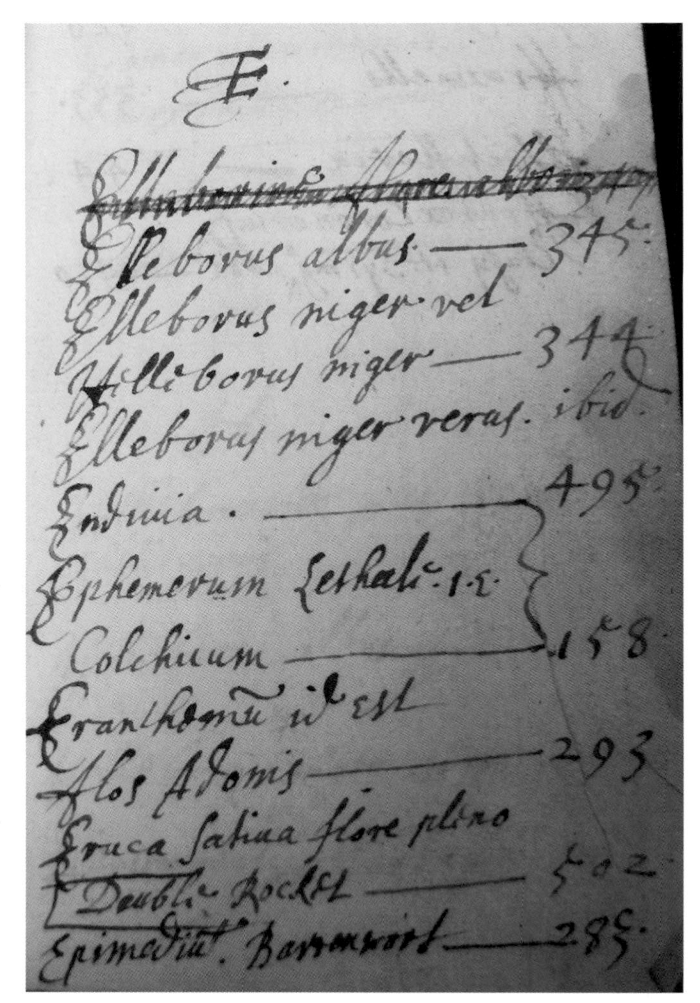

E.

Elleborus albus — 345.
Elleborus niger vel
Helleborus niger — 344.
Elleborus niger verus. ibid.
Endiuia. — 495.
Ephemerum Lethale. 1.5.
Colchicum — 158.
Eranthemu id est
Flos Adonis — 293
Eruca Satiua flore pleno
Double Rocket — 502.
Epimedium. Barrenwort — 285.

Figure 10 The writing of Sir John Reresby's plant catalogue 'Omnium stirpium que in horto neo continentur Thribergh', dated 11 April 1642, within the Garden Notebook, is in a firm hand, italic in style, and displays varied types of seventeenth-century abbreviations. Depicted is Folio 28. *Courtesy West Yorkshire Archive Service, Leeds*

availability of plants at that time. It also highlights the dedication of Sir John, a man with limited knowledge and means who during turbulent times was still determined to increase his plant collection. This can be summarised in the words of his son's description of him in 1668:

Sir John Reresby, my father, was exactly curious in his garden, and was one of the first that acquainted that part of England (so far north) with the exactness and nicety of those things – not only as to the form or contrivance of the ground, but as to excellency and variety of fruits, flowers, greens, in which he was rather extravagant than curious, for his pleasure not only innocently but pleasantly in it.[75]

[75] Cartwright, p. 78.

FIGURE 5 The Mausoleum, James Gibbs, 1739–40. *Photo: the author, 2008*

on Warburton's map[8] of 1720, the park is not shown. In Thomas Jefferys' atlas[9] of Yorkshire it is shown, located well to the south on the high ground beyond the village of Yearby (see Figure 2). This would appear to have been its position by the 1760s, and it may well have always been located there. There is also a hint in Knyff and Kip's view, for what appears to be a track that runs around the north part of this area may well have been meant to represent a park wall or pale. What Jefferys' surveyors also recorded in the park was a temple and an area of formal (?) water apparently to its front. Since Arthur Young[10] also mentions a temple in the park it would appear that it had appeared by this latter date: but who built it and when? There seems to be no evidence of its building amongst estate accounts held at the North Yorkshire County Record Office. According to Philo,[11] a rocky dell could also be found in the park with two pools where water cascaded from one to the other. This was known as Neptune's pool and was used to supply water to the village. The location and the connotations of the pools' name do not seem to align with Charles Turner's work on the estate later in the century: could this be part of Cholmley Turner's landscaping?

To return to Knyff and Kip's view – the village itself consists of straggling groups of low cottages along the road in a landscape that was to become further dominated by the Turner presence, since the Free School and the Mausoleum were yet to be added when the perspective was taken. But by the 1760s and 1770s, the village itself was to disappear under the improvements of Sir Charles Turner, the first baronet.

SIR CHARLES TURNER (1726–1783)

Charles Turner was the son of William and Jane Turner. William had succeeded to the estate on the death of Cholmley Turner in 1757, and although William himself did not die until 1774, it would appear from contemporary accounts such as Arthur Young's[12] that his son Charles was already running the estate by the 1760s. This may also be the explanation of both William's and Charles's names appearing against Kirkleatham on the Jefferys' map alluded to earlier. Charles had all the attributes associated with the son of a landed family of the eighteenth century: educated, he maintained an art collection at Kirkleatham Hall and had employed the architect John Carr; Turner was also an ardent sportsman, a local magistrate, an agricultural improver and became a Member of Parliament. It is the latter two callings in particular that formed and set in train his ideas about how the Kirkleatham estate should be managed and were ultimately to shape its surroundings. If previous generations of the Turners had already left the stamp of paternalistic and dynastic ambitions on the village, Charles Turner was to extend this, taking the work to the limits of his grounds.

Turner's changes at Kirkleatham and its surroundings cannot be fixed with precision, but there is good evidence of the years over which this took place. He commissioned the

[8] John Warburton, *A New and Correct Map of the County of York* (1720).

[9] Thomas Jefferys, *The County of York Surveyed in 1767, 1768, 1769, 1770* (London, 1775).

[10] Arthur Young, *A Six Month's Tour through the North of England*, 2nd edn, 4 vols (London, 1771), II, 112.

[11] Phil Philo, *Kirkleatham: A History of the Village, Estate and Old Hall Museum* (Kirkleatham: Langbaurgh on Tees Museum Service [n.d.]), p. 17.

[12] Young, II, 98–143.

architect John Carr, for example, to remodel the house in a gothic style. According to Wragg,[13] Carr appears in the Kirkleatham accounts from 1764 and particularly in 1766 and 1767. However, he was probably consulted slightly before this date, for the accounts for 1763 show that Carr had been paid £129 for 'work measured of[f]'.[14] Young was able to comment that the house was 'an excellent living house' which did 'great honour to the abilities of Mr Carr',[15] suggesting that it was completed when he visited the estate around 1769. Perhaps by this date also the formal gardens around the house had been remodelled either by Charles or his father. An estate plan of 1774 by Thomas Atkinson shows the house with open land or garden to the north and an area described as the 'Long Lawn' to the south.[16] This latter was bordered on its eastern side by a long pond with cascades. The plan is also interesting in that it depicts the area to the north of the house as containing castellated buildings. According to Wragg,[17] Carr continued to work for Turner until 1779–1780, the implication being that these constructions in the gardens may also be to Carr's designs. They survive in part and comprise angle bastions (Figure 6) connected perhaps to a length of wall; possibly another wall connected the latter to a rugged medieval gatehouse (Figure 7) across the approach to the house from the east to form a sort of quadrangular enclosure. This medievalising was given further effect by constructing a moat (Figure 8) between the bastions – all features that survived into the nineteenth century and were recorded on the Ordnance Survey six-inch sheet that was published in 1857.

What Atkinson's plan does not record is a further gothic building of some importance. This was the pigeon cote and consisted of a central tower with three satellite towers spaced equidistantly around it and connected to it by arcaded wing walls (Figure 9). This was located towards the far end of the Long Lawn and probably acted as an eye-catcher within the view of the south front of the house where an octagonal gothic temple was also built. This raises some further questions. Was the pigeon cote really intended as a pigeon cote, an unusual feature for an improving agriculturalist such as Turner, given the nuisance that such birds can be, or did it have some deeper significance? This building needs to be set within the context of Turner's other landscaping and the architecture he employed. All of this, as outlined above, was in a simple castellated gothic style, as was Turner's remodelling of Kirkleatham Hall itself. The underlying question that this raises, then, concerns gothic architecture and the meanings that it might hold in the eighteenth century.

The conceptualisation of 'gothic' in the eighteenth century is a complex one.[18] It ranges from terror, darkness and superstition, to traditions of constitutional democracy. The latter is a perhaps surprising notion, but it derives from widely held eighteenth-century views that the origins of England's democratic institutions could be found in

[13] Brian Wragg, *The Life and Works of John Carr of York*, ed. by Giles Worsley (York: Oblong, 2000), pp. 166–68.
[14] NYRO, Turner of Kirkleatham, ZK 6564 (account for 1763).
[15] Young, II, 98–99.
[16] Thomas Atkinson, *A Plan of the Manor and Parish of Kirkleatham*, NYRO, Turner of Kirkleatham, ZMI 71.
[17] Wragg, p. 168.
[18] For an introduction, though in a literary context, see Angela Wright, *Gothic Fiction* (London: Palgrave Macmillan, 2007).

FIGURE 6 Remains of the western bastion. *Photo: the author, 2008*

FIGURE 7 The gatehouse. *Photo: the author, 2008*

FIGURE 8 The remains of the moat and the eastern bastion

FIGURE 9 The pigeon cote, the Turner's Arms just visible in the background (undated, but before 1964). *Courtesy Kirkleatham Old Hall Museum*

Anglo-Saxon England and in particular in the Witan. The Witan, it was held, where king, bishops, eorls and theigns consulted and decided policy or law, was an ancestor of the constitutional settlement between monarch, Lords and Commons. It was, moreover, the Anglo-Saxon peoples who had liberated England from Roman oppression, although after 1066 they in turn were to suffer the yoke of Norman Conquest. However, this brought into play a further idea: that of liberty and liberation. This was inherent in the Anglo-Saxon character, and nowhere was this better displayed than in what were regarded as the iconic events associated with the signing of the Magna Carta by King John at Runnymede in 1215, and its reassertion in 1217 after the conclusion of the Barons' War. Magna Carta took on a significance out of all proportion to what it actually conferred, for it came to be seen as the guarantee of the liberties of every free-born Englishman.[19]

Gothic architecture might be associated with all of this. It can be observed in some Yorkshire landscape monuments where the political becomes known through inscriptions such as that on the ruined castle (now demolished) erected for Jeremiah Dixon of Leeds on Tunnel Howe Hill. It was dedicated to King Alfred and characterised him as a preserver of law and liberty. It also appears in more literary forms such as the series of verses that appear below a print of the gothic tower and ruins at Wimpole Hall, Cambridgeshire. There were probably several motives behind the construction of this ruin for the Earl of Hardwick, but one of them is clearly quite political judging from the verses that appear below a print of it issued in 1777 and which compare the zeal for liberty amongst medieval aristocrats with the perceived lack of concern of their counterparts in the eighteenth century, for while

> Freedom's cause once rais'd the civil broil,
> And Magna Charta clos'd the glorious toil

today:

> Spruce modern Villas different Scenes afford;
> The Patriot Baronet, the courtier Lord,
> Gently amused, now waste the Summers day
> In Book-room, Print-room, or in Ferme ornée[20]

– the implication being that ardour for a liberty hard-won, had become dulled by the distractions of modern living and the careless attitude of contemporary aristocracy.

While it may be easy to see the association between gothic architecture and events at the beginning of the thirteenth century when such architecture was developing, the case seems less easy to make for the Anglo-Saxon period – until one realises that to many in the eighteenth century the Anglo-Saxons were seen as the progenitors of gothic architecture. While very few Anglo-Saxon structures had survived, yet, as Batty Langley argued in his influential pattern book of gothic designs, it was reasonable to suppose that the gothic architecture of the Middle Ages was 'taken from Fragments found among Saxon

[19] For a thorough discussion of these ideas and their development see: R. J. Smith, *The Gothic Bequest: Medieval Institutions and British Thought, 1688–1863* (Cambridge: Cambridge University Press, 1987).
[20] See Gervase Jackson-Stops, *An English Arcadia 1600–1990* (London: National Trust, 1992), pp. 86–89.

Ruins'; furthermore he would have that style of architecture denominated Saxon rather than gothic, but for the latter term having gained popular currency.[21]

While the foregoing is a rather compressed account of political beliefs and their association with eighteenth-century architecture, such ideas were under discussion among contemporaries. These views informed the political discourse of men such as Henry St John, Viscount Bolingbroke, accorded with the social and economic thought of some of the Scottish enlightenment writers such as Adam Ferguson, or, as we have seen, appeared in less well-articulated forms to support the architectural writing of men such as Langley. If other philosophers and politicians such as Hume or Burke took a rather more rigorous view of the Middle Ages, they were ready to accept Magna Carta as a warrant of English liberty. Whatever view was formed of the Middle Ages, gothic theory was, nevertheless, important in seventeenth- and eighteenth-century England in giving legitimacy to a democratic constitution and civil law, the model of the Witan or Magna Carta represented as historical traditions or events that would aid this end.

The Kirkleatham landscape as remodelled by Charles Turner should be read with the above politicisation of the gothic in mind, and Turner had decided political views. This is perhaps not surprising given that he came from a politically active family. Sir William Turner, as we have seen above, was caught up in London politics in the seventeenth century. As an alderman of London he was removed from office for refusing to support James II and did not return until after the Revolution of 1688. He became a Tory Member of Parliament for the City of London in 1690, yet was an unorthodox and independently minded Tory, supporting the interests of commerce rather than country.[22] Cholmley Turner had represented Northallerton between 1715 and 1722, and then Yorkshire from 1727 to 1747. He stood as a Whig and supported the Hanoverian succession.[23]

Charles Turner became MP for York in 1768 and represented that city until the year of his death in 1783. This was a calling that he had keenly pursued for a number of years. As Lord Fitzwilliam wrote to his mother on Turner's success in 1768, 'Charles Turner must be delighted with being at last in Parliament, it has long been the object of all his wishes, and he esteems it a greater honour to be a Member of a British Parliament than to be the Grand Monarque.'[24] He stood with the support of the Rockingham Whigs and often voted with them, yet he declared himself an independent and would not join the York Rockingham Club because of what he considered aristocratical interference and told Rockingham so.

This episode gives some idea of Turner's principles, which accorded more with radical Whiggism than Rockinghamite opposition. Turner supported parliamentary reform and annual parliaments; was against clerical intrusion in politics and spoke against the Sabbath Bill in 1781; he was against pressing and an opponent of the war in America. Sir Nathaniel Wraxall, a contemporary political diarist and commentator, regarded Turner

[21] Batty and Thomas Langley, *Ancient Architecture Restored and Improved in the Gothick Mode* (London, 1742), 'Dissertation' [no pagination].

[22] Cruickshanks et al., *House of Commons*, v, 708–09.

[23] Romney Sedgwick, *The House of Commons 1715–1754*, 2 vols (London: HMSO, 1970), II, 487.

[24] Quoted in *The House of Commons 1754–1790*, ed. by Sir Lewis Namier and John Brooke, 3 vols (London: HMSO, 1964), III, 568.

FIGURE 10 Kirkleatham Hall taken from an engraving in Ord's *History and Antiquities of Cleveland* (1846)

as an eccentric, but acknowledged his 'love of liberty and detestation of encroachment on the comforts, pleasures, or enjoyments of his fellow subjects',[25] a principle that even led him to speak against the game laws. Wraxall also recognised Turner as a man of 'benevolence, probity, philanthropy and general humanity'.[26] In a debate on electoral reform in 1782 Turner summed up his political position as wishing 'the constitution to be so established that no administration, however bad, may be able to convert it to the injury of the people'.[27] In other words he was an upholder of personal freedoms and a defender of liberty. This comes across strongly in the speech quoted in Ord of which the following extract gives the flavour:

Corruption and tyranny can never stand against the virtuous efforts of a free people. Be firm, be zealous, be unanimous, assert your birthright – annual parliaments and an equal representation – a privilege inherent in the constitution [...] with spirit and resolution insist upon your privileges, and I will meet you at Runnymede. I love the poor; I have divided my fortune with them. The poor man's labour is the rich man's wealth; and without your toil the kingdom is worth nothing. While I am free, you shall never be slaves.[28]

[25] *The Historical and Posthumous Memoirs of Sir Nathaniel William Wraxall, 1772–1784*, ed. by Henry B. Wheatley, 5 vols (London, 1884) II, 268.
[26] Ibid., 269.
[27] Ibid., 305.
[28] Ord, pp. 377–78.

The landscape and architecture of Kirkleatham need to be interpreted in the light of such principles. While the changes that Turner brought to the landscape were an embellishment of the grounds around his house, they also served as an introduction to the estate along the road from the east, which in Turner's day passed through fields; next the visitor would pass beneath a medieval-looking gatehouse before arriving at the house, itself rebuilt from an early classical design to one of castellated gothic, the whole of the lawned areas being protected by bastions. Yet the house retained a classical entrance portico and largely classical interiors despite hood moulds, pointed arches and tower-like wings to the exterior (Figure 10). It was the gothic brought up to date to provide what Young considered that 'excellent living house, in which the agreeable part of convenience is consulted'.[29] That is, a living house as opposed to a show house; not built for the glory of its owner, but as the house of an English gentleman and convenient for his family. And it was one where the architectural principles of republican Rome met the architectural traditions of the Middle Ages and all that was associated with them.

The works in the gardens round about must be seen in this light also, for they were not separate items added on a whim, but, I would contend, represented that imagined spirit of Old England and the defence of liberty. If this line of argument is accepted then the pigeon cote becomes susceptible of a similar interpretation. While it was certainly an eye-catcher and may have been a pigeon cote, it seems also to have held other meanings: could the central tower standing firm and higher than the others represent that spirit of resistance and the defence of rights? The attached towers perhaps represent the three kingdoms (England and Wales, Ireland, Scotland) united around this ideal; or could this tripartite configuration represent the constitutional settlement following the Revolution of 1688 – monarch, Lords and Commons, a guarantee of civil democratic government?

Turner's views on democracy and government may have been no more than the extreme end of Whig ideals, yet even so they were unusual in their day. To have expressed them in the landscape of Kirkleatham – if that is what his landscaping represents – also gives evidence of how deeply he held such convictions. But it would be a mistake to think that Turner was a socialist before his time. On the contrary, despite his statements concerning parliament's following the people's wishes, concerns about the nobility and monarchical meddling in politics, or declarations about the relationship between labour and capital, it is also clear that he believed that the political and moral lead should be taken by the aristocracy. This becomes evident when we consider the other important contribution made to the Kirkleatham landscape by Turner: his agricultural improvements.

It is uncertain when the first phases of agricultural improvement occurred at Kirkleatham in terms of the enclosure of its open fields, but it can have been no later than 1774, since the Kirkleatham estate plan[30] shows the area completely enclosed by that date. Furthermore the view of the village by Knyff and Kip suggests that there were already some enclosed fields by 1707. In addition to this, much of nearby Coatham's open fields

[29] Young, II, 98.
[30] NYRO, Turner of Kirkleatham, ZMI 71.

and part of its commons were enclosed in the mid-eighteenth century,[31] which may have been a later stage of improvement. Whatever the precise date of enclosure, the big agricultural changes of the eighteenth century came about under Charles Turner. The principal evidence concerning this comes from Young's Tour, in which he devotes a good deal of space to Kirkleatham (fifty-seven pages). Turner experimented with soil fertility, cropping, and improvements in the breeding of cattle, while at the same time encouraging his tenants to follow his example. Young says he had consolidated their holdings (by enclosure?) and had rebuilt farms and outbuildings.[32] But while such agricultural activity led in itself to a re-ordering of the landscape, further changes were to take place, for there is a yet more intricate meaning that improvement assumed in the eighteenth century. As Nigel Everett has commented in analysing such developments:

In the landscape of benevolence the gentleman occupies an estate where resources are used to stimulate morality as much as prosperity. He seeks to realize the underlying harmony of a nature valued for its variety and instructive analogies rather than merely exploited for use or made subject to the desire for display.[33]

Turner's improvements had such moral implications, also, and these in turn had further spatial consequences for the landscape and the way it was peopled. The enclosure and consolidation of strips and the reconstruction of farms is one, but another was the almost entire removal of the village. Again Young supplies the details,[34] for according to him, the village cottages were 'wretched hovels' which were taken down and their occupants transferred to newly built accommodation at nearby Yearby. But this was not the end of it, for the 'neighbourhood was much pestered with a collection of little blackguard alehouses, which not only encouraged idleness and drunkenness among the villagers, but were constant receptacles of smugglers'.[35] These Turner had closed (his position as a justice must have helped) and he replaced them with two inns: one on the coast at Coatham and the Turner's Arms near to Yearby, a gothic design that harmonised with other of his gothic work in the landscape and around the house. A further aspect was ensuring a sufficient supply of labour, which Turner did by taking boys from the foundling hospital at Ackworth whom he apprenticed to his tenants. In addition, while other local gentlemen and vestry officials were keen to eject the poor from their parishes, Turner allowed them to reside at Kirkleatham and put them to work, but:

the idle strolling part of the poor that can work, but will not, he has as little mercy on; but is sure to punish them in such a manner as the law allows in his acting capacity as a justice of the peace.[36]

To accommodate this increase in population further cottages were built, according to Young, although one should be wary of this statement, since neither Yearby nor Coatham

[31] Barbara English, *Yorkshire Enclosure Awards* (Hull: University of Hull, 1985), p. 34.
[32] Young, II, 99.
[33] Nigel Everett, *The Tory View of Landscape* (New York: Yale University Press, 1994), p. 21.
[34] Young, II, 100–01.
[35] Ibid., 101–02.
[36] Ibid., 129–30.

seems to have grown much during Charles Turner's management of the estate, suggesting that no very great numbers were attracted to these places. Nevertheless, by the 1770s changes had taken place at Kirkleatham, and its appearance had altered. The landscape had now become entirely enclosed to the north, east and west between Kirkleatham and Coatham, the 1774 estate plan alluded to above recording numerous small enclosed fields, and the village itself had all but disappeared with Turner's tenants re-housed as discussed above. This left Kirkleatham 'village' as a sort of monument to the Turner dynasty and their paternalistic project.

Picture a traveller passing through this spot in the 1770s. He or she would have first encountered the baroque Free School, by this date no longer a school, but a library and museum; next would come Sir William Turner's Hospital; a short distance away was the church and the Turner Mausoleum, and across from this Charles Turner's new country house – and very little else for, apart from the vicarage and some cottages for the gardening staff, there was little left of the former village. Should the traveller wish to journey on toward the sea, then Turner's Lobster Pot Inn at Coatham could provide accommodation; on the other hand, if the traveller's journey were south towards Guisborough, then the Turner's Arms provided a further place of residence for the night. All seems overwhelmingly paternalistic, all behaviour readily under surveillance and the Turner presence everywhere.

This is certainly one view, and it tends to indicate how the interests of an individual could impose an ideal, a means of obtaining social and moral order, over the beliefs of others. Yet in adopting this position, could it also be that one misses some of the optimism in such schemes? Certainly some contemporaries and near contemporaries such as Graves, read this as an enlightened landscape reflecting a paternalism that extended a more tolerable means of living to tenants or labourers while attempting to improve social and moral conditions. Young was of this mind, and standing in the temple in the park above Yearby gave a synoptic account of these ideas in describing the prospect before him:

> From the temple, upon the hill in the park, is a most noble prospect of the country around these edifices; you look down upon them in the midst of a fine extensive vale intersected with enclosures, and bounded by the sea and the river Tees; the higher lands of Durham filling the distant view: The new farmhouses raised by Mr. Turner, render the prospect neatly pleasing.[37]

There are further implications to be taken into account also. One might characterise Turner's landscaping as motivated by ideas about British liberty and a monument to the continuity of the Turner line, yet this was as much a landscape of improvement and benevolence. It was achieved through the creation of an agricultural landscape which promised plenty both through the application of rational techniques of farming and through unceasing labour. In this respect it might almost be seen as a georgic vision of landscape, and, given the broader political issues which were incorporated into this vision, one might even say Virgilian. If this seems fanciful, yet the writings of Virgil or

[37] Ibid., 112.

the Roman agriculturalists could be found on many a gentleman's bookshelves,[38] and georgic notions of the countryside as a place of beauty, yet a place maintained by farming and the hard work that this involved, aligned well with paternalistic ideologies of dependence.

Turner fitted this mould and was portrayed in this way by at least one contemporary and neighbour, John Hall of Skelton Castle, who in his poem 'A Cleveland Prospect' alludes to Turner in language that represents him as a latter day Cincinnatus, the general of Roman myth-history, who was persuaded to leave the retirement of his farm to save Rome from the onslaught of the Sabines and who returned to the rural life after completing this.

> Observe, – nor let those stately piles below,
> Nor *Turner's* princely realms unnoticed go;
> Forc'd, like Rome's consul, with reluctant brow,
> To leave his oxen, cabbages, and plough.[39]

Charles Turner died in 1783, a year after receiving a baronetcy from the Rockingham administration. His son, Sir Charles, was the last of the male line of the Turners, and the estate passed during the nineteenth century to the Vansittarts and the Newcomens.

Today, while some of the major works remain, such as the Free School, Hospital and Mausoleum, others have been demolished: most seriously the house, the garden temple and the pigeon cote; the temple in the park seems to have disappeared some time ago, whilst the park itself is agricultural land. If it is still possible to glimpse something of the view that Young described while standing in the park in 1769, the remnants of this eighteenth-century landscape of benevolent improvement now take second place to the urban-industrial growth of twentieth-century Middlesbrough and refineries along the Tees in which they have become ossified and isolated relics.

[38] Joan Thirsk, 'Sixteenth-Century Agriculture and the Classical Tradition', in *Culture and Cultivation in Early Modern England*, ed. by Michael Lesley and Timothy Raylor (Leicester: Leicester University Press, 1992), pp. 15–34.

[39] Re-printed in Graves, pp. 36–37.

Jacobite Patronage: Lord Strafford, James Gibbs, Wentworth Castle, and the Politics of Dissent

PATRICK EYRES

The fashionable architect, James Gibbs, was a Scot and secretly both a Jacobite and Catholic. Who better to be commissioned by the deposed Tory minister and Jacobite conspirator, Lord Strafford? It has long been known that in 1724 Gibbs designed Strafford's Long Gallery at Stainborough Hall, outside Barnsley in south Yorkshire.[1] This epic space runs the length of the first two floors of the 180-foot-long baroque palace that was erected between 1709 and 1714 as the east wing of an earlier house (Figure 1). Just as the new mansion and gardens neared completion in 1731, the place was renamed Wentworth Castle to emphasise the dynastic status of Thomas Wentworth, first Earl of Strafford (second creation, 1672–1739). However, as this paper demonstrates, it is now emerging that James Gibbs (1682–1754) was involved at Wentworth Castle from 1717 into the mid-1730s, and that he designed much of the mansion's interior as well as Strafford's garden buildings. Moreover, by designing the mock-mediaeval Stainborough Castle for the summit of the estate (Figures 1 and 2), Gibbs not only created the pioneering genre of garden building that I shall refer to as Saxon Gothic,[2] but also coded it as a Jacobite symbol. He subsequently developed the genre for members of the alliance between Tories and dissident Whigs that formed the parliamentary opposition to the Whig government of Sir Robert Walpole. This discussion will consider Gibbs's Jacobite symbolism at Wentworth Castle as well as his Saxon Gothic garden buildings at Hartwell and Stowe in Buckinghamshire.

The Jacobite defeat at Culloden in 1746 confirmed that the Whig party had backed the Hanoverian winner in the battle for the British crown. Consequently the inheritors of

[1] The Strafford Papers, British Library, London, Additional Manuscripts (hereafter Add. MSS), record that Gibbs's joiner, Charles Griffith, was contracted 'to wainscout ye Gallery at Stainebourough as Desined by Mr Gibbs', 28 July 1724, Add. MSS, 22, 239, fol. 128.

[2] Michael Charlesworth established the Saxon-ness of Stainborough Castle in the *New Arcadian Journal* (hereafter *NAJ*); see 'Elevation and Succession: The Representations of Jacobite and Hanoverian Politics in the Landscape Gardens of Wentworth Castle and Wentworth Woodhouse', no. 31/32 (1991), 7–65, and 'Thomas Wentworth's Monument: The Achievement of Peace', no. 57/58 (2005), 31–63 (reprinted in no. 63/64 (2008), 49–79). Richard Wheeler uses the term Saxon Gothic to describe Gibbs's gothic buildings at Hartwell and Stowe; see Wheeler, 'Prince Frederick and Liberty: The Gardens of Hartwell House, Buckinghamshire, in the Mid-Eighteenth Century', *Garden History*, 34.1 (2006), 80–91, and also Wheeler, 'The Role of Garden Statuary in the Eighteenth Century as exemplified by the Garden of Sir Thomas and Sir William Lee at Hartwell', in *Talking Heads: Garden Statuary in the Eighteenth Century* (Aylesbury: Buckinghamshire Gardens Trust, 2007), pp. 7–14.

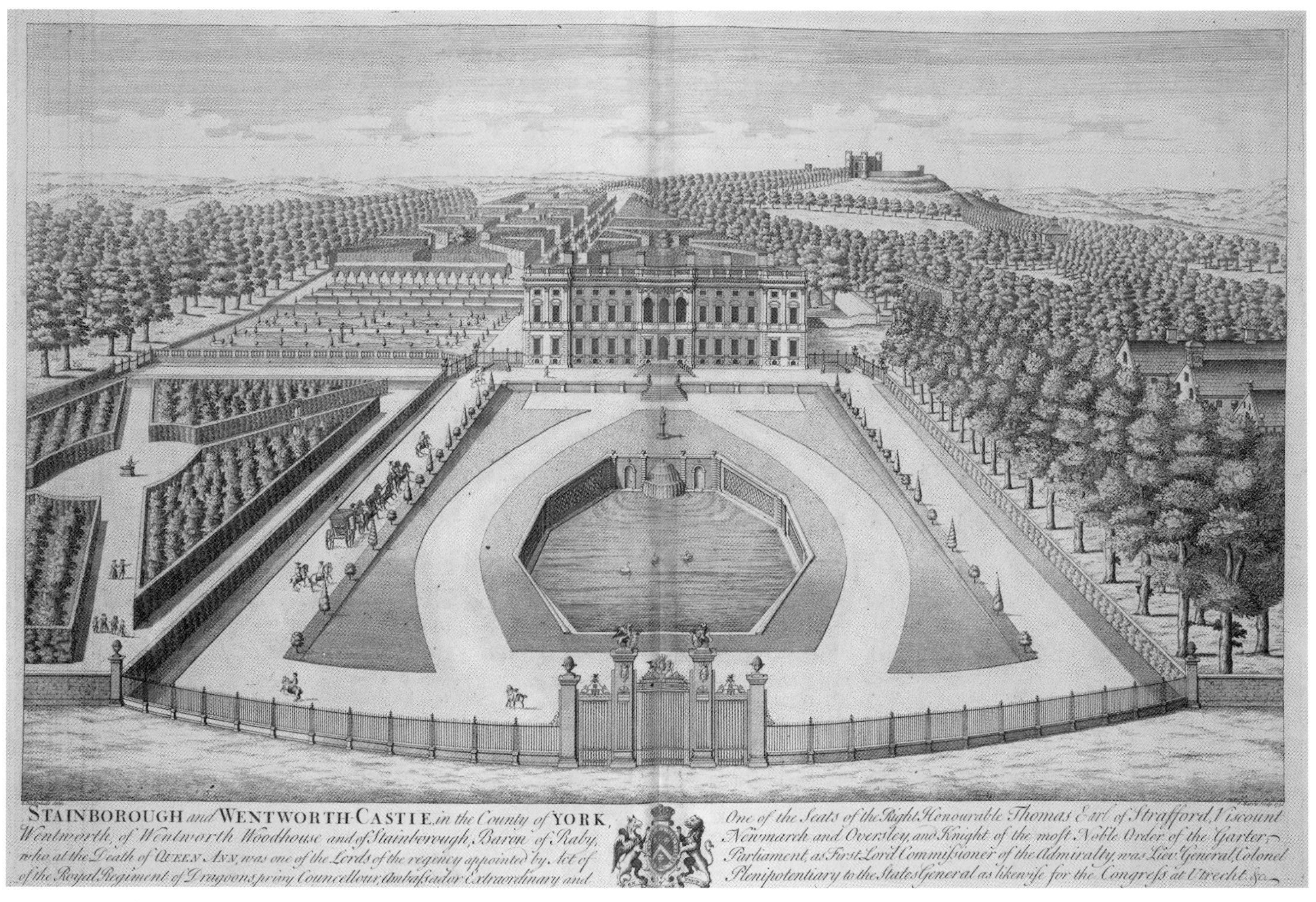

FIGURE 1 Thomas Badeslade and John Harris, *Stainborough and Wentworth Castle*, engraving, 1730 (from the east). *Wentworth Castle Heritage Trust*

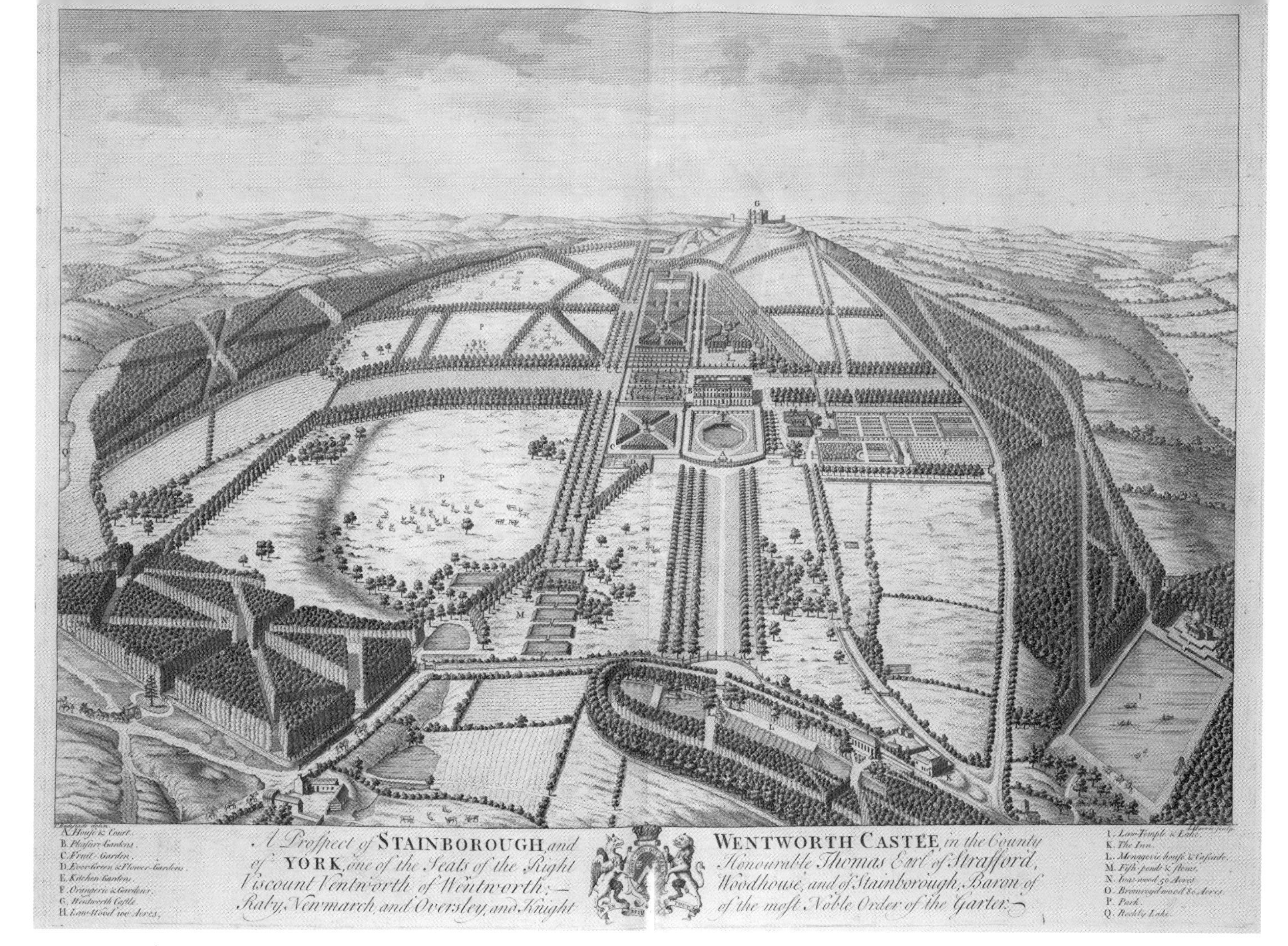

FIGURE 2 Thomas Badeslade and John Harris, *A Prospect of Stainborough and Wentworth Castle*, engraving, *c.* 1730.
Wentworth Castle Heritage Trust

Jacobite estates would adroitly invest in the political correctness of removing any symbolism that might suggest an embarrassing affiliation. This process of self-censorship has contributed to the perception that early Georgian political gardening was a Whig phenomenon, and it has rarely been considered from a Tory, let alone Jacobite, perspective.[3] However, we are fortunate that the inheritors of Wentworth Castle failed to remove Strafford's politically incorrect Jacobite symbolism. As a result Wentworth Castle provides a splendid case study of country house building and landscape gardening by those marginalised in politically volatile and uncertain times.[4] Please note that although Thomas Wentworth did not acquire his earldom until 1711 he will be referred to as Strafford throughout.

Before discussing the mansion and gardens it is useful to consider the crises in the royal succession that enabled the Whig party to monopolise government from 1714 to 1760. These years are referred to as the Whig Ascendency and the phenomenon is usually explained by the preference of Kings George I and II for their north German electorate of Hanover rather than their island kingdom of Britain. Nonetheless the term is also a good example of the way that history is written by the victors. The Whigs held power for so long because they had used their initial parliamentary majority to neuter opposition by proscribing Tories from all public offices, whether civil, ecclesiastical or military. Moreover, by 1746 the Whig-backed Hanoverian monarchy had triumphed in the thirty-two-year struggle against the rival and Tory-favoured claim to the throne from the exiled Stuart King James III. The terms Whig and Tory had been coined during 1679–81 to describe the opposing sides in parliament: those who favoured a Protestant constitutional monarchy were branded as Whigs, after the name of certain fanatical Scots Covenanters; and those who preferred the existing hierarchy of king, Anglican Church and parliament were dubbed Tories, after the extremist and eponymous Irish Catholic rebels.

Matters came to a head in 1688 when the Catholic Stuart King, James II, was exiled through the Glorious Revolution in favour of establishing a Protestant constitutional monarchy. Jacobite became the term used for supporters of the Catholic Stuart claim because both the exiled King and his male heir were named James: in Latin, *Jacobus*. James II's Protestant Stuart daughters succeeded as Queen Mary II, consort of the Dutch Prince of Orange who was imported to become King William III, followed by Queen Anne. As all of Anne's children had predeceased her, it seemed natural to Jacobites that on her death in 1714 the Queen's younger half-brother would succeed her as James III. However, he had proved to be as resolutely Catholic as his father and, to ensure the Protestant Succession, parliament had arranged that the Elector of Hanover would be imported as King George I. Thus the nation's loyalties were divided for over thirty years. Although known to Hanoverians as The Pretender, his Jacobite designation of King

[3] While Nigel Everett's *The Tory View of Landscape* (New Haven & London: Yale University Press, 1994) usefully concentrates on the later eighteenth and early nineteenth centuries, a welcome discussion of Tory and Whig gardening in the early Georgian era is provided by Tim Richardson's *The Arcadian Friends: Inventing the English Landscape Garden* (London: Bantam Press, 2007).

[4] This paper complements the extensive discussion of the politics and iconography of Strafford's mansion, garden and park in *The Georgian Landscape of Wentworth Castle: New Arcadian Journal*, no. 63/64 (2008), hereafter *Wentworth Castle NAJ* 63/64; see the chapters by Patrick Eyres, Michael Charlesworth, Jan Woudstra, Christopher Margrave, Jane Furse and Wendy Frith.

James III will be used herein. Jacobite efforts to restore the Stuarts would generate numerous plots and four armed insurgencies, of which the 1715 and the 1745 are the most familiar. It was not until the defeat of James's son, Prince Charles Edward (a.k.a. Bonnie Prince Charlie), on the battlefield of Culloden in 1746 that the Stuart cause was irrevocably vanquished and Hanoverian security guaranteed. Consequently, the anti-Hanoverian political and social turbulence of the first half of the eighteenth century tends to be overlooked.

As a pragmatic career soldier, Strafford had eschewed affiliation to either Whigs or Tories. He had fought as a cavalry officer in the campaigns of William III against the Jacobites in Scotland and Ireland (1689–91) and against the armies of Louis XIV in Flanders (1692–97). On the outbreak of the War of Spanish Succession in 1702, he fought alongside the Duke of Marlborough and was promoted to Major-General in 1704 and Lieutenant-General in 1707. However, by dedicating himself to the quest for peace, Strafford became a key player both in British politics and European diplomacy. After eight years of war, the Tory agenda for peace won a landslide victory in the 1710 general election, and in 1711 Strafford accepted the posts of ambassador to the Dutch government in The Hague and joint British negotiator at the peace conference convened at Utrecht. It was also in 1711 that he became a privy councillor and managed to acquire the revived title, Earl of Strafford. In 1713 the Peace of Utrecht was ratified by parliament; Strafford was appointed First Lord of the Admiralty and inaugurated as a Knight of the Garter. Yet, on the premature death of Queen Anne in 1714, his political career evaporated.

The triumphantly elected Whig parliament began to purge the Tories through proscription from public office and, especially after defeat of the Scottish insurgency in 1715, demonised all Tories as treacherous Jacobites. To make matters worse, the new King, George I, was displeased with the peace negotiator because Hanover was among the allies excluded from the Tories' unilateral treaty, and was thus obliged to negotiate a separate concordat with France. Moreover the Whigs excoriated the treaty as contrary to the national interest and, also in 1715, the government began proceedings to impeach the principal Tories responsible for the peace: Bolingbroke and Ormonde fled abroad, Strafford and Oxford were arrested. Yet in 1717 proceedings against them were dropped. Although he survived this brutal assault, Strafford was so alienated that by 1717 he had switched his allegiance to the Jacobite cause of the exiled King, James III, and began to work actively towards restoration of the Stuart monarchy.

THE SYMBOLISM OF THE INTERIOR DECORATION AT WENTWORTH CASTLE

It was also in 1717 that his cousin, Lord Bathurst, acknowledged Strafford's determination to make the Yorkshire estate his monument.[5] Even though a political exile, Strafford was very well aware that his dynastic elevation and diplomatic triumph had been achieved under the auspices of the Stuart Queen Anne. As a deposed Tory minister, he was concerned to assert both the status of his dynasty and his role as the Queen's peacemaker. As

[5] Bathurst, letter to Strafford, 31 August 1717: 'since ye design'd itt for y^r^ monumen^t^'; Add. MSS, 31, 141, fol. 194.

a Jacobite conspirator, he would also encode his Stuart allegiance in the fabric of his mansion, gardens and park. It is becoming clear to the author that it was the architect, James Gibbs, who created the iconography of Strafford's monument. Paradoxically both fashionable and a Jacobite, Gibbs was just the man for Strafford; equally, Strafford was representative of the Tory and Jacobite patronage network enjoyed by Gibbs. It is not difficult to appreciate that the political affiliation of patron and architect had a significant bearing on their approach to the design of interiors and garden buildings. However, to be a Jacobite in Hanoverian Britain was a clandestine, treasonous activity and the symbolic references to this at Wentworth Castle are appropriately discreet. In order to excavate the visual clues of their shared allegiance, we must first consider the way that Gibbs embellished Strafford's baroque palace.

Strafford had been ambitious to revive the earldom that became extinct when the second Earl of Strafford died in 1695. Unexpectedly the Earl's legacy of the ancestral seat at Wentworth Woodhouse was not passed on to him, but to his cousin. Thus Strafford had also been motivated by the desire to eclipse this rival branch of the family through superior status as well as the conspicuous display of mansion building and landscape gardening.[6] A country estate was regarded as the prerequisite for social elevation into the aristocracy, and Strafford managed to buy the neighbouring Stainborough estate in 1708. He also chose to befit his status as British ambassador to Berlin (appointed 1706) by commissioning the design of his country mansion from the Prussian court architect, Jean Bodt (a.k.a. Johannes Bodt).[7] However the new mansion was not built exactly to Bodt's design. Strafford was at the height of his power during 1711–14, and it should not be surprising that he obtained the services of an eminent British architect to undertake modifications. Thomas Archer is favoured on stylistic grounds by architectural historians,[8] and is the only professional architect that Strafford records as offering advice.[9] Erected between 1709 and 1714 under the supervision of Edward Reeves, the building was then illustrated in Colen Campbell's prestigious *Vitruvius Britannicus* (1715).[10] Needless to say interior decoration was delayed by the tumultuous political upheaval of 1714–17. By the time work began in 1717 Thomas Archer had retired and to modify Bodt's design Strafford had turned to the fashionable architect and fellow Jacobite, James Gibbs. Hence

[6] See Patrick Eyres, 'The Rivalry between Wentworth Castle and Wentworth Woodhouse, 1695–1750', *Wentworth Castle NAJ*, 63/64, 15–47. In 1695 Wentworth had inherited the title, Lord Raby, and was known as such until he acquired the earldom in 1711.

[7] Michael Charlesworth notes that Jean Bodt and 'Monsieur Eosander' were both architects to the Prussian Court in Berlin and collaborated over the design of Stainborough Hall; see 'Thomas Wentworth's Monument: The Achievement of Peace', *Wentworth Castle NAJ*, 63/64, 49–79 (p. 53).

[8] See John Harris and Nikolaus Pevsner in *Architectural Review*, 130.773 (July 1961), 34–35; James Lees-Milne, *English Country Houses: Baroque 1685–1715* (London: Country Life Books, 1970), pp. 236–42; Marcus Whiffen, *Thomas Archer: Architect of the English Baroque* (Los Angeles: Hennessy & Ingalls, 1973), pp. 14–17, 54, 79; and Whiffen, *Thomas Archer* (London: Art and Technics, 1950), pp. 15–17.

[9] Strafford, letter to Archer, 17 April 1714; Add. MSS, 31, 141, fol. 150.

[10] The revised elevation is also shown in the Kip and Knyff overviews (1711 and 1714) and the Holzendorf print (1713). An extra bay was added at each end of the building, all the window surrounds were altered and the roof was concealed with a balustrade; in particular, the first storey's central windows were enlarged in height and width and curved at the top to complement the new segmental arches of the pediments above all the twelve flanking windows, which created a lively rhythm along the façade of the widened, fifteen-bay elevation.

the 1724 contract for the Long Gallery would mark yet another phase in the on-going programme of embellishment.

As the architect patronised by the Tory elite, the Whig putsch of 1714–17 had jeopardised Gibbs's career. He was tainted by the patronage of at least three of Strafford's government colleagues: Lords Bingley, Mar and Oxford. Nonetheless he also enjoyed the cachet of being the first British architect to be professionally trained in Rome (1704–08) and he provided a distinctive interpretation of antique and contemporary Roman architecture that appealed to the Whig magnates who ran Hanoverian Britain. Thus, against the odds, he became fashionable. One of Gibbs's most significant Whig patrons was John Campbell, second Duke of Argyll. Gibbs had begun work on Argyll's Surrey villa, Sudbrook House, on the very eve of the Battle of Sheriffmuir in November 1715. Here Argyll, commanding government troops, confronted the Jacobite army raised by the deposed Tory minister and Gibbs's chief patron, Lord Mar. Through his victory, Argyll secured the Hanoverian succession. As it was doubtless Argyll who had dissuaded the architect from joining Mar's army in Scotland, he also saved Gibbs's career. Later, while Master of the Ordnance in 1727, Argyll obtained for Gibbs his only official sinecure, the government post of Architect of the Ordnance. Thus in 1728, Gibbs appreciatively dedicated his *Book of Architecture* to Argyll. The Duke also enjoyed a longstanding friendship with Strafford, which had originated during their military service, and it is likely that it was Argyll who recommended Gibbs to Strafford.[11] Nonetheless Strafford would also have witnessed the architect's embellishment of a property adjacent to his own in Twickenham.[12] Between 1716 and 1721 Gibbs had augmented the new house of fellow Scot and retired politician, James Johnston, with an octagonal garden pavilion (now the Orleans House Gallery) which was immediately hailed as a triumph of architectural and interior design.

At Wentworth Castle Gibbs addressed the entire interior, operating as the design coordinator who provided ideas as well as craftsmen and artists,[13] for example: the joiner

[11] The relationship between the two soldiers was so close that Strafford's son William would marry Argyll's daughter Anne. Indeed in 1744 William would dedicate the Argyll Column at Wentworth Castle to the posthumous memory of his father-in-law. For the Argyll Column, see Jane Furse, 'The Gothick and Picturesque Landscape of William Wentworth', 115–43 (pp. 116–18), and Wendy Frith, 'Sappho and the Speckled Monster: Lady Mary Wortley Montagu, Smallpox Inoculation and Eighteenth Century Bodies', 145–70 (pp. 150–52), *Wentworth Castle NAJ*, 63/64.

[12] Strafford had a London town house and a retreat up the Thames at Twickenham. In 1699 he had bought a house on Twickenham Common (later called Gifford Lodge), but in 1701 moved to another on the riverside, later known as Mount Lebanon; see 'Isabella Lady Wentworth', <http://www.twickenham-museum.org.uk> [accessed 9 September 2008]. He also had estates in Northamptonshire and Suffolk.

[13] William Thornton, the York builder-joiner, and his men fitted the windows and floors throughout the building. He may have supervised the interior work until his death in 1721. The doorcases and mural woodwork of the South or Queen Anne suite of ground floor rooms bear the hallmarks of Thornton's work at Beningborough, and especially that of his associate, the York carver Daniel Harvey. Thornton had been consulted in 1714 about the windows and glass: letters to Strafford, Add. MSS, 22, 238, fol. 10, 28 March; fols 145–46, 20 April; fol. 150, 5 May; fol. 165, undated (August); fol. 169, 14 September. Arnold (head gardener), letter to Strafford, 16 June 1717; Add. MSS, 22, 239, fols 28–29: 'Mr Thorton [*sic*] is here and 7 or 8 men at worke.' Strafford's account (1716–31), Child's Bank (Royal Bank of Scotland Group Archives), payments to William Thornton: 23 November 1716, 23 September and 10 December 1718, CH/194/13, fol. 303. I am grateful to Jane Furse for drawing my attention to this archive.

Charles Griffith,[14] the stuccoist Francesco Vassalli,[15] the artist Giacomo Amiconi,[16] and the builder-joiner Edward Reeves, along with their assistants.[17] By September 1724 an anonymous visitor found the ground floor rooms and the Long Gallery finished,[18] while in 1725 Strafford's cousin Bathurst wrote appreciatively of the gallery's magnificence.[19]

[14] Charles Griffith signed the 1724 contract that acknowledges Gibbs as the designer of the Long Gallery. He was involved as early as 1718 and through to *c.* 1730, simultaneously working for Gibbs on the interiors of Johnston's Octagon and St Martin-in-the-Fields (1716–21, 1722–29). Strafford's account (1716–31), Child's Bank, payments to Griffith, 1718–1730: 2 October and 10 December 1718, CH/194/13, fol. 303; 30 September and (to Mrs Griffith) 17 October 1719, CH/194/13, fol. 75; 8 August 1724, CH/194/14, fol. 76; 5 September 1730, CH/194/15, fol. 241. Griffith's bills: Add. MSS, 22, 258, fol. 31, 28 June 1721; fol. 42, 15 June 1722; fols 95–96, 15 June 1724; fols 125–30, 26 November 1726 and 22 August 1727; and Add. MSS, 63, 430, fol. 3, 8 June 1728.

[15] Francesco Vassalli was one of the numerous Italian-speaking Swiss *stuccatori* employed by Gibbs and undertook the decorative plasterwork at Wentworth Castle.

[16] Giacomo Amiconi executed the oil painting, *Morpheus and Endymion*, for the centre panel of the Great Hall ceiling. He was employed by Gibbs throughout his sojourn in London. See Terry Friedman, *James Gibbs* (New Haven and London: Yale University Press, 1984), pp. 215, 324. The title of the painting is confirmed by 'An Account of Pictures', in John Robinson's *The Inventory of Furniture*, 1804, Vernon-Wentworth Muniments: 145, Sheffield Archives (hereafter V-WM).

[17] Edward Reeves seems to have been involved at Wentworth Castle between 1711 and 1734. He had worked for Strafford in Twickenham since *c.* 1703 and supervised the building of the new mansion in Yorkshire. Strafford's account (1716–31), Child's Bank, payments: to Edward Reeves, 13 September 1716, CH/194/13, fol. 303; Bell and Reeves, 26 March 1729, and Thomas Reeves, 16 July 1730, CH/19415, fol. 241; Thomas Reeves, 4 March 1731, CH/194/15, fol. 242. I am grateful to Rob Shepperd, email to author 30 October 2008, for confirming that Edward and Thomas were brothers who worked together, and that Bell could be John Bell, a gardener in Twickenham; see also 'Edward Reeves', <http://www.twickenham-museum.org.uk> [accessed 9 September 2008], which suggests that Strafford's mother, Lady Isabella Wentworth, might have recommended him. Strafford, letter to Bromley (steward), 6 November 1712, records his involvement at Stainborough: 'I shall speak to Reeves, as you desire', V-WM, 77, fol. 14. Among numerous other tasks, Reeves implemented Gibbs's alterations to the pre-existing Cutler House (*c.* 1670). A collection of drawings by Reeves, associated with letters to Strafford from Draycott in London *c.* 1728–30, combined with payments to him by Gibbs between 1731 and 1734, indicate that he was the draughtsman for the architect's design ideas: V-WM, LD 1121, fols 178–79, fols 184–87, fol. 192, fols 196–97. Reeves also owned a copy of Gibbs's *Book of Architecture* (1728). See Gibbs's account (opened in 1723) at the Jacobite Drummond's Bank (Royal Bank of Scotland Group Archives), payments to Edward Reeves, 1731–34, presumably for work at Wentworth Castle: 28 May and 7 December 1731, DR/427/11, fol. 165; 3 February 1732, DR/427/12, fol. 191; 27 April, 14 January, 4 July, 11 September, 21 October and 29 January 1734, DR/427/14, fol. 215.

[18] Anon., 'Account of my Journey begun 6 Aug 1724', entry dated 11 September, Yorkshire Archaeological Society Archives, MS 328, p. 59, pl. 92; transcribed by Karen Lynch. In the Great Hall Harvey carved the four Ionic capitals in wood for the central columns, and Griffith installed the wooden panelling of the wainscot around the walls. Harvey's bills: Add. MSS, 22, 241, fol. 20, 22 October 1725; fol. 22, 4 June 1726; fol. 25, 25 December 1726; fol. 26, 4 December 1727; fol. 28, 16 September 1727. Like the wainscot, Amiconi's ceiling painting was executed in London and shipped up to Yorkshire where it was installed during 1734 as the final flourish of the interior; Add. MSS, 22, 258, fol. 359, stables accounts, 10–25 February 1734, for 'Shipping Endymion', and fol. 426, 14 June 1735, for Amiconi's receipt for Strafford's payment of £52 10*s.* for the painting.

[19] Letter, Bathurst to Strafford, 26 October 1725, cited in Joseph Wilkinson, *Worthies, Families and Celebrities of Barnsley and the District* (London: 1883), p. 379. The revised plans for the Long Gallery were illustrated in *Vitruvius Britannicus* (1715). The space was dramatised by the addition of two pairs of columns that screened the square pavilions at each end. These had been created by extending the thirteen-bay elevation to fifteen, and each pavilion comprised two window bays. Preoccupied with political events, it was not until after the death of Queen Anne in August 1714 that Strafford ordered from Italy the four marble columns and associated pilasters and pedestals. Strafford, correspondence with Christopher Crowe, British Consul in Leghorn (Livorno), Add. MSS, 22, 221, fols 259–64, 10 August, 3 and 30 September 1714. But the Whig purge prevented any more being done until 1717 when the marble work became a priority. Letters to Strafford, Add. MSS, 22, 239, from Arnold, fols 28–29, 16 June 1717: 'the marble man I never hard any thing of him', and Hargreaves (steward), fols 90–91, 8 June 1719: 'I writ to Mr. Thornton concerning ye marble pedestals.' In August 1720 Daniel Harvey was contracted to produce in Roche Abbey stone eight capitals for the imported columns: four

Gibbs had replaced Bodt's baroque murals with a scheme that displayed Strafford's 'curious Collection of Painting, Sculpture and other excellent Decorations'[20] so that the Long Gallery emulated the Palazzo Colonna in Rome.[21] Such an overt reference to Rome in a Jacobite mansion would not be missed by a sympathiser for it was there that the King-in-waiting's exile was endured. Strafford must have rued the irony that it was the terms of the Peace of Utrecht that had obliged James III to quit France and settle in Rome. Strafford's baroque palace was dedicated to conspicuous display,[22] and the plasterwork of the Italian Staircase forms the centrepiece of the mansion's, indeed the estate's, Jacobite symbolism. Moreover the stuccowork coincided with the completion of Strafford's most significant garden building, Stainborough Castle.

The stairwell of the cantilevered Italian Staircase is lit throughout the day by clerestory windows high in the north and west walls.[23] Thus it is the most strategic location for symbolic decoration in the whole of the east-facing mansion. During 1729–1731 Gibbs's *stuccatori* embellished two ground floor ceilings and the entire stairwell; hence the designation, Italian Staircase, in honour of the craftsmen. Terry Friedman has reflected that the Italophile Gibbs had such confidence in his *stuccatori*, who were specialists in iconographic representation, that he would brief them on the patron's agenda and the key design elements, and allow them to interpret the theme as they saw fit.[24] Contrary to received wisdom, the plasterwork was executed by Francesco Vassalli,[25] probably assisted

---

Corinthian to top the columns and four Composite for the pilasters. Harvey's contract, 29 August 1720, Add. MSS, 22, 241, fol. 11. Harvey's bills: Add. MSS, 22, 241, fol. 25, 25 December 1726; fol. 26, 4 December 1727; fol. 28, 16 September 1727. Payment for 6 letters 'from Mr. Harvey the Carver', Stainborough Rent Roll, 1724, V-WM, LD 1121, fols 7–8.

[20] Colen Campbell, *Vitruvius Britannicus*, 3 vols (London: 1715–25), I, pp. 6–7, and pl. 92 (and 93–94). Strafford had acquired the paintings in Rome during 1709. Strafford acquired volumes 1–3 (1715–25) of *Vitruvius Britannicus* and perhaps the 1739 edition by Badeslade and Rocque. The earlier volumes published subscriber lists but the 1739 edition did not.

[21] Alec Cobbe, in conversation with author, 31 August 2008, regarded the Long Gallery as characteristic of Gibbs's mission to bring Rome to Britain. The floor, ceiling and coving were executed between 1721 and 1723; Hargreaves, letters to Strafford, Add. MSS, 22, 239, fols 102–03, 26 November 1721, and fol. 136, 8 January 1723. The plain plastering was complete by the end of 1724; Huss received part payment 'for ye: Gallery', Stainborough Rent Roll, 1723, V-WM, LD 1121, fols 5–6. Morgan (steward), letter to Strafford, 13 November 1724: 'Mr. Huss the Plaisterer is here & proposes finishing by Monday next', Add. MSS, 22, 239, fols 157–58. Huss's bills: Add. MSS, 22, 241, fol. 19, 22 October 1725; fol. 22, 4 June 1726; fol. 24, 25 December 1726; fol. 26, 4 December 1717; fol. 28, 16 September 1727. Griffith's contract, 'to wainscout ye Gallery at Stainebourough as Desined by Mr Gibbs', 28 July 1724, Add. MSS, 22, 239, fol. 128. The wooden panelling of the wainscot comprised the total environment of the space; not only did it accommodate each painting, it also formed the architrave that surrounded the gallery just below the coving, as well as the Composite pilaster columns that punctuated the mural space, framed the windows and complemented the marble pilasters of the pavilions. All the wainscoting was made in London and shipped up to Yorkshire by sea; Add. MSS, 22, 239, fol. 128, Griffith's contract, 28 July 1724, and fols 157–60, Morgan, letters to Strafford, 13 and 17 November 1724.

[22] The older Cutler House (*c.* 1670) was retained as the residence and improved to suit the domestic requirements of Strafford and his family.

[23] For the construction of the Italian Staircase, see Stephen Jones, 'The Politics of Plasterwork in the Italianate Staircase at Wentworth Castle' (unpublished BA dissertation, School of Fine Art, University of Leeds, 2007), pp. 27–39.

[24] Terry Friedman, conversation with author, 16 August 2007.

[25] Payments to Vassalli, 26 March and 29 November 1729, Strafford's account (1716–31), Child's Bank, CH/194/15, fol. 241; letter to Vassalli, 5 October 1731, Add. MSS, 63, 470, fol. 40; William Addinell, bill, 'To sashes in y^{e} Staircase att Stainborough after y^{e} Stucco men have done', 18 December 1731, Add. MSS, 22, 241, fol. 50.

FIGURE 3 Francesco Vassalli, Perseus Medallion, Italian Staircase, postcard, *c.* 1950. *Wentworth Castle Heritage Trust*

by Martino Quadri.[26] It was previously thought that the work was undertaken *c.* 1715 by Guiseppe Artari and Giovanni Bagutti.[27]

The splendid allegory of Peace conquering War on the walls and ceiling of the Italian Staircase displays Strafford's triumphant celebration of the Stuart monarchy and his own achievements in that service. For Jacobites, fertility was a key image of the Stuart restoration.[28] By commemorating the Peace of Utrecht, Strafford's entire decorative programme symbolically aspired to the golden age ushered in by the returning monarch accompanied by the fertility of Ceres. In view of Michael Charlesworth's detailed analysis elsewhere, a summary will suffice.[29] Medallions of Fame and Perseus articulate the classical myth wherein the goddess Minerva despatches the hero Perseus to slay the snake-haired Gorgon, Medusa (Figure 3). Thus the allegory creates associations between Queen Anne and Minerva, Strafford and Perseus, Medusa and the war. The theme is complemented by the ceiling figures of Minerva, Perseus, Heroic Virtue and Fortitude that surround the symbol of Strafford's cherished Order of the Garter Knights, as well as by the clerestory plasterwork busts of Roman emperors and trophies of arms. Gibbs further linked Strafford's peacemaking with Roman imperial precedent through the subtle

[26] W. John and Kit Smith, *An Architectural History of Towneley Hall, Burnley* (Nelson: Heritage Trust of the North West, 2004), p. 60, also attribute the Italian Staircase to Vassalli and Quadri on the grounds of stylistic similarity to their documented work at Towneley Hall; see pp. 56–62, for the suggestion that Vassalli might have acquired engravings by Gaetano Brunetti while in Italy during 1730. So it is possible that the Italian Staircase was completed with the benefit of these fresh designs. Brunetti later published in England *Sixty Different Sorts of Ornament* (London: 1731).

[27] Geoffrey Beard, *Georgian Craftsmen and their Work* (London: Country Life Publications, 1966), p. 50, and Beard, *Craftsmen and Interior Decoration in England, 1660–1820* (London: Bloomsbury Books, 1986), p. 168. Subsequent authors have thus cited Artari and Bagutti, for example: James Lees-Milne, *English Country Houses: Baroque*, p. 241; Friedman, *Gibbs*, pp. 14, 125; John Cornforth, 'Of Gods, Grapes and Monkeys', *Country Life* (11 March 1993), pp. 58–61. Even though he dated the Italian Staircase prematurely, Beard (1986, pp. 243–45) also demonstrates that between 1729 and 1735 Artari and Bagutti were employed in London and the Home Counties: at Cavendish Square (1729), Moulsham Hall (1730–31), Moor Park and Wimpole (1732) and Clandon Hall (1731–35). Between 1730 and 1734, Vassalli and Quadri were engaged at a number of other mansions in Lancashire and Yorkshire: at Aske Hall (1730), Towneley Hall (1730–31), Gisburn Hall (1731–32), Parlington Hall (1732–33) and Duncombe Park (1734); see Beard, *Craftsmen* (1986), p. 288, for Aske, Towneley and Parlington; W. J. and K. Smith, *Towneley Hall*, p. 62, for Towneley and Gisburn; Add. MSS, 31, 142, fol. 128, 5 May 1734, for Duncombe.

[28] Murray G. H. Pittock, 'The Aeneid in the Age of Burlington: A Jacobite Text?', in *Lord Burlington: Architecture, Art and Life*, ed. by Tony Barnard and Jane Clark (London and Rio Grande: The Hambledon Press, 1995), pp. 232–49 (p. 243).

[29] See Charlesworth, *Wentworth Castle NAJ* 63/64, 53–61.

inclusion within the mural borders of floral motifs that derive from the *Ara Pacis Augustae*, the Altar of Augustan Peace.[30] Excavated fragments of this monument were on display in Rome and had doubtless been seen by Gibbs and Strafford. As at Wentworth Castle, these sinuous motifs had been intended to celebrate the fertile prosperity of triumphant peace.

The complementary theme of the interior plasterwork, the relief sculpture on the mansion's façade, and the garden statuary are also detailed elsewhere so, again, it will suffice to say that all these elements signify the fame and plenty of peace and the elite status of the soldier-peacemaker.[31] Thus the profusion of fruits and vegetables signify the fecundity of a peaceful land and allude both to national and dynastic prosperity: on the ground floor ceilings stuccoed by Vassalli this imagery accompanies personifications of Fame (with trumpets) and Plenty (with cornucopia); on the façade relief, carved with an exuberant flamboyance by Daniel Harvey,[32] profuse vegetation frames Strafford's coat of arms, the motto of his beloved garter knighthood and a trophy of arms; the garden statues by John Nost not only signified regeneration and prosperity, but were also symbolic of restoration. Minerva, Ceres and Venus were complemented by The Blackamoor. Figured as a kneeling African, The Blackamoor doubtless embodied the Stuart cipher of the Black Boy which, since the days of Charles II, had personified the exiled monarch. Moreover Jane Clark, in her recent study of Lord Burlington, also emphasises that Stuart supporters often used an early form of masonic symbolism, in which the black skin of Africans was used to signify the darkness that represented hidden knowledge; the Latin motto *Lux e tenebris* ('light from darkness') would clarify the symbol. Bearing a sundial on its head, The Blackamoor reveals knowledge of time through the illumination of light.[33]

So it was amidst the fulsomeness of peace that Gibbs embedded specific symbols of Strafford's illicit affiliation. Those within the mansion were derived from Jacobite propaganda smuggled into Britain, in particular from the miniature, discreet and portable designs on medals. The keystone over the entrance to the Great Hall would prepare a fellow-traveller for the interior, and also register a covert snub to the Whig censorship of the popular practice of decorating the lintels of doorways on Restoration Day (29 May) with oak sprigs to demonstrate support for the Stuarts.[34] Amongst garlands of flowers and a 'fanfare' of trumpets, the keystone clearly sports oak leaves growing afresh from the stump of a severed tree (Figure 4). The oak had been adopted as a Stuart symbol following defeat in the English Civil Wars. The Italian Staircase also displays two medallions

[30] Terry Friedman, letter to author, 17 August 2007.

[31] See Eyres, *Wentworth Castle NAJ* 63/64, 19–24.

[32] Beard, *Craftsmen* (1966), p. 50. Harvey was a Huguenot who had anglicised his name from Hervé; see Rupert Gunnis, *Dictionary of British Sculptors, 1660–1851* (London: Abbey Press, 1968), pp 190–91.

[33] Jane Clark, 'Lord Burlington's Here', in Barnard and Clark, p. 290. For The Blackamoor, the Peace of Utrecht and the Slave Trade, see Eyres, *Wentworth Castle NAJ* 63/64, p. 24.

[34] Charlesworth, in *Wentworth Castle NAJ* 63/64, p. 63, draws attention to Paul Monod's discussions in *Jacobitism and the English People, 1688–1788* (Cambridge: Cambridge University Press, 1989), pp. 182, 183, 204, 209, 215. From 1715 to as late as 1777, oak boughs, sprigs or leaves were used to adorn houses and clothing to demonstrate Jacobite allegiance. During 1717 and 1718 the Whig authorities began to arrest perpetrators and this became standard practice throughout England for the next forty years. In 1760 Restoration Day, commemorating Charles II's accession, was renamed Oak Apple Day.

Figure 4 Daniel Harvey, relief and keystone above entrance to Great Hall of the baroque mansion. *Photo: the author*

whose portraits are assumed to represent father and son, Strafford and his heir William. Although decorative to most eyes, the sprigs of oak leaves below the uppermost would enable Jacobites to read these medallions as a Stuart king and the King-over-the-water. This might be achieved through a similarity to the restored King, Charles II, and the young and yet-to-be restored James III; or through resemblance to the Jacobite double portrait medals, struck to promote the legitimacy of the Stuart succession, which bear the exiled James II on one side and his heir, James III, on the other.[35] In a cause rife with symbolism,[36] it is likely that the eight imperial busts around the clerestory would have reinforced the legitimacy of the Stuart succession: from James I to Charles I, Charles II, James II, Mary II and Anne to the Kings-in-waiting, James III and Charles III.

JACOBITE POLITICAL GARDENING AT WENTWORTH CASTLE

Despite the political upheaval, work on the gardens had continued apace and the key features of this discussion can be seen in the bird's-eye prints of 1730 by Thomas Badeslade and John Harris, which were subsequently reproduced in the 1739 edition of *Vitruvius Brittanicus* [*sic*] (Figures 1 and 2). They can also be seen in the recent overview by Chris Broughton which was drawn to commemorate the epic Phase One restoration of the estate during 2004–2008 (Figure 5). Ever since 1713, Strafford's head gardener, John Arnold, had been implementing the design that had been obtained from the former royal gardener, George London, for the wilderness gardens, parterre, octagon pool and walled kitchen garden.[37] In 1716 Robert Bakewell of Derby had been contracted to provide the

[35] For these medallions, see Charlesworth, pp. 62–64, and Eyres, pp. 27–30, *Wentworth Castle NAJ* 63/64.

[36] For the wealth of Jacobite symbolism, see Michael Charlesworth, 'The Garden of the Lost Lover', *New Arcadian Journal*, no. 31/32 (1991), 67–74.

[37] See Jan Woudstra, 'The Early Eighteenth-Century Wilderness at Stainborough', pp. 81–99, and Christopher Margrave, 'The Early Eighteenth-Century Walled Kitchen Garden at Stainborough', pp. 101–12, in *Wentworth Castle NAJ* 63/64.

FIGURE 5 Chris Broughton, drawing: *Overview of Wentworth Castle*. Note the Union Jack wilderness gardens above the mansion and the Gun Room immediately to the right (the avenue of trees ascending the garden is a twentieth-century feature); the Lady Mary Obelisk is just below Stainborough Castle and the Queen Anne Obelisk is in the foreground. *New Arcadian Journal, 2008 (New Arcadian Press)*

iron gates and pallisading around the Octagon Court in front of the mansion, and these were installed in 1717.[38] During 1720 and 1721 sculpture purchased from the London statuary yard of John Nost was installed in the gardens and park.[39] By 1725 the Octagon Pool was complete,[40] and also the cascade in distant Menagerie Wood (Figure 2,

[38] Bakewell's contract, 10 September 1716, Add. MSS, 22, 241, fol. 7; design, V-WM LD 1121, fols 196–97; installation, Arnold, letter to Strafford, 16 June 1717, Add. MSS, 22, 239, fol. 29; payment, Strafford's account (1716–31), Child's Bank, 13 July 1730, CH/194/15, fol. 241.

[39] William Addinell, bills for painting the sculpture, Add. MSS, 22, 241, fol. 14, 28 September 1720; fol. 16, 2 September 1721. Payment to Nost, Strafford's account (1716–31), Child's Bank, 7 June 1728, CH/194/14, fol. 316.

[40] Arnold, letters to Strafford (design and detail), Add. MSS, 22, 239, fols 9–10, 10 March 1713; fols 11–12, 16 June and 7 July 1714. Thackwray's annotated plan of water storage in cellar of house for octagon pool, August 1714, V-WM LD 1121, fol. 180. Hargreaves, letters to Strafford (collapse and repair), Add. MSS, 22, 239, fols 96–97, 10 November 1721; fols 102–03, 20 November 1721.

foreground).[41] These two features have been attributed to Thomas Archer:[42] the Octagon Pool was designed in 1714 but the date for the design of the cascade in Menagerie Wood remains uncertain. However, in the light of Archer's retirement in 1715, Menagerie House (1717) may well have been the first garden building that Gibbs designed for Strafford. The Law Lake temple and the mock-mediaeval castle would follow. The Gun Room and the two obelisks were erected after 1730.

James Gibbs has acquired an impeccable reputation for the design of garden buildings, and even for garden design. John Dixon Hunt and Peter Willis have acknowledged him as one of the 'landscapists' who created the English landscape garden.[43] Terry Friedman has attributed Gibbs's knowledge of garden design to the collaborations with Charles Bridgeman during the 1720s at places such as Wimpole and Stowe.[44] Friedman and Willis concur that, despite little documentation of Bridgeman-Gibbs collaborations, there is enough evidence to accept that the two formed a gardening partnership. They were also neighbours in London and members of the exclusive St Luke's Club for artists and connoisseurs.[45] Friedman has also pointed out that, when Gibbs was called in to complete a mansion, he frequently went on to design garden buildings, as at Hartwell and here at Wentworth Castle.[46] Gibbs is thought to have designed most of the buildings as well as the garden at Hartwell, which was composed of Bridgeman's hallmark elements: canalised water and terraces.[47] It is these features that characterise the Law Lake (also Law Wood) garden at Wentworth Castle (Figure 2, bottom right). Although in the early nineteenth century it would be overtaken by mining, the Law Lake temple (Figure 6) was set on terraces adjacent to a rectangular pool and is similar to garden buildings illustrated

[41] Bathurst's letter to Strafford, 26 October 1725, records completion of the octagon and menagerie; cited in Wilkinson, *Worthies of Barnsley*, p. 379.

[42] For their attribution to Thomas Archer, see Woudstra, Wentworth Castle NAJ 63/64, 81–82, and 'Wentworth Castle Gardens and Stainborough Park: Conservation Plan' (internal document, Hilary Taylor Landscape Associates Ltd, August 2005), pp. 10–15 (Archive: Wentworth Castle Heritage Trust). In the light of these attributions it is interesting that Joseph Bower's plan for the 'cascade in ye menagerie', Add. MSS, 31, 141, fol. 155, November 1723, is lodged amidst Archer's 1714 correspondence with Strafford.

[43] *The Genius of the Place: The English Landscape Garden, 1620–1820*, ed. by John Dixon Hunt and Peter Willis (London: Paul Elek, 1975), p. 11.

[44] For Gibbs's garden buildings, see Friedman, *Gibbs*, pp. 156–200; see Peter Willis, *Charles Bridgeman and the English Landscape Garden* (Newcastle: Elysium Press, 2001), pp. 44, 74, 79–88, 436, for the Gibbs-Bridgeman collaborations at Cannons, Dyrham, Gubbins, Hackwood, Kedleston, Badminton and Tring, and possibly Dawley and Down Hall, in addition to Stowe and Wimpole.

[45] See Willis, *Bridgeman*, pp. 30 and 37, for Bridgeman and Gibbs as neighbours (Bridgeman at no. 8 Henrietta Street from 1725, Gibbs at no. 5 from 1730) and clubmen in London (Gibbs was elected in 1716, Bridgeman in 1726, possibly engineered by Gibbs).

[46] Terry Friedman, conversation with author, 4 September 2008. At Hartwell Gibbs was called in to remodel the Jacobean house and, between 1723 and 1738, designed buildings in the garden which was probably by Charles Bridgeman. Their collaboration at Hartwell is proposed by Sir Roy Strong, *The Artist & the Garden* (New Haven & London: Yale University Press, 2000), p. 230, and cited in Willis, *Bridgeman*, pp. 429–30, as also is Eric Throssell's preference for Gibbs as designer of both garden and buildings.

[47] The design of garden and buildings is attributed to Gibbs by Eric Throssell, see: 'Hartwell House, Buckinghamshire: A Lost Formal Garden, A Classical Idyll – And a Myth Dispelled', *Follies Journal*, no. 2 (2002), 37–52 (p. 37); 'Hartwell House: The Late Sixteenth- and Early Seventeenth-Century Gardens and Parterres of the Lee Family', *Garden History*, 34.1 (2006), 92–111 (p. 95); and reiterated by Sarah Rutherford and Eric Throssell, 'Gibbs in the Garden at Hartwell', Hartwell Seminar 2008.

FIGURE 6 Law Lake Temple, detail of Badeslade and Harris, *A Prospect of Stainborough and Wentworth Castle*, engraving, *c.*1730. *Wentworth Castle Heritage Trust*

FIGURE 7 George Bickham, The Temple of Friendship, engraving, *The Beauties of Stowe*, 1750. *Private collection*

by Gibbs in *A Book of Architecture* and used at Chiswick Park and Hartwell, and much later at Stowe in the form of the Temple of Friendship (Figure 7).[48]

Tim Richardson has observed that Gibbs's *Book of Architecture* (1728) was the first comprehensive pattern book of designs for garden buildings and ornaments.[49] Strafford was among the subscribers. Other architectural publications to which he subscribed include John James's translation of Claude Perrault's *A Treatise of the Five Orders of Architecture* (1708) and the first three volumes of Colen Campbell's *Vitruvius Britannicus* (1715, 1717, 1725); Badeslade and Rocque's 1739 edition does not list subscribers. Of these only Gibbs's book was in the library at Wentworth Castle.[50] The others must have been in the London collection. This suggests that Gibbs's book was being used practically for the design of garden features,[51] perhaps for the 'two little obeliss' referred to by the mason Joseph Bower in 1732.[52] One of these might have been the Sun Monument (Figure 5, top left), now popularly known as Lady Mary's Obelisk, which was repaired in 1746 but may well have been built earlier.[53] The other was the Queen Anne Obelisk (Figure 5, bottom left), which was erected in 1734 across the park at the junction with the public road. The evidence for Gibbs as the designer of Strafford's garden buildings has been marshalled elsewhere, and so this discussion focuses on the garden's Jacobite symbolism.[54]

The Queen Anne Obelisk commemorated the Stuart cause in particular ways. It marked defeat of the government's candidates in the 1734 Yorkshire election, which had proved to be one of the most hotly contested of the century. This victory had been achieved through collaboration between Strafford and the dissident Whig taste-maker Lord Burlington, who is also considered to have been an active and senior Jacobite

[48] Friedman, letter to author, 17 August 2007. See Friedman, *Gibbs*, pp. 164–66, for the group of domed buildings designed, though not necessarily realised, for Down Hall, Chiswick, Stowe, Hackwood, Cliveden, Tring, Badminton, Kiveton and Wrest Park. See also p. 166, pl. 179–80 (temple at Chiswick, *c.* 1719); p. 187, pl. 209 (Menagerie, Hartwell, *c.* 1723–38); and p. 191, pl. 214 (Temple of Friendship, Stowe, 1739–42). See also James Gibbs, *A Book of Architecture, Containing Designs of Buildings and Ornaments* (London: 1728), pl. 67 (elevation), pl. 69 (for Down Hall), and pl. 83. The Temple of Friendship exemplifies the way that Gibbs recycled his designs. This was a point emphasised by Alec Cobbe, 'Newbridge, Gibbs and Garden Ornament', Hartwell Seminar 2008. Numerous examples are cited in Alec Cobbe and Terry Friedman, *James Gibbs in Ireland: Newbridge, his Villa for Charles Cobbe, Archbishop of Dublin* (Dublin: The Cobbe Foundation/The Irish Georgian Society, 2005), pp. 9–13.

[49] Richardson, *The Arcadian Friends*, p. 299; see also pp. 192 and 221, for the observation that Gibbs was the 'architect to the Tories in their wilderness decades' and that the Gibbs-Bridgeman partnership formed 'a Tory designer "dream team" '.

[50] V-WM 146, Inventory of Books, 1801.

[51] For numerous drawings of unrealised garden buildings, see V-WM, LD 1121, fols 181–83, 191, 192, 195 and 198; see also Furse, *Wentworth Castle NAJ* 63/64, 118–19 and notes 23, 24. Great excitement followed the loan in March 2009 to the Wentworth Castle Heritage Trust of a postcard (*c.* 1900) of the two-storeyed garden building at Constantine's Well, which was presumed long vanished. The postcard revealed the building as it was probably built in the 1730s, with window surrounds and quoins reminiscent of those illustrated, for example, by pl. 68 and pl. 78 in Gibbs's *A Book of Architecture*; see also Susan Kellerman herein.

[52] Cited in Neville Whittaker, 'A History of the House, Gardens and Landscape Park at Wentworth Castle, Yorkshire, with Notes on the Principal Persons Connected with it' (unpublished MA dissertation, University of Durham, 1964), p. 17. See Gibbs, *A Book of Architecture*, for obelisks, pl. 85–87, and Joseph Bower's letter to Strafford, 19 February 1733, Add. MSS, 22, 239, fol. 203, for the mason's drawing for the Queen Anne's Obelisk.

[53] It is likely that the radiant sun emblem and the inscription were added by William to his father's obelisk. For the pioneering medical technique commemorated by the Sun Monument, see Frith, pp. 145–70, and for the dating, p. 147, n. 14; see also Furse, p. 118, n. 21, both in *Wentworth Castle NAJ* 63/64.

[54] See Patrick Eyres, 'Wentworth Castle: Gibbs and Garden Buildings', in *The Bucks Gardener*, no. 29 (forthcoming, summer 2009).

FIGURE 8 James Gibbs, The Gun Room (restored) in relation to the mansion. Note the relocated Strafford memorial statue to left of mansion. *Photo: the author*

conspirator.[55] However, the obelisk primarily celebrated Strafford's royal and Stuart patron. Twenty years after Queen Anne's death, the Jacobite resonance of this memorial is marked by the inscription's absolute refusal to acknowledge 'The Successor'; neither George I nor his successor George II are named.[56] Indeed 'The Successor' could not be named because he was the exiled James III. Although some commentators prefer to be wary about the Jacobite iconography at Wentworth Castle, it is salutary to note that even the restrained Tim Richardson has conceded that 'the Queen Anne Obelisk is the only explicit Jacobite garden feature on British soil'.[57]

Nevertheless the contemporary view uphill from the banqueting house now known as the Gun Room (Figure 8)[58] would have warmed the cockles of a Stuart aficionado

[55] For the election alliance of Strafford and Burlington, in company with other Tory and dissident Whig lords, see Eveline Cruickshank, 'The Political Career of the Third Earl of Burlington', pp. 201–15 (p. 212); for the evidence of Burlington's Jacobitism, see Jane Clark, 'Lord Burlington's Here', pp. 251–310, both in Barnard and Clark, *Lord Burlington*.

[56] See Charlesworth, *Wentworth Castle NAJ* 63/64, 49–53.

[57] Tim Richardson, 'The Politics of the Garden', *Country Life*, 22.50 (10 December 2008), pp. 42–47 (p. 46). This feature on Georgian Wentworth Castle reiterates his earlier reflection that the Queen Anne Obelisk 'is the only example of Jacobite sentiments expressed in a landscape setting', in Richardson, *The Arcadian Friends*, p. 334.

[58] It is known as the Gun Room on account of its use during Victorian shooting parties. The pavilion's cruciform or Greek Cross plan, its Venetian window and vestiges of the original interior have encouraged Terry Friedman to consider that its design derives from a group of garden buildings published by Gibbs in *A Book of Architecture*, and that it functioned as a banqueting house; Friedman, letter to author, 17 August 2007. There are plentiful designs for garden buildings with a cruciform plan, dome and Venetian features (such as porticos or windows). Of the two temples designed for Hackwood Park, one has a Venetian portico akin to the Gun Room's window; see Gibbs, *A Book of Architecture*, pl. 73–74, and pl. 68 (for Down Hall), also pl. 70 (for Kedleston Hall), pl. 77 (for Stowe), and pl. 67; see also Friedman, *Gibbs*, pp. 164–65, pl. 174 (for Hackwood), and p. 168, pl. 183 (for Down Hall). It may not be coincidence that the garden pavilion designed by Gibbs for his consistent patron and Strafford's longstanding friend, the Duke of Argyll, at Adderbury sports a Venetian façade and frieze similar to the Gun Room. The Adderbury pavilion, designed 1734–40, was probably inspired by the Renaissance tempietto at Bomarzo; see Friedman, *Gibbs*, pp. 162–63, pl. 172; another temple, designed for Kedleston Hall (p. 172, pl. 189), sports only the window, not the frieze.

because it encompassed the wilderness gardens massed to the left, and Stainborough Castle on the skyline (Figure 5). As it was Vassalli who undertook the castle's interior plasterwork, it is likely that he also stuccoed the Gun Room.[59] Although neither scheme survives, it is tantalising to wonder whether oak sprigs and double portrait medallions graced these interiors. Had this been the case, the decoration would have triangulated this banqueting house with the wildernesses and castle as Jacobite features. Jan Woudstra has noted that contemporary evidence demonstrates the variety of designs used to shape wildernesses in English gardens.[60] Yet at Wentworth Castle it was the double cross pattern that was chosen and planted in 1713. Although this was a traditional design, it coincidentally replicated the shape of the recently formed Union flag which combined the crosses of St Andrew and St George (Figures 1 and 5). For Strafford the double cross wildernesses may well have been conceived as a Stuart symbol to celebrate the Union of Scotland and England under Queen Anne in 1707 and, especially, the Tory defeat on 13 May 1713 of the Whig parliamentary attempt to dissolve the nascent Union.[61] In the years after 1717, this resemblance may have been seen as a prescient symbol of his continuing Stuart allegiance.

Crowning the summit of the gardens, Stainborough Castle (Figures 1, 2 and 5, top) is the Saxon Gothic structure that not only accommodated banqueting but also, by referring to dynastic longevity and, covertly, to Jacobite virtue, stood as the most symbolic of all Strafford's garden buildings. Although a miniature replica of a mediaeval castle, the design of this monumental garden building was an innovative architectural hybrid intended to invoke the Saxon past as a reflection on the present. Erected between 1726 and 1730, it was named Stainborough Castle in 1731 to emphasise the ancient name of the estate. 'Re-built', as Strafford's inscription claims, on the site of what was understood to be an ancient fortification, the castle was recognized by contemporaries as Saxon. Although destroyed by the partial collapse of the structure in 1961, it has been recorded that Vassalli's stuccowork in the banqueting room was 'similar in style and quality to that of the east wing [Italian] staircase, and included similar medallions'.[62] Perhaps these medallions also alluded to the Jacobite double portrait medals and, in conjunction with oak leaves, signalled the Stuart resonance of the building's Saxon Gothic form. Strafford's will ordained that his memorial should stand inside the bailey. Once the portrait statue by Michael Rysbrack was posthumously installed during 1744, the inscription summarised the monument that Strafford had set out to create in 1717

[59] Whittaker, 'A History of ... Wentworth Castle', p. 19, described (*c.* 1964) the interior plasterwork as 'contemporary with that in the Italian staircase'. If so, the Gun Room was probably erected between 1731, when Vassalli was at work on the staircase, and 1734 when he stuccoed the banqueting room in Stainborough Castle. Friedman, in conversation with author, 4 September 2008, emphasised that the presence of Vassalli's craftsmanship within these two garden buildings corroborates the evidence that Gibbs was the designer.

[60] Woudstra, *Wentworth Castle NAJ* 63/64, 83–84.

[61] Charlesworth, *Wentworth Castle NAJ* 63/64, 61–62.

[62] Whittaker, 'A History of ... Wentworth Castle', p. 16. For Vassalli, see Wardman (steward), letters to Strafford, 1734, Add. MSS, 31, 142, fol. 128, 5 May; fol. 135, 6 May; fol. 157, undated. I am most appreciative of Michael Charlesworth and Jane Furse for sharing their archive references to Vassalli.

FIGURE 9 James Gibbs, gatehouse-keep, Stainborough Castle, postcard, *c.* 1920, with Michael Rysbrack's Strafford memorial statue, in its original position. *Wentworth Castle Heritage Trust*

(Figure 9).[63] The synthesis of sculpture, text and landscape architecture enshrined his restoration of dynastic status, proclaimed his achievements under Queen Anne, and encoded his Stuart allegiance within the castle that invoked Saxon liberties as Jacobite virtues.

Before the rise of a scientific approach to history in the late eighteenth and early nineteenth centuries, Saxon and Gothic were unspecific, interchangeable architectural terms. Nonetheless they were used by political interests to invoke ancient virtues and liberties as a means of defining notions of Britishness, and were consequently polemical in proposing alternative identities to Hanoverian Whiggery. While Michael Charlesworth has noted that these interests were opposed to the government of Sir Robert Walpole,[64] the dynastic and Jacobite symbolism of Stainborough Castle was established by his

[63] Friedman, conversation with author, 18 May 2007, pointed out the likelihood that Gibbs was instrumental in the second Strafford's commissioning of Michael Rysbrack in 1742 to sculpt the memorial statue of his father. Rysbrack was Gibbs's favourite sculptor and had regularly worked for him. There was also the long-standing association between Gibbs, Rysbrack, Argyll and Strafford which might have contributed to the second Earl's decision. See also Furse, *Wentworth Castle NAJ* 63/64, 116–118. The statue was relocated in the late 1970s.

[64] Michael Charlesworth, *The Gothic Revival 1720–1870: Literary Sources and Documents*, 3 vols (Robertsbridge: Helm Information, 2002), I, Introduction, 5–51 (pp. 14–17).

pioneering articles in the *New Arcadian Journal*.[65] This discussion will emphasise that it was James Gibbs who created Saxon Gothic as a genre of garden building to symbolise Jacobite dissent from Hanoverian rule. Hence Gibbs gave physical form to the Jacobite association between the virtues of Saxon kingship and the Stuart monarchy. Furthermore, Gibbs subsequently introduced this genre into the gardens of dissident Whig politicians, thus enlarging the repertoire of architectural styles within Georgian political gardening.

Gibbs was well aware of the symbolic preference for mediaeval or Gothic architecture by Tory and Jacobite politicians. In a letter of 1716 to his exiled patron the Earl of Mar, another deposed Tory minister and commander of the ill-fated Jacobite insurgency during 1715, Gibbs commented: 'Our brothers of the brush [Jacobites] go on in the same style of building as formerly.'[66] However, it may have been membership of the Society of Antiquaries that stimulated his active interest in medieval architecture; his election, in 1726, coincided with the design of Stainborough Castle. George Clarke has observed that 'Gibbs designed more mock-Gothic than is generally realised',[67] and the Gothic Tower at Hartwell (1738) has prompted Terry Friedman to consider that 'this work offers the possibility of Gibbs having designed similar buildings with less securely documented histories'.[68] Friedman has recently proposed that the Jacobite symbolism of Stainborough Castle is underpinned by the primitive sophistication of the Saxon architecture. Curved windows and crenellations are used throughout, while rustications surround the 'triumphal' archway through the gatehouse-keep and the windows of the first floor banqueting room.[69] Moreover each of the four bailey wall turrets contains quatrefoil windows (Figure 10). This feature seems to have been a gothic revival pioneered by Gibbs, and he used it as a signature motif so that the three quatrefoil windows of Hartwell's tower

[65] See Michael Charlesworth in the *New Arcadian Journal*: 'Elevation and Succession', pp. 7–65, no. 31/32 (1991), and 'Thomas Wentworth's Monument', pp. 31–63, no. 57/58 (2005), reprinted, pp. 49–79, no. 63/64 (2008).

[66] Friedman, *Gibbs*, p. 198. Mar was also an amateur architect and in exile at the Stuart court in France. Friedman, conversation with author, 4 September 2008, considered it possible that Gibbs was acting as Mars's spy, and reiterated that Strafford's Jacobitism accounts for his continuing patronage of Gibbs. See also Bryan Little, *The Life and Work of James Gibbs, 1682–1754* (London: Batsford, 1955), pp. 42–43, who refers to the 'Jacobite business' of Gibbs's correspondence with Mar, 1716–18, and who states Gibbs had attempted to win Argyll to the cause during the building of Sudbrook. In the light of the chapters by Eveline Cruickshank and Jane Clark in Barnard and Clark, Gibbs may well have been successful.

[67] George Clarke, Michael Gibbon, Laurence Whistler, *Stowe: A Guide to the Gardens* (Buckingham: 1956, 1968 and 1974), p. 23.

[68] Friedman, *Gibbs*, p. 200; for his discussion of Hartwell, see pp. 182–89.

[69] For attribution of Stainborough Castle to Gibbs, see Terry Friedman, 'Romanticism and Neoclassicism for Parlington: the Tastes of Sir Thomas Gascoigne', *Leeds Arts Calendar*, no. 66 (1970), 16–24 (p. 19). Friedman's papers (unpublished) indicate that in the early 1980s he had considered that Gibbs may have provided a sketch for the castle, which was executed by Joseph Bowers and his team of estate masons. Friedman, in conversation with author, 16 August 2007, noted that Stainborough Castle incorporates elements that feature in other garden buildings created by Gibbs, as well as in numerous designs within his book. For curved windows in garden buildings, see Gibbs, *A Book of Architecture*, pl. 71, pl. 77 and pl. 81, and for curved windows and entrances with rusticated surrounds, see pl. 68, 70, 73, 75, 76, 78, 79, 80, 83 and 84. For triumphal arches, see Friedman, *Gibbs*, p. 162, pl. 173, the rusticated triumphal arch for Ditchley; p. 186, pl. 207, the rustic arch at Hartwell; p. 199, pl. 223, the crenellated and rusticated gothic arch at Gubbins; see also p. 199, pl. 224, for the proposed gothic arcade, Kiveton Park, 1741.

FIGURE 10 James Gibbs, turret and bailey wall (pre-restoration), Stainborough Castle, postcard, *c.* 1920. *Wentworth Castle Heritage Trust*

FIGURE 11 James Gibbs, The Gothic Tower, Hartwell. *Photo: the author*

(Figure 11) are identical to those of Stainborough Castle,[70] and to those of Gibbs's gothic buildings at Stowe.

The pioneering Saxon Gothic garden building, Stainborough Castle, was immediately followed by a companion. Alfred's Hall in Cirencester Park was built by Strafford's cousin, fellow Tory and Jacobite, Lord Bathurst. Completed during 1732, it replaced a smaller retreat designed by Bathurst and the poet Alexander Pope in 1721. Bathurst was one of the dozen Tories elevated to the peerage in January 1712 to ensure a majority in the House of Lords for the government's peace treaty. After the death of Queen Anne he contributed £1000 to Lord Mar's ill-fated 1715 insurgency. Both cousins were conspirators in the Atterbury plot and, in preparation, James III had appointed Strafford commander of his forces north of the river Trent, and also elevated him in the Jacobite peerage as Duke of Strafford. Bathurst became conspicuous in his support for Bishop Atterbury, leader of the Jacobite conspiracy betrayed in 1722,[71] and renowned for his criticism of Walpole's government. Influenced by Stainborough Castle, Bathurst designed Alfred's Hall himself.[72] During 1731 he wrote asking to see the plans for Strafford's castle and discussed a Saxon Gothic structure which he proposed to erect as a terminus of the grand avenues in Cirencester Park. There is an echo of Strafford's building in Bathurst's castle, which is a fascinating synthesis of the ornamental, political and utilitarian: a square enclosure comprising crenellated walls with a tower at each corner, subdivided into equal halves by two battlemented farm buildings linked by another tower that rose over a central archway. Each half of the enclosure would be planted with 'Scotsch firs & Beach trees',[73] probably as an arboreal symbol of a Stuart Britishness. It is uncertain whether this idea and its accompanying sketch is a prototype for the final form of Alfred's Hall or an unrealised proposal.[74] Nevertheless it is important to note that neither Stainborough

[70] Charles Boot and Sarah Rutherford drew my attention to this during the Hartwell Seminar 2008.

[71] Although both were conspirators, there was insufficient evidence to implicate either Bathurst or Strafford; see Charlesworth, *Wentworth Castle NAJ* 63/64, 52, 68–69. Strafford would destroy all his correspondence with James III; see J. J. Cartwright, *The Wentworth Papers*: 1705–39 (London: W. Yorman, 1883), p. 35. Bathurst's son would later burn his father's incriminating letters; see, for the Jacobite Bathurst, James Lees-Milne, *Earls of Creation: Five Great Patrons of Eighteenth-Century Art* (London: Hamish Hamilton, 1962), pp. 5–7.

[72] Bathurst's letters to Strafford confirm his interest in design. Michael Charlesworth, in email to author, 6 October 2008, emphasised that Stainborough Castle was Bathurst's example. He also confirmed that Alfred's Hall was completed in 1732, and cited Maynard Mack, *Alexander Pope: A Life* (New Haven & London: Yale University Press, 1977), p. 383, to document the building's evolution from 'a house in the woods designed by Bathurst and Pope in 1721 ... [which was] later extended and gothicized into a structure called Alfred's Hall'. See also Timothy Mowl, *Gentlemen and Players: Gardeners of the English Landscape* (Stroud: Sutton Publishing, 2000), p. 101, in which Mowl confirms Bathurst as the designer of the structure completed in July 1732, and casts doubts on Pope's participation. Mowl reiterates this important point in his *Historic Gardens of Gloucestershire* (Stroud: Tempus Publishing, 2002), p. 69.

[73] Bathurst, letter to Strafford, 17 August 1731, Add. MSS, 31, 142, fols 24–25, which includes a sketch plan of his proposed battlemented farm as a parkland feature.

[74] Bathurst, letter to Strafford, 28 July 1731, Add. MSS, 31, 142, fol. 22. Bathurst was particularly taken with the gothic and urged Strafford to build a mediaeval south wing to his mansion at Wentworth Castle: 'built up yr south front of yr old House & put Battlements at top and a projection to answer yr projection of yr new House with some proper ornaments in ye Castle stile wch is not so expensive as y^{t} Italian manner.' The collection of drawings in V-WM, LD 1121 includes a plan and elevation (fol. 178) surprisingly entitled: 'Plan of Stainborough of Mr Reeves for the South front to be considered'. This drawing and Bathurst's letters (fols 22, 24, 25) confirm Strafford's interest in a classical south front to complement the baroque east front. However, the Palladian south front was eventually designed and built *c.* 1760 by his heir.

Castle nor Alfred's Hall was erected as a ruin and that both were built for banqueting. Named after the legendary Saxon monarch perceived to be the heroic champion of British liberties, Alfred's Hall exemplifies the way that both structures symbolise the Jacobite discourse of Saxon political virtue.

SAXON GOTHIC AND THE POLITICS OF DISSENT

It is particularly illuminating to consider Stainborough Castle in relation to Gibbs's Saxon Gothic garden buildings at Hartwell and Stowe, where his patrons were Whig members of the opposition alliance: respectively Sir Thomas Lee and Viscount Cobham. It might seem ironic that Gibbs appeared to oversee the Whig appropriation of the Tory-Jacobite use of Gothic for politically symbolic garden architecture. However, Gibbs was instrumental in a far more subtle process. Paul Monod has emphasised that betrayal of the Jacobite Atterbury Plot in 1722 plunged the Tories into such chaos that the party was only able to regroup during the 1730s by allying with dissident Whigs opposed to Sir Robert Walpole's government.[75] This alliance became enlarged after the 1733 crisis over the Excise Bill that drove so many Whigs into opposition, including Viscount Cobham and his circle. Indeed Stowe became the epicentre of the political gardening that symbolised Tory-Whig dissent. As a Tory, Gibbs was acceptable to the dissidents and it was through this alliance that he enabled opposition Whigs to deploy the Saxon Gothic style to symbolise ancient British history as an alternative and dissenting ideology to Walpolean Whiggery.

By the 1730s, the Saxons and their legendary King Alfred had become synonymous with opposition gardening. Whereas Strafford's Stainborough Castle and Bathurst's Alfred's Hall invoked Saxon political virtue, Hartwell's Gothic Tower was 'probably a memorial to the Saxon King Alfred',[76] and the Gothic Temple at Stowe would be dedicated to 'The Liberties of Our Ancestors'. Alfred's Saxon virtues were hailed anew as those of a Patriot King, and associated with Frederick, Prince of Wales. Frederick was not only heir to the throne, but also alienated from his father George II, and had become the titular head of the opposition; in 1735 Frederick erected a statue of Alfred in the garden at Carlton House, London. The Prince was anticipated by Tory and dissident Whig alike as the Patriot-King-to-be. While Frederick was groomed by Viscount Bolingbroke through his Tory journal, *The Craftsman*, James Thomson's Whiggish poem *Liberty* was dedicated to the Prince. Not surprisingly, both Thomson's *Works* and *The Craftsman* were in Strafford's library at Wentworth Castle.[77] Thomson also provided the libretto for Thomas Arne's *Masque of Alfred* which was performed in Frederick's garden at Cliveden in 1740.[78] During 1737 Prince Frederick had been fêted at Hartwell and Stowe (and also at Cirencester Park by Bathurst), and in 1738 Gibbs provided the Gothic Tower for Lee at

[75] Monod, *Jacobitism and the English People*, pp. 344–45.
[76] Wheeler, 'Prince Frederick and Liberty', p. 83; see also Wheeler, 'The Role of Garden Statuary in the Eighteenth Century', p. 10.
[77] V-WM 146, Inventory of Books, 1801.
[78] Co-authored with David Mallet; see Paul Whiteley, 'Images of Empire: James Thomson's "Rule Britannia"', *New Arcadian Journal*, no. 35/36 (1993), 48–59.

Hartwell and the eye-catcher, Stowe Castle, for Cobham. The two other Gothic features at Stowe were both designed by Gibbs: Keeper's Lodge, later known as the Bourbon Tower, and the sumptuous Gothic Temple (a.k.a. the Temple of Liberty). The conception of these two buildings was intimated by the bust of Alfred that had been installed in Stowe's Temple of British Worthies by 1739.

Keeper's Lodge contained all the characteristics of Stainborough Castle (Figure 12). Erected in 1741, it was crenellated and has quatrefoil windows on the ground floor; these and the curved windows above, as well as the rounded doorway, are surrounded with primitive rustications.[79] The triangular Gothic Temple is the most original and spectacular of Gibbs's buildings at Stowe (Figure 13). It was also built during 1741 in richly russet ironstone with three corner turrets, pointed windows and battlements, and is rife with 'understated medievalisms including simple quatrefoil windows'.[80] Indeed there is a plethora of Gibbs's signature quatrefoil motifs: nine in the tracery of the first floor windows and three variants above. They also feature within the painted vaults of the ceiling. These form Saxon frames that contain eighteen of the fifty-four shields bearing the heraldic arms of Cobham's spurious ancestors; the apex of the vault is marked with a single quatrefoil.[81] However, although erected in 1741, the temple was completed between 1744 and 1748 after the fall of Walpole's government.[82] Nonetheless it is no coincidence that Gibbs designed Keeper's Lodge and the Gothic Temple for Cobham in 1741; nor that in 1741 Bathurst emulated Strafford by raising a monument to Queen Anne in Cirencester Park. It was during the 1741 parliamentary session that the opposition alliance, led by Strafford's lifelong friend Argyll, fatally undermined Walpole's premiership. To be precise, it was in 1741 that James III mobilised Tory participation and was thus instrumental in Walpole's downfall.

Significant members of the parliamentary alliance were enshrined within the Temple of Friendship that Gibbs had designed for Cobham in 1739 (Figure 7); the building stands in relation to two of the architect's Saxon Gothic buildings: Stowe Castle beyond the garden and the Gothic Temple within. Remember, a prototype of the Temple of

[79] Friedman, letter to author, 17 August 2007.

[80] Friedman, letter to author, 17 August 2007. See Friedman, *Gibbs*, pp. 192–98, and pl. 217–19, IX, X; see also John Martin Robinson, *Temples of Delight: Stowe Landscape Gardens* (London: National Trust, 1994), pp. 98–103.

[81] There are six groups of three armorials (eighteen), each group accompanied by a similar quatrefoil motif and all are set on a gilded mosaic background. The attribution of the Gothic Temple to Gibbs by Clarke et al., *Stowe*, p. 23, Friedman, *Gibbs*, p. 196, and Willis, *Bridgeman*, p. 123, is sustained in the National Trust's subsequent publications on Stowe. Wheeler, 'Gibbs and Liberty', Hartwell Seminar 2008, emphasised that Stowe Castle, Keeper's Lodge and the Gothic Temple were among the garden buildings designed by Gibbs at Stowe. However, Michael Bevington suggests that the Gothic Temple might mark the beginnings of the career of Capability Brown as an architect, or it may even be the work of Leoni; see Michael Bevington, 'The Bourbon Tower & The Second Duke's Obelisk', *Templa Quam Dilecta: Stowe*, no. 10 (1991), p. 8.

[82] See Jonathan Marsden, 'Description of the Gardens', in *Stowe Landscape Gardens* (London: National Trust, 1992 and 1997), pp. 8–50 (pp. 36–37); and Michael Bevington, in *Stowe: The Garden and The Park* (Stowe: Capability Books, 1994), pp. 102–04. In 1745 the seven statues of Saxon gods by Michael Rysbrack were relocated from the Saxon Temple (1737) to complement the Gothic Temple's theme of liberty; see also John Kenworthy-Browne, 'Rysbrack's Saxon Deities', *Apollo* (September 1985), pp. 220–27. These deities gave their names to the days of the week: Mona, Tiw, Woden, Thuner, Friga, Seatern, Sunna.

FIGURE 12 George Bickham, Keeper's Lodge and Stowe Castle, engraving, *The Beauties of Stowe*, 1750. *Private collection*

FIGURE 13 George Bickham, The Gothic Temple, engraving, *The Beauties of Stowe*, 1750. *Private collection*

Friendship had been erected by 1730 as the Law Lake temple at Wentworth Castle.[83] As the Stowe temple was equipped with a basement kitchen and cellar it was clearly intended to be used for the convivial entertaining of Cobham's political cronies. While interior murals castigated the alleged corruption of Walpole's government, the place of Frederick Prince of Wales was confirmed among the opposition. The Prince's portrait was among the ten busts that dignified these chums as political friends, contemporary British Worthies and heroes of the anti-Walpole alliance. Clearly all the men portrayed had a vested interest in gaining power through membership of the post-Walpole government. To this end the flexibility of their allegiance reflected the uncertainty of the times. Although celebrating Frederick as the Patriot-King-in-waiting, most of them would enter into secret negotiations with representatives of James III. Consequently these Stowe 'friends' are symptomatic of the perception that the Stuart restoration was a possibility and thus that it was sensible to insure political careers by ensuring a foot in both camps.

The potency of the Stuart claim had consistently destabilised the security of Hanoverian rule. After their disarray during the 1720s, the Tories had been rallied into the alliance with dissident Whigs in 1730 by the direct exhortation of James III. After his resignation

[83] Michael Bevington has also suggested this provenance, see 'The Temple of Friendship', *Templa Quam Dilecta: Stowe*, no. 7 (1990), p. 9.

early in 1742 Walpole acknowledged that his downfall had become inevitable during 1741 due to the way that James had re-mobilised Tory participation in the opposition.[84] The Jacobite plan for a peaceful Stuart restoration had been approved by James in 1731 and was directed in England by Strafford, his cousin Bathurst and two other Tory lords, Gower and Arran,[85] who would later be joined by the Whig Lords Cobham and Westmorland. The plan required the formation of a post-Walpole ministry comprising leading Tories and dissident Whigs who would invite James to take the throne. However, on Walpole's resignation the opposition alliance had crumbled and Argyll's attempt to achieve the government favourable to James III was frustrated by Carteret and Pulteney who formed an exclusively Hanoverian Whig ministry.[86] Yet the apparent imminence of the Stuart restoration was such that by 1743 most of the Stowe 'friends' were effectively Jacobites in that to achieve power they pragmatically connived at the return of James III.

By 1743 the Jacobite aim to create a restoration parliament was supplemented by a council of regency to welcome the Stuart Prince of Wales, Charles Edward, who would be accompanied by a French army. While Cobham and Westmorland, along with six Tories, were to be the regents,[87] most of the political 'friends' represented by the temple's portrait busts were named in the Jacobite list of those who would support the restoration. These were the Tories Bathurst and Gower, and the Whigs Chesterfield, Westmorland and Lyttelton as well as William Pitt. It is likely that the un-named Lords Marchmont and Temple were of the same persuasion.[88] In view of the commitment of Cobham and his 'friends' to the Stuart restoration, it is reasonable to describe his Saxon garden buildings at Stowe as Jacobite Gothic and place them alongside their progenitor at Strafford's Wentworth Castle and their companion at Bathurst's Cirencester Park.[89]

Needless to say, these clandestine and self-serving allegiances would evaporate after the Jacobite defeat at Culloden in 1746. Indeed this proved to be the catalyst for the shift in the use of gothic to articulate an exclusively Whig agenda (Figure 14). The key moment was when, in the wake of the '45, Cobham ordained that an additional inscription should be carved into the Gothic Temple at Stowe. This had nothing whatsoever to do with

[84] Eveline Cruickshank, *Political Untouchables: The Tories and the '45* (London: Gerald Duckworth, 1979), pp. 27–28.

[85] Ibid., p. 12.

[86] Ibid., pp. 27–33.

[87] Ibid., p. 46.

[88] Ibid., Appendix 1, pp. 115–38. Although Cobham's Jacobitism remained a secret to his kinship Whigs, two are named in the 1743 list: George and James Grenville.

[89] Gibbs is also associated with the triangular and castellated Gothic Tower at Whitton Park for the silviculturalist, Archibald Campbell, Earl of Islay and brother of the Duke of Argyll. Erected by 1748, long after the fall of Walpole, this is post-Saxon Gothic and lacks definitive attribution to Gibbs even though, like Stowe's Gothic Temple, it has turrets at each angle and they are pierced, high on each ground floor storey, with his signature quatrefoil windows; see Willis, *Bridgeman*, pp. 72–78, Friedman, *Gibbs*, pp. 162–65, and Michael Symes, Alison Hodges, John Harvey, 'The Plantings at Whitton', *Garden History*, 14.2 (1986), 138–72 (p. 143). Whitton's Gothic Tower represents the time (mid-to-late 1740s) when gothic garden buildings were no longer a rarity. As pattern books began to be published, the features used earlier by Gibbs had become evident in the designs of other architects. The presence of the quatrefoil in Batty Langley's *Ancient Architecture* (1742) and William Halfpenny's *Rural Architecture in the Gothick Taste* (1752), derived from these authors' own researches. For example, the Gothic Temple built at Painshill, *c.* 1745, was derived from Langley's pl. lvi. Moreover, the threat posed by the Jacobite army's march on London in 1745 had amplified the patriotic associations of the now fashionable gothic folly as, doubtless, was the case at Whitton.

FIGURE 14 James Gibbs, The Gothic Temple, Stowe, with tower as enlarged by Sanderson Miller, *c.* 1756. *Photo: the author*

Figure 1 Gipton Spa (Grade II), Gledhow Valley, Leeds. The door gives access to the dressing room, from where an internal door leads through to the open-air bath (behind the wall, to the right). An inscription on a stone set into the inner wall records the builder as Edward Waddington of Gledhow (1671), but the present building may be wholly or partially of a later (eighteenth-century) date. *Photo: Dick Knight, 2008*

Figure 2 Gipton Spa, Leeds. The bath house is built against a slope (a former quarry), where the spring which still supplies water to the cistern is located. *Photo: Dick Knight, 2008*

cisterns, offering the contrast of a warm and cold plunge; such double baths might also point to the more social side of bathing.[8]

Bathing appears to have been predominantly but not exclusively a male activity, but this impression may, to some extent, result from available records rather than reflect reality. It is evident from the separate facilities at some bath houses that women did go into the bath. Although some instances will be touched on here, the role of gender in bath-house use is outside the scope of this paper.

Beyond bathing, the building might also serve a number of other purposes. As an ornamental feature in the wider landscape, it might serve as an eyecatcher; or it might terminate a vista along a canal, beautify walks through the garden or pleasure grounds, or punctuate a carriage drive through the park. Some bath houses would have additional facilities, such as a room for playing cards, for banqueting, or taking tea (with the requisite kitchen facilities); or bathing might be combined with other polite activities, adjacent to a bowling green or boathouse.

Most of the bath houses and plunge pools that survive, or for which we have documentation, were built and used during the long eighteenth century, *c.* 1688–1815. Little is currently known about bath houses constructed pre-1700, and of the few that survive, hard facts are elusive. After 1800, the interest in bathing shifted from the private cold plunge to the commercially run spas, which offered not only more sophisticated hydrotherapy treatments but social networking and a programme of entertainment. The baths discussed here were primarily intended for private use, that is, for family and friends, and possibly servants (as was probably the case at Stockeld). There are some, particularly those where the water source was reputed to have specific therapeutic properties, which seem to have offered limited 'public' access (mostly a public of a certain social class, that is), and some which were later developed into commercial establishments, to exploit the popularity of spas, particularly in the early nineteenth century.[9] Baths of a clearly commercial nature are excluded from this study: this includes spas and public *bagnios*, both of which offered a greater variety of facilities and services, the latter often boasting a reputation as houses of ill-repute.[10]

The terminology used for baths can be somewhat confusing. The designation *spa* (or *spaw*), from the town of that name in Belgium, usually denotes a mineral spring, and may indicate that an eighteenth-century bath house exploited an ancient spring known for its therapeutic qualities. The use of *well* often also indicates an ancient site. But *spa*, *well* and *bathing well* appear to have sometimes been used interchangeably and somewhat loosely (cf. Gipton Spa/Well in Leeds). The term *bagnio* seems to have been used of buildings on a grander scale, more luxuriously appointed, and was no doubt adopted to suggest something of the exotic, the emphasis perhaps being on hedonism as much as

[8] The Green House at Wanstead, Essex, boasted a double bath in the early 1700s; my thanks to Andrew Skelton for this information.

[9] Sir William Chaytor of Croft Hall (in the North Riding of Yorkshire) transformed a cold bath in a field into Croft Spa Baths; Ignatius Bonomi designed later buildings, c. 1827. Bonomi also designed spa buildings for Sir William Worsley at Hovingham, but the enterprise did not take off. See also Phyllis Hembry, *British Spas from 1815 to the Present* (London: Athlone Press, 1997), pp. 75–76.

[10] Cf. illustrations by Rowlandson, and Hogarth's *The Bagnio* in his *Marriage à la Mode* series.

health.[11] The terms *bath* and *bath house* will be used here, where the focus is on the building's function in garden design.

Bath houses, or evidence of them, can be found across the British Isles and beyond: in France, Switzerland, Germany, Slovakia, Finland, Russia, Cuba, and Greece, some modest, others exotic or opulent. The bath complex by the Scottish architect, Charles Cameron, for Catherine the Great at Tsarskoye Selo (1779–92) is perhaps the grandest of all.

Although the emphasis here is on the bath house as garden building, a proper understanding of its purpose and status extends beyond the obvious domain of architecture and garden design. The bath house concretises the *mores* of polite eighteenth-century society; it embodies developments in science, medicine, engineering, and technology; and even religion plays a part in the history of bathing – so something of this historical background, as well as a brief account of the architecture, is needed to contextualise the bath house in the garden.

HISTORICAL CONTEXT

Antiquity and Superstition

The spring or well feeding an eighteenth-century bath house was often known to have existed for centuries. Some sources had sacred associations dating back to pagan times, and it is likely that some would have been exploited by the Romans for both public and private bath houses. Subsequently, some took on Christian significance, arising from supposed therapeutic qualities of the water and claims for the occurrence of miraculous cures – hence designations such as Holywell, or Lady Well, or dedication to a named saint.[12] After the break from Rome, both Church and Government tried to suppress the cult of water and associations with miracles, and to discourage pilgrimages to such sites, which might be a gathering point for Catholic subversion.[13] Throughout the eighteenth century, writers recalled the earlier religious associations of wells currently used for bathing or dipping. Sir John Floyer MD (1649–1734), one of the most celebrated advocates of cold bathing, recorded the association of St Mungo and St Winifred with miracles at wells and springs in his seminal work *Psykhroloysia, or the History of Cold-Bathing* (first published *c.* 1702); and he dedicated his own bath near Lichfield to St Chad, the patron saint of springs. Yet, as a physician, Floyer was advocating the benefits of cold bathing from a medical and scientific, not a religious, standpoint.[14] In the early 1730s, John Macky, a Whig sympathiser and fervent anti-Catholic, recorded that St Winifred's Well

[11] An example would be Lord Burlington's *Bagnio* at Chiswick (1717, gone).

[12] In Yorkshire, there are many examples of wells dedicated to St Helen, probably a reference to the mother of the Roman Emperor Constantine the Great, who brought Christianity to this country.

[13] See Janet and Colin Bord, *Sacred Waters: Holy Wells and Water Lore in Britain and Ireland* (London: Paladin Books, 1986), pp. 44–47.

[14] John Floyer, *Psykhroloysia or, the History of Cold-Bathing*, 4th edn (London: 1715), p. 170. See also Richard Kentish, *An Essay on Sea-Bathing and the Internal Use of Sea-Water* (London: J. Murray, 1787), p. 7; *Englishmen at Rest and Play: Some Phases of English Leisure 1558–1714*, ed. by R. V. Lennard (Oxford: Clarendon Press, 1931), p. 10.

Figure 3 (above) The cistern at Gipton Spa. This has recently been cleared of the rubbish which had collected over many years, and the water still runs clear. *Photo: Dick Knight, 2008*

Figure 4 (left) Gipton Spa, showing the steps leading down into the water and the door through into the dressing room. *Photo: Dick Knight, 2008*

at Holywell, Flint, which began life as a medieval well chapel, dedicated to a seventh-century Welsh saint, remained a place of pilgrimage for Catholics;[15] and writing of Ewel, in Surrey, Macky seized on the opportunity to deride the old superstitions:

> Yet the Cold Bath, lately erected on the bottom of this pretended Miracle, meets with little Encouragement, as the old Story it self doth with Belief; it not being the Fashion in this, as in some other Countries, to have salutiferous waters under the Inspection of the Parson, or the Protection of a Saint.[16]

The Leeds antiquarian, Ralph Thoresby, wrote in the early 1700s of Gipton Well, at Gledhow in Leeds: 'At this Place a very curious *cold Spring*, which in a *Romish* Country could not have miss'd the Patronage of some Saint.'[17] Thoresby himself records visits to Gipton and to St Mungo's Well at Copgrove, Yorkshire, a popular bathing establishment.[18]

It is possible that the association with ancient water sources was exploited by builders of bath houses to add gravitas to the building, and to intimate the antiquity of the family and its seat, in much the same way that ancient sites were chosen for sham castles or mausoleums. A bath house designed in 1741 by James Gibbs for the 4th Duke of Leeds at Kiveton, South Yorkshire, was to be located 'over St Nicolaus's Well', and the elevation bears the name in Latin, 'Fons St Nicolai'.[19] Even if the spring or well had no demonstrable pedigree, this could be created, in the same way that the artificial ruin or sham castle, both essential garden features, suggested antiquity.

One further important aspect of history associated with bath houses was their classical tradition, familiar to the eighteenth-century nobleman or gentleman through his travels in Italy on the Grand Tour, or through the paintings, prints, and drawings by architects and artists such as Palladio, William Kent, Robert Adam, and Charles Cameron. Just as the triumphal arches and temples of Rome were transplanted to British estates, so might the ancient bath houses have inspired, in some instances, their northern offspring. The distinctive domed roof, pierced with an oculus and rectangular apertures in the stone to admit the light, as described by Vitruvius and Cameron,[20] was sometimes copied into the

[15] John Macky, *A Journey through England. In Familiar Letters, from a Gentleman here, to his Friend Abroad*, 5th edn, 2 vols (London: 1732), II, 156. For a further account of St Winifred's see P. R. Angerstein's *Illustrated Travel Diary, 1753–1755: Industry in England and Wales from a Swedish Perspective*, trans. by Torsten and Peter Berg (London: Science Museum, 2001), p. 323.

[16] Macky, I (5th edn), 153.

[17] Ralph Thoresby, *Ducatus Leodiensis*, 1st edn (London: Maurice Atkins, 1715), p. 113.

[18] *The Diary of Ralph Thoresby*, FRS, *1677–1724*, ed. by Revd Joseph Hunter, 2 vols (London: Henry Colburn and Richard Bentley, 1830), I, 12 July 1694, 8 July 1693; II, 19 July 1708.

[19] Terry Friedman, *James Gibbs* (New Haven: Yale University Press, 1984), p. 190, Plate 212. The reason for this dedication is unclear.

[20] Vitruvius, *Ten Books on Architecture*, trans. by Ingrid Rowland (Cambridge: Cambridge University Press, 1999), V. 10, p. 72; Charles Cameron, *The Baths of the Romans* (London: 1775), p. 13. Cameron's illustration of the *caldarium* at Pisa (p. 48) shows a domed ceiling, lit by an oculus and rectangular lights cut around it.

British bath house design, thus invoking the occasional designation 'Roman'.[21] Such a true 'Roman-style' bath would, of course, have a pedigree, reflecting the education and taste of its owner. The St Nicolaus's Well bath house at Kiveton was to have 'facilities like those recommended in descriptions of Laurentinum' (the villa of Pliny the Younger).[22]

Enlightenment and Empiricism

In the seventeenth and early eighteenth centuries, claims for the benefits of immersion in cold water migrated from the realms of religion (particularly the superstition and miraculous intervention associated with Catholicism) to natural philosophy (science) and medicine, with a growing reliance on empirical knowledge. Cold bathing was recommended for maintaining and improving health generally, and also for treating specific ailments, the benefits emanating from immersion in water that was simply cold and 'pure', or with specific mineral content.

Those advocating the benefits of cold bathing (physicians and apothecaries) felt it necessary to distance themselves from religion and demonstrate rationality. A very early example of this can be seen in Michael Stanhope's *Newes out of Yorke-shire* (1626), where he contrasts 'iugling imposturing, Romish Priests' and their 'Mountebank trickes', attracting crowds to their 'Sainted Wells', to the 'reall, vertuall [efficacious] Spring' at Knaresborough;[23] and in 1652, the physician John French said of these medicinal wells:

> Let not any one judge me to be a Catholick by this my approbation of this Sainted Well [St Mungo's Well], for I am none [...] I do not out of any superstitious account attribute any medicinal virtues to the Sainted Well [...] The reason of my vindication of it, is grounded upon some notable cures, which I have seen effected thereby.[24]

Although the latest scientific method was applied, and 'evidence' was adduced for the healing properties of water, it is clear that not all the results were verifiable, or repeatable; nor could cause and effect be demonstrated – although it must be recognised that false beliefs should not necessarily be equated with irrational beliefs. New approaches continued to rub shoulders with old ideas, as demonstrated by Sir John Floyer, whose

[21] Such architectural features could be found in Richard Payne Knight's bath at Downton, Herefordshire (which survives, albeit ruinous), sometimes referred to as 'Roman'; the 'Roman bath' at Painshill, Surrey (gone); and the cold bath at Wrest Park, Bedfordshire. It seems that some bath houses may also have acquired the name 'Roman' due to a belief, plausible or otherwise, that the site dated back to Roman times. In other cases, any rationale for the epithet has been lost in the mists of time; or has been misapplied, due to lack of information and access: cf. the underground bath at Northowram Hall, Northowram, West Yorkshire, described as being in 'pseudo Roman style', in P. W. Robinson, 'Commercial, Hydropathic and Private Baths in Calderdale in the Eighteenth and Nineteenth Centuries', *Transactions of the Halifax Antiquarian Society*, n.s. 3 (1995), 1995, 71–89 (p. 84).

[22] Friedman, p. 189.

[23] Michael Stanhope, *Newes out of Yorke-shire* (London, 1626), pp. 28–29.

[24] John French, *The York-shire Spaw* (London, 1652), pp. 123–24.

prolific writings displayed a simultaneous enthusiasm for research and inquiry, and adherence to old notions of physiology, such as 'the Fermentation of the humours'.[25]

While bathing was undoubtedly a modish activity (gravitating towards hedonism, for some individuals), and building a bath house on one's estate served as yet another vehicle for displaying status, it was nevertheless the case that immersion in cold water was widely believed to promote general well-being and to cure particular ailments. In a letter to Floyer, Dr Nathaniel Ellison distinguishes between 'the Healthful that go in for Pleasure' and 'distemper'd People'.[26] Henry Hoare clearly found unalloyed pleasure in his grotto bath at Stourhead, during the hot summer of 1764: 'A souse in that delicious bath and grot, filld with fresh magic, is Asiatick luxury, and just too much for mortals, or at least for subjects.'[27]

As for the vast range of specific distempers that immersion was claimed to alleviate or cure, these included leprosy, eczema, rabies, rickets, rheumatism, gout, asthma, deafness, and infertility. While some claims were grounded in the state of medical knowledge at the time, it is evident that many such claims were grossly exaggerated, and some strayed into quackery. Bath houses known for having water with particular qualities (such as chalybeate wells, containing iron), whether private, public, or semi-public, would have been sought out for such ailments. In Leeds, Ralph Thoresby 'dipped' his son to cure his lameness (1708),[28] and Lady Mary Wortley Montague had her son dipped in the cold well at Water Fulford, near York, while living at nearby Middlethorpe Hall.[29]

The prevailing belief in the efficacy of cold bathing is demonstrated by the presence during the eighteenth century in many gentlemen's libraries of literature on the medical benefits, and the many references in personal correspondence between family and friends. Robert Molesworth (later Viscount Molesworth) wrote to the Hon. Mrs Molesworth in June 1707 from his estate at Edlington, near Doncaster: 'On Monday I began to use my own cold bath. All I can tell you is that it has done me no hurt.' And in July, he reported:

> On Wednesday last I first began to bathe in St. Catherine's Well, and have been twice in it, and once in my own in the cow pasture over head and ears; as yet I can only tell you that it does me no harm, and, I believe will do me a great deal of good.[30]

Molesworth owned estates in Ireland, and had acquired the small Edlington estate some seven years previously; it appears from his comment here that he had not embarked on any landscaping for his bath 'in the cow pasture'.

[25] 'A Letter from the Late Sir John Floyer to Mr King of Bungay, Suffolk' (dated 21 April 1728), in *Gentleman's Magazine*, 4 (1734), 197–98 (p. 197). Correspondence from the Husbands Bosworth estate, Leicestershire, shows that a copy of Floyer's *Psykhroloysia* was purchased in 1787, suggesting it was still consulted many decades later (Leicestershire, Leicester and Rutland Record Office, DG39/708). See *Oxford Dictionary of National Biography* for a full account of Sir John Floyer.

[26] Floyer, *Psykhroloysia*, p. 127.

[27] Kenneth Woodbridge, *The Stourhead Landscape*, 2nd edn (London: National Trust, 2002), p. 23.

[28] Thoresby, *Diary*, II, pp. 8–9.

[29] *The Complete Letters of Lady Mary Wortley Montague*, ed. by Robert Halsband, 3 vols (Oxford: Clarendon Press, 1965–67), I, pp. 209, 211 (letters to Wortley, 26 and 30 July 1714).

[30] Historic Manuscripts Commission, *Report on Manuscripts in Various Collections*, VIII (London: HMSO, 1913), pp. 237–38. St Catherine's Well is probably the site still marked on the OS map between Edlington Wood and Loversall, at the intersection of the A1(M) and M18.

The practice of cold bathing, together with claims for the benefits accruing from it, were closely linked to advances in scientific methods, the development of scientific and medical instruments, and increased understanding of human physiology. A persistent and consistent water supply, of a reliable quality and at a constant temperature, was fundamental to bathing, and so developments in measuring temperature, analysing content, and recording results were of great significance. Floyer described how, *c.* 1701, he had identified the coldest spring water for his own bath using a 'Portable Thermometer' and a 'Minute-Glass';[31] and in a letter to Floyer, apothecary John King reported that he measured the coldness of the water with a portable thermometer and 'try'd its Weight with a Hydrostatic Balance' before erecting his cold bath at Bungay.[32]

Another prominent figure associated with cold bathing was Dr Thomas Short of Sheffield, who published two volumes in 1734 and 1740, giving locations of springs and wells across the English counties, together with detailed analysis of mineral content and medical applications. He corresponded at some length on the subject with Dr Richard Richardson FRS of North Bierley, West Yorkshire, celebrated antiquary and botanist, whom Short described as 'a most valuable friend', and samples from sources in the neighbourhood were collected with Richardson's cooperation.[33] Short dedicated his first volume (on Yorkshire and adjoining counties) to Sir Hans Sloane and the Royal Society, and his subscribers were drawn from the nobility and gentry, and from physicians, surgeons, and apothecaries.[34]

The rationale for cold water bathing was that immersion followed by raising body temperature stimulated the circulation, opened the pores, and encouraged perspiration: hence the fireplace in the dressing room of bath houses, where the bather would rub down the body and take a warm drink.[35] Common advice to the healthy was to bathe regularly, in the morning, mainly but not exclusively in summer, and to remain in the water only briefly. Dr Cheyne's observations on how bathers should proceed explains much of the design of the bath house:

I cannot approve the precipitant Way of jumping in, or throwing the Head foremost into a Cold bath [...] The Natural Way is, holding by the Rope, to walk down the Steps as fast as

[31] John Floyer, *Psykhroloysia*, p. 17.

[32] John King, *An Essay on Hot and Cold Bathing* (London, 1737), pp. x–xi. A hydrostatic balance was used to obtain specific gravity. Accurate measurements of temperature were problematic until Gabriel Fahrenheit developed first the alcohol thermometer in 1709, and then the mercury version, and his eponymous scale, in 1714: see John Gribbin, *Science: A History 1543–2001* (London: Penguin Books, 2003), pp. 242–43.

[33] John Nichols, *Illustrations of the Literary History of the Eighteenth Century*, 8 vols (London: printed for the author by Nichols, Son, and Bentley, 1817–58), I, 794–98 (correspondence dated 1731–46).

[34] Thomas Short, *The Natural, Experimental, and Medicinal History of the Mineral Waters of Derbyshire, Lincolnshire, and Yorkshire* (London: printed for the author, 1734); and *An Essay towards a Natural, Experimental, and Medicinal History of the Principle* [*sic*] *Mineral Waters of Cumberland, etc.* (Sheffield: printed for the author, 1740). Subscribers from Yorkshire or with local estates included the Earl of Burlington; Samuel Buck of Rotherham; the Earl of Carlisle; John Dickson of Leeds, gent; John Grimston of Burlington, esq; William Hillary, MD, Leeds; Samuel Ibbertson of Denton, esq; Richard Richardson MD, of North Byerley; Hon. Sir Thomas Robinson; Hon. Sir George Saville, bart; Hon. Sir William Strickland; William Spencer of Bramley Grange, esq; Sir William Wentworth, bart; Ben Wynne, surgeon, Leeds.

[35] See George Cheyne, *An Essay of Health and Long Life* (London: printed for George Strahan, 1724), pp. 100–02; also Kentish, pp. 24–27; Adam Hunter, *An Essay on Two Mineral Springs at Harrogate; and on the Springs of Thorp-Arch and Ilkley* (Leeds: Robinson, 1819), pp. 117–20.

one can, when got to the Bottom, bending their Hams (as Women do when they Curt'sy low) to shorten their Length, so as to bring their Heads a good Way under Water, and then popping up again to take Breath, and thus alternately for two or three Times, and out again, rubbing and currying well before they are dress'd.[36]

However, medical advice was sometimes treated with scepticism: in a letter to Thomas Wentworth, 1st Earl of Strafford, his cousin Lord Bathurst tells him he is 'more likely to find benefit' to his poor health from the pleasures of his estate at Wentworth Castle than by 'all Dr. Cheney's prescriptions'.[37]

ARCHITECTS AND CRAFTSMEN

As with all garden buildings, some owners commissioned architects, craftsmen and landscape gardeners of renown to design, ornament, and landscape the bath house: Sir John Vanbrugh, William Kent, James Gibbs, James Paine, Sanderson Miller, Robert Adam, Lancelot 'Capability' Brown, John Carr of York, Richard Woods, Humphry Repton, Sir James Thornhill, Francesco Vassalli – all worked on bath houses. For those patrons of lesser means, the estate mason could work from examples in pattern books. And, as with other garden buildings, some bath houses would have been designed by the owner, 'gentleman' architects or landscape gardeners such as John Evelyn, Lord Burlington, Alexander Pope, and Richard Payne Knight. In some cases, interior decoration might have been created by family members or friends, as at Walton Hall, Warwickshire, where Mrs Delany and the ladies of the house were responsible for the shell work.[38] But too often, it is impossible to establish authorship: garden buildings of this kind rarely merited the presentation drawings provided for the main house, and the working plans would have been discarded, mislaid, or destroyed.

While celebrated architects, landscape gardeners and craftsmen worked on other projects in Yorkshire, evidence for them working on bath houses here is sadly lacking or inconclusive. Vanbrugh, for example, designed bath houses at Stowe and at Eastbury (Dorset), but not, as far as we know, at Castle Howard; we have nothing as magnificent as Robert Adam's Fishing Pavilion at Kedleston Hall, Derbyshire, with cold bath, boat houses, and fishing room. Gibbs's design for a bath house at Kiveton was unexecuted.[39] Stuccoist Francesco Vassalli, one of 'Gibbs's *stuccatori*' at Wentworth Castle, worked on the Italian staircase and ceilings in the mansion (*c.* 1730), and at Gibside (Co. Durham), he was responsible for elaborate plasterwork in the bath house (built 1733–36); but if he worked on a bath house at Wentworth Castle or elsewhere in Yorkshire, this has yet to be discovered.[40]

[36] Cheyne, pp. 102–03.
[37] *The Wentworth Papers 1705–39* (London: Wyman, 1883), p. 523 (letter dated 17 July 1736). It seems likely that Dr Cheyne and Dr Cheney are one and the same.
[38] William Hawkes, 'The Walton Bath House, Warwickshire', *Follies Journal*, 1 (2001), 29–34 (p. 29).
[39] Friedman, p. 321.
[40] For Vassalli's involvement at Wentworth Castle, see the paper by Patrick Eyres in this volume. For the bath house at Gibside, see Margaret Wills, *Gibside and the Bowes Family* (Society of Antiquaries of Newcastle upon Tyne, 1995), pp. 18–21.

We know that John Carr of York designed a number of bath houses. At Harewood House, near Leeds, Carr presented a bill for eight guineas for: 'All day there [22 August 1778] to view the situation proposed for a Bath by Mr Lascelles order. And afterwards making the plan and Elevation for the bath.' It is not clear whether this design was accepted, for in November 1778, William Belwood, architect and surveyor from York, also produced plans, and presented his bill: 'Finish'd designs for a bath vizt a plan, the elevation of one end, two elevations of the sides, & a section.'[41] A bath house was indeed built, since references to work at 'the Bathing Place' and 'the new Bathing Place' occur in the accounts in 1796,[42] and a surveyor's notebook of *c.* 1812 shows 'Bath', an L-shaped building, on or near the site of Nun's Well, at Arthington Nunnery, part of the Harewood estate;[43] but who designed the building cannot be determined.

Carr also produced a design for a Doric bath house at Kilnwick Hall, Kilnwick-on-the-Wolds, probably at the time when he was engaged by John Grimston to carry out alterations to the house in the 1770s. This drawing was in the possession of the architect Francis Johnson until his death in 1995, but all attempts to trace its current whereabouts have so far failed. This bath house may have been intended for a site in the garden known as 'Lady's Well'.[44] A report of another drawing by John Carr, for a 'Bagnio or Bath-house for his Lordship' (2nd Marquis of Rockingham) at Wentworth Woodhouse, has so far been impossible to substantiate: the bath may have been located in a building to the rear of the north tower of the house; however, despite extensive searches and inquiries, this drawing has also not been found.[45] At Denton Hall, near Ilkley, where Carr was responsible for the house, stables, and church (1770s), a small building which could be a bath house (or possibly a well house) is very much in the Carr style; its location to the north of the house suggests it could have served as an eyecatcher.[46] A bath at Wetherby Grange may have been by Carr, possibly based on a design by James Wyatt.[47]

As for other sites, we can only speculate that the architect responsible for the house or other garden buildings might also have designed the bath house. We do not know who designed the bath house at Stockeld, but James Paine designed the house, and designed bath houses elsewhere, including a particularly fine Doric example (built *c.* 1745) at Hardwick Hall, in County Durham, the foundations of which can still be seen.[48] John Platt, architect of Thundercliffe Grange, near Rotherham, might also have designed the bath

[41] West Yorkshire Archive Service, Leeds (hereafter WYL), WYL 250/367 and 364, bills dated 6 September 1780 and 3 August 1779 respectively. These plans have not been found or identified in the Harewood archives.

[42] WYL 250/407.

[43] WYL 250 Survey 20/Book 9.

[44] 'Lady's Well' is shown on Francis Johnson's 1951 reconstruction of the gardens in 1750, based on a contemporary survey: see David Neave and Deborah Turnbull, *Landscaped Parks and Gardens of East Yorkshire* (Bridlington: Georgian Society for East Yorkshire, 1992), p. 47. Only remnants of the gardens remain.

[45] This drawing was seen in the 1960s, and the elevation matched a building which was subsequently used as a fives court, and then as a store for the groundsmen in the 1960s when Wentworth Woodhouse was a teacher training college. Unfortunately, the member of the teaching staff who saw the plan has since died.

[46] George Sheeran, *Landscape Gardens in West Yorkshire 1680–1880* (Wakefield: Wakefield Historical Publications, 1990), p. 211, also identifies this as a possible bath house.

[47] See further discussion on this below.

[48] See *The Reawakening of Hardwick Park, Sedgefield* (The Friends of Hardwick, 2002), pp. 15–16; and http://www.friendsofhardwick.org.uk for more information.

there (Figure 5), for in 1783 he records that he was 'At Grange wth Lady Effingham & set out a build^{g} for a Dairy'.[49]

LANDSCAPE SETTING

The siting of the bath house was largely determined by a suitable water source, but whatever the nature of that source (spring or well, diverted stream, or seawater), the building would be incorporated into an existing designed landscape, or a new design would be created around it, just as with other garden buildings. In formal gardens and parks of the late 1600s and early 1700s, the bath house might terminate a vista along an *allée*, as at Chiswick House, where the *bagnio* (designed by Lord Burlington, 1717) terminated the *allée* on a *patte d'oie*; or along a canal, as at Rufford Abbey, Nottinghamshire, where the Bath-Summerhouse (1729) formed part of 'an axial vista' along a serpentine stream and tree-lined canal.[50] In later, more informal landscapes, the bath house might form part of the pleasure grounds, set on a path amidst lawns and ornamental plantings: at Four Ashes Hall, Enville, Staffordshire, a circular perambulation, the Bath Walk, created between 1807 and 1838 and planted with a variety of hollies, incorporated the eighteenth-century bath house and adjoining pools.[51] In the park, the bath house might punctuate a drive or ride, perhaps nestling in a sequestered corner, or offering a prospect over a river, lake, or distant countryside. George Bowes placed his bath house at Gibside on a revetted shelf seventy feet (21 m) above the River Derwent. Valentine Morris's bath house at Piercefield, Chepstow, was set on a path offering spectacular, Gilpinesque views over the River Wye. An existing bath house on the estuary at Antony in Cornwall was to be incorporated into a winding walk in Humphry Repton's proposed improvements (1792). A setting on a river bank, overhung by trees, could create a quintessentially Picturesque or romantic scene: Richard Payne Knight's bath on the banks of the Teme at Downton Castle, Herefordshire, is a perfect example of this.[52] So the bath house would offer pleasant surroundings not only for those plunging into the bath itself, but also for those taking tea there; and, for those doing the tour of the estate, it would serve as an ornamental interlude en route.

In the sixteenth and seventeenth centuries, the bath would be found in the gardens close to the house. In Yorkshire, at Leconfield Castle, near Beverley, a 1537 survey recorded a banqueting house used for bathing, in the garden.[53] Such a (detached) banqueting house would provide a view down over the garden or out over the deer park from the

[49] Sheffield Archives (SA), A116, John Platt's journal, 1763–96 (microfilm).

[50] The *bagnio* at Chiswick was pulled down in 1778: see John Harris, *The Palladian Revival: Lord Burlington, his Villa and Garden at Chiswick* (New Haven and London: Yale University Press, 1994), p. 57. For the Bath-Summerhouse at Rufford Abbey (restored), see Alice Dugdale, 'John Hallam: "A Poor Country Joiner"?', *Georgian Group Journal*, 7 (1997), 37–42 (p. 41).

[51] Both bath house and walk survive. My thanks to Dianne Barre and owner Stephen Thompson for documentary evidence for this site.

[52] Only traces of the Gibside bath house survive (but the dramatic setting can still be appreciated); the Piercefield bath is nothing more than a boggy pile of stones; that at Downton survives as a ruin.

[53] See David Neave and Edward Waterson, *Lost Houses of East Yorkshire* (Bridlington: Georgian Society for East Yorkshire, 1988), p. 41.

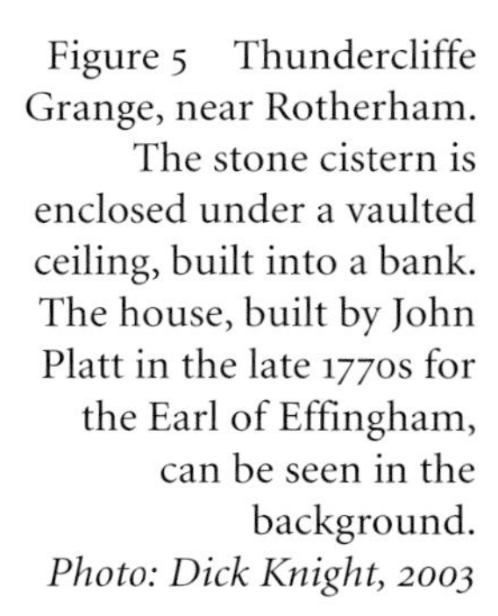

Figure 5 Thundercliffe Grange, near Rotherham. The stone cistern is enclosed under a vaulted ceiling, built into a bank. The house, built by John Platt in the late 1770s for the Earl of Effingham, can be seen in the background. *Photo: Dick Knight, 2003*

upper floor, where the 'banquet' would be laid out, and the bath would most likely have been at ground floor or basement level.[54] A tower at Heath, near Wakefield, is a slightly later example of a belvedere or viewing tower with what may have been a bath in the basement: known as Dame Mary Bolles's Well, and originally belonging to Heath Old Hall, this Grade II* building is described by English Heritage as an early to mid-seventeenth-century water tower, housing a nineteenth-century water wheel.[55] A large cistern, carved out of the bed rock, is fed by a spring; it is thought the building supplied water to the Hall and to a nearby ironworks.

Moving into the late 1600s and early 1700s, we still find some baths relatively close to the house.[56] Sometimes, they would be combined with a summerhouse. At Sowerby Croft in Sowerby Bridge, near Halifax, a two-storey stone gazebo (Grade II), possibly dating from around 1700, stands at the corner of what could have been a small formal garden of the late seventeenth or early eighteenth century. The upper room, originally reached by an external staircase, has evidence of ornamental plasterwork; on the ground

[54] A sixteenth-century banqueting house at Weston, Otley, has evidence of water at ground level, suggesting the possibility of it once housing a bath. However, at Theobalds, Hertfordshire, a German traveller, Paul Hentzner, described (1598) a summerhouse where 'the upper part of it is set round with cisterns of lead, into which the water is conveyed through pipes, so that fish may be kept in them, and in summer time they are very convenient for bathing': quoted in Jennifer Potter, *Strange Blooms: The Curious Lives and Adventures of the John Tradescants* (London: Atlantic Books, 2006), pp. 15–16.

[55] Sheeran, pp. 213–14. Dame Mary Bolles owned Heath Old Hall 1635–60. See English Heritage (EH) 'Images of England' (IoE) website, <http://www.imagesofengland.org.uk/> IoE no. 342391, for listing information [accessed 9 February 2009]. All future references giving IoE number can be accessed through this website.

[56] One such example is at Packwood House, Warwickshire, where an open-air plunge pool, some fifty metres from the house, is dated to 1680: *Packwood House* (National Trust, 2000), p. 25; IoE no. 308307.

floor ('semi-subterranean, with a small "mezzanine" window') is a small stone-lined bath.[57]

A 1758 lease of property in Beverley records a 'messuage' on the north side of Flemingate, with 'a bathing house built by John Hoggard at North end of the garden'.[58] In a similar lease of 1761 for the same property, John Hoggard was described as 'gentleman'. Hoggard later became an alderman, and then mayor of Beverley; if this was the same John Hoggard who was described as a tanner in 1749, then this would be an example of upward social mobility, with the construction of a bath house demonstrating his status as a gentleman in polite society.

On a grander scale, at Wentworth House (now Wentworth Woodhouse) in South Yorkshire, Thomas Wentworth, Lord Malton (later 1st Marquis of Rockingham), built a 'Greenhouse and Bagnio' (1725–27). A 1731 plan[59] shows the building at right angles to the west front of the house; to the north, it forms one side of a walled garden, laid out with parterres; its southern façade looks out across a lawn, divided into quarters, each set with a large obelisk, towards lines of what appear to be pleached fruit trees, and a bowling green, set along the vast terrace bordering the park. The greenhouse and *bagnio* form part of the late 1720s formal garden layout.[60] Thus we see a conjunction of three of the polite activities indulged in by gentlemen of taste, centring on the greenhouse, bath, and bowling green.[61] A similar combination of greenhouse and bath (pre-1713) could be found at Wanstead in Essex, and at Buckingham House, London. In *c.* 1710, the Duke of Buckingham described 'a little square garden that has a fountain in the middle and two green houses on the sides, with a convenient bathing apartment in one of them; and near another part of it lies a flower garden'. Interestingly, the Duke also mentions a 'little closet of Books at the end of that green-house', and, under the windows of the closet and greenhouse, 'a little wilderness full of blackbirds and nightingales' – perhaps we haven't fully appreciated that the sound of birds singing might also have been a pleasure afforded by garden buildings.[62] The idea of a bath incorporated into a complex of gentlemanly activities perhaps reached its apogee in an unexecuted garden temple (*c.* 1770) at Chartley, Staffordshire, for the 5th Earl Ferrers, connoisseur and virtuoso, which

[57] The EH listing (IoE no. 339346) states the gazebo stood in a former tentercroft, and suggests a date of mid-eighteenth century, which seems somewhat late for the style; it makes no mention of a garden, and does not describe the interior of the ground floor (so no mention of the bath). I am grateful to George Sheeran for sharing his field notes on the garden and the interior of the gazebo; and see Sheeran, pp. 20 and 22.

[58] East Riding of Yorkshire Archives and Record Service, Beverley, Beverley Borough Records, DDBC/16/181. The site is now much changed, and the bath house has probably gone.

[59] SA, WWM Add. 204, Plan of the garden, park ..., Seat of the Rt. Hon. Thos. Lord Malton (inscribed: 'Latitude of this Seat taken by Mr. Gordon June 21st 1731').

[60] In the General Rent Roll 1723–1750, the 1st Marquis of Rockingham (formerly Lord Malton) records that the obelisks were installed 1728–29: SA, WWM/A/1273.

[61] The greenhouse would house a gentleman's collection of exotics, which could be shown to visitors.

[62] Letter to the Duke of Shrewsbury, quoted in Peter Coats, *The Gardens of Buckingham Palace* (London: Michael Joseph, 1978), p. 37. At Wanstead, the greenhouse had two end pavilions, that to the west housing a bathing chamber and adjacent bedchamber. My thanks to Andrew Skelton for bringing these examples to my attention. At Carshalton, the grand, lavishly-appointed 'Water Tower' (c. 1718), standing originally at the end of a canal designed by Charles Bridgeman, included a bathing chamber and greenhouse (restored). See Jean Irvine Knight, 'The Greenhouse and Bagnio at the Bottom of the Garden: The Water Tower, Carshalton, Surrey', *Follies Journal*, 4 (2004), 27–40.

combined an observatory, hot and cold baths, study, rooms for billiards, music, and mathematical instruments, and a walk for conversation.[63]

Thundercliffe Grange, near Rotherham, a country house begun in the late 1770s by John Platt for the Earl of Effingham, retains a bath barely one hundred metres west of the house (see Figure 5). Siting a bath near the house itself at this date was more unusual: a 1773 survey by William Fairbanks shows a 'well' at this location,[64] so perhaps the sheer convenience of a suitable water source was exploited. The bath is set into a slope in the pleasure grounds, facing across ponds and a water course towards an area marked as 'Shrubbery' on OS maps between 1893 and 1935. The gardens are now much reduced, cut off to the immediate south west by the M1. So far, no documentation has been found regarding the construction and original appearance of the bath, although it is likely that it was built at the same time as the house, possibly also designed by John Platt. What survives today is a stone tank beneath a smooth ashlar, semi-circular vaulted ceiling; the roof is now covered in vegetation. If the front archway of the bath has always been open, perhaps with just an iron gate across the entrance for security (evidence of a gate or door survives), a bather would have had a pleasant view out across the gardens. The current shape and state of the roof invites speculation that the vaulted ceiling might once have carried the floor of an upper chamber, perhaps similar to the mid-eighteenth-century bath house at Walton Hall: here, also set on a sloping site, a banqueting room surmounted a cyclopean rock-work base, with the bathing chamber inside the low rock-work vault at ground level, thus affording the bather a view across the valley.[65]

In the town of Wetherby, a Grade II-listed bath house that once stood in a modest garden on the banks of the River Wharfe has not only survived but was handsomely restored in the 1990s, and recently landscaped (Figures 6 and 7). The property, like most of the town, was originally part of the Devonshire estate, and sold as Lot 37 in the great Wetherby sale of 1824:

A very comfortable DWELLING HOUSE in WestGate, most delightfully situate in a Paddock on the Banks of the Wharfe, with Flower Garden, and Kitchen Garden [...] A valuable Paddock and Croft, in which is a convenient Bath and Dressing Room, near the River.[66]

An example of a surviving bath house with a long history that was incorporated into an eighteenth-century ornamental landscape is Gipton Spa in Gledhow Valley, Leeds (see Figures 1–4). The spring was noted in a survey for James I,[67] and an inscription on a stone built into the wall records: HOC FAECIT EDVARDUS WADDINGTON DE GLEADOWE ANNOQVAE DOMINI 1671 (*Built by Edward Waddington of Gledhow AD 1671*). The current building has, however, probably undergone some restoration at various times. Ralph

[63] Leicestershire, Leicester and Rutland Record Office, 26 D 53/2138. My thanks to Dianne Barre for bringing the drawings for the temple to my attention.

[64] Information from residents and archaeologists working at the site in 2004.

[65] The pool in the grotto at Stourhead offered the bather an entrancing view out across the surface of the lake to the bridge and church.

[66] WYL 160/98/12, sales particulars for 'The Whole Town of Wetherby', 1824. For a history of the bath house and its restoration, see Peter H. Thornborrow, 'The Bath House, Wharfedale Lawn, Wetherby, West Yorkshire', *Follies Journal*, 1 (2001), 35–40.

[67] See Karen Lynch, 'Gipton Spa, Leeds', *Follies Journal*, 1 (2001), 43–44 (p. 43).

Figure 6 (above) The bath house (listed Grade II) at Wharfedale Lawn, Wetherby, overlooking the River Wharfe. The building (no date known, but probably eighteenth century) was restored in the 1990s after the roof and most of the front wall had collapsed. The door leads into an upper room with a fireplace. *Photo: Dick Knight, 2003*

Figure 7 (left) The bath house at Wetherby. The door leads down into the bathing chamber at ground level. *Photo: Dick Knight, 2003*

Thoresby stated in 1715 that this bath was 'frequented by Persons of Honour', i.e. it had limited public access.[68] When Jeremiah Dixon FRS, a Leeds merchant, bought Gledhow Hall estate in 1764, he redesigned the pleasure grounds and woods, incorporating the bath house. Like many extant bath houses, the fairly plain little classical structure we see today has a rather forlorn air about it: it is roofed with corrugated iron, and has been fenced off by the council against vandals and other 'undesirables';[69] but when it featured

[68] *Ducatus Leodiensis*, p. 113.
[69] It is now in the care of the Friends of Gledhow Valley Woods, who have considerably improved the state of the building, and organise open days.

along one of the rides, it was undoubtedly an attractive, well-maintained building. With the adjoining quarry probably exploited as a picturesque backdrop, it would have been an embellishment to the park. And no doubt, as an antiquarian, Dixon considered it an embellishment with added historical value – his interest in antiquarianism could be seen at nearby King Alfred's (sham) Castle, on Tunnel How Hill, Meanwood, built *c.* 1770 to the memory of 'Alfred the Great, the pious and magnanimous, the friend of science, virtue, law and liberty'.[70]

Another bath in a quarry setting is Lady Eglintoun's Well, built into the rock face at Bretton Hall, South Yorkshire, home to a branch of the Wentworth family. The ashlar façade has engaged columns with fluted capitals, and the entablature has 'vase- or pedestal-like fragments' and 'a sculpted limestone owl'.[71] The well, or bath, is now concealed behind a locked door. An inscription over the entrance records its construction by Lady Eglintoun in 1685.[72] Nineteenth-century OS maps suggest a later bath house may have stood further west, near the southern edge of the Upper Lake, in 'Bath Wood'. This may have been a feature added in the landscaping of this part of the park in the second half of the 1700s by Sir Thomas Wentworth, which included creating the lakes, with a menagerie on an island, and a ship, the 'Aurora'.[73]

As many bath houses were features on the drives and rides through estates, they would naturally have been commented on by visitors in the many travel diaries, journals, and letters written in the eighteenth century. Such personal accounts provide another invaluable source of evidence, particularly for those bath houses that have since disappeared or taken on new identities. The well-known writings of Ralph Thoresby, Bishop Pococke, John Byng (Viscount Torrington), Thomas Pennant, William Bray, the Duchess of Northumberland, Mrs Philip Lybbe Powys, Mrs Delany, and Anna Seward all contain mention of bath houses; but there are also many other lesser-known or unpublished personal accounts which are equally valuable.

Sometimes, a reference to a bath is irritatingly brief, but might be the sole surviving record. While living at Wighill Park, near Tadcaster, Lady Mary York (daughter of Edward Lascelles, 1st Earl of Harewood) records, on 1 July 1812: 'we walked to look at the Bath.' There are further references to walking in the Bath Walk – but regrettably no further details.[74] Nineteenth-century OS maps and a 1920s plan of the Wighill estate show 'Bathingwell Walk', leading south west from the shrubbery near the house towards Walton Wood.[75] The only reminder of the bath now is Bathingwell Cottage (probably not

[70] From a plaque on the building; only traces of the structure remain. See <http://www.leodis.net/display.aspx–resourceIdentifier=9054> [accessed 4 November 2008].

[71] These details, as given in the EH listing, are now difficult to make out due to weathering and vegetation: IoE no. 334276.

[72] In 1678, Lady Wentworth, widow of Sir Thomas Wentworth, married Alexander Montgomerie, 8th Earl of Eglintoun, thus becoming the Right Honourable Grace Countess of Eglintoun. The well now stands near the Lower Lake, but this was not formed until much later, in the eighteenth century.

[73] Letter from Sir Thomas Wentworth to his sister Annabella, 29 November 1782, formerly held in the archives at Bretton Hall.

[74] Borthwick Institute, University of York, York of Hutton Wandesley papers (uncatalogued), Diaries of Lady Mary York. My thanks to Karen Lynch for this reference.

the bath house itself), adjacent to Home Farm.

Several visitors to Studley Royal mention the bath house in the water gardens, but although it was clearly a feature on the standard tour of the water gardens, we learn little of its appearance from visitors' journals. Amelia Clark, great-niece of the architect John Carr, noted in 1796: 'Near the first entrance into this charming scenery is the cold bath; from thence you are led to the Temple of Piety.'[76] In September 1793, Lady Polwarth was taken on a tour round Studley Royal:

Was at last a fine Day & Mr Waddilove shew'd Studley to us & to Ldy Grey beginning from the Chinese Seat down in the Valley below then up again into the Meadows which overhang it, then into the garden, then to Fountains Abbey, then back into the garden, the Upper walk to the Banqueting House, then to the Cold Bath & out of the Garden cross the Park to the House.[77]

We have no record of the construction of the bath house at Studley, only that it was already in existence in the year 1737: a letter to John Aislabie from his steward, William Hallot, dated 1 January 1737/8, gives an account of men 'cutting hassells [hazels] on the right of Kelders walk and in that Quarter betwixt the Bathing well and the grass walk looking down from the green house [Banqueting House] to the high fall'.[78] It was situated on a walk (marked as Well Walk on the 1910 OS map, although the building had gone by then), just below the Banqueting House, opposite Moon Pond. It faced south south east, and so would have commanded a vista along the Upper Canal to the Rustic Bridge, and up to the Temple of Venus (on Tent Hill, as it later became known), until this was demolished in 1768.

There are three illustrations of the bath house. An 1848 print by William Westall shows the building in the distance, framed by trees (Figure 8); an 1834 sketch by J. R. Walbran presents a closer view of the building, set amongst mature trees (Figure 9);[79] and an early nineteenth-century view by Dunning gives a considerable amount of architectural detail.[80] The building was in typical early Palladian style: a central pedimented section and symmetrical wings either side coming forward, housing the bath and dressing room. A central half-glazed double door under a fanlight had a rusticated surround, and rectangular sash windows appeared to bear prominent keystones. We learn something of the interior from a description in Ely Hargrove's *History of Knaresborough*: 'A neat little building, consisting of two rooms. The bath is ten feet long and eight feet wide, four feet

[75] Brotherton Library, University of Leeds, Brotherton Collection Yorkshire, D-3.1 q WIG, The Wighill and Bilton Estates ... Particulars with plans and conditions of sale of the attractive country mansion situate and known as Wighill Park, 1920.

[76] *Uncle John Carr: The Diaries of his Great-nieces, Harriet and Amelia Clark*, ed. by Corita Myerscough (York: York Georgian Society, 2000), p. 37.

[77] WYL 150/2299, MS Diaries of Amabel Yorke 1769–1827 (37 vols). My thanks to Karen Lynch for this reference.

[78] WYL 150/5566 parcel 288/3 (Vyner MSS). I am grateful to Bill Barber for alerting me to this letter.

[79] York Minster Archives, Hailstone QQ25, Walbran Notebook no. 36, 'Cold Bath, Studley'.

[80] Private collection.

Figure 8 The bath house at Studley Royal, shown in an 1848 print by William Westall. *Courtesy Bill Barber*

Figure 9 'Cold Bath, Studley', detail from an 1834 sketch by J. R. Walbran (York Minster Library and Archives, Hailstone QQ25, Walbran Notebook no. 36). *Reproduced by kind permission of the Dean and Chapter of York*

six inches deep. Dressing room is thirteen feet long, ten feet broad and seven feet tall. – Furniture green and white.'[81]

The disappearance of the building can be dated to *c.* 1850: it was marked on the 1st edition OS map (surveyed *c.* 1849), but a newspaper report of June 1856 refers to the place 'where the Bath House once stood',[82] and it was not shown on an estate map of *c.* 1870.[83]

At Wentworth Castle, near Barnsley, there is documentation for two or three cold baths on the estate. There is currently no evidence to substantiate the suggestion by English Heritage that the small classical building now known as the Gun Room (Grade II), just to the north-west of the house, might have been a bath house.[84] There is, however, firm map evidence to locate a cold bath south of the house, on Stainborough Lane, opposite Cold Bath Farm, at the end of an avenue leading south from Archer's Hill Gate. This first appears on an estate map of *c.* 1730 as two large rectangles: these appear to denote water, which might indicate open-air plunge pools.[85] The cold bath survived, in

[81] Ely Hargrove, *History of Knaresborough*, 5th edn (York: Wilson, Spence and Mawman, 1798), p. 209.
[82] *Ripon and Richmond Chronicle*, 7 June 1856. My thanks to Bill Barber for this reference.
[83] Information from Mark Newman, Territory Archaeologist, North, National Trust.
[84] See EH listing information, IoE no. 333919.
[85] SA, VWM/Maps/63R, Estate plan of Wentworth Estates *c.* 1730, possibly by Badeslade.

some form, for a further 200 years: the same rectangles, marked 'Old Cold Bath', appear on OS maps published between 1855 and 1948; and a plan of 1882 for 'a water course from Cold Bath to Wentworth Castle', suggests the same source was then supplying water to the house.[86] Nothing more is known at present about this cold bath: today, it survives only in the name of the farm, and indications in the adjacent field of some kind of underground water source or course; but the view from the site across the Wentworth Castle landscape and its architectural features is breathtaking.

The most detailed evidence for a bath house at Wentworth Castle is a site in Old Park, in the south-eastern corner of the estate, near Birdwell. This comes in part from a travel journal kept by Dorothy Richardson (1748–1819), grand-daughter of Dr Richard Richardson of North Bierley. Dorothy travelled widely, and her journals show her to be a perceptive and reliable recorder of eighteenth-century architecture and landscape. She visited Wentworth Castle in 1761 and 1767, and her account of her second visit gives enough detail of her route and the features she observed, including the bath house, for us to locate the site with some accuracy. From 'the new Front' of the house (i.e. the south front, built by William, 2nd Earl of Strafford), she records the vista across to Queen Anne's Obelisk, and then continues through the park,

> between two Woods, thro a long Avenue; at the end of which is an open Lawn, with a fine piece of Water [Rockley Dam], and a bridge over it – over the Water on a little Hill side, at a small distance is a Building with two Wings; a Tower in the middle & under it an open Colonade of three Pillars.

This was Rockley Woodhouse, built *c.* 1756.[87] She passes along a 'Gloomy Lane', and then 'an open takes in the Ruin upon Barnsley Common; & Rockley Abbey, at about a fields breadth from the Road'. Next, through another wood – Richardson would now be in Old Park (as named on nineteenth-century OS maps) – and

> by a Square Bath, built upon four Arches with a Spire at each Corner, over the Arches is a Dressing Room with an Egyptian [i.e. Diocletian] Window – We passed under a large Arch by the Side of the Bath; and thro a pair of gates out of the Park. To the right, on the side of a Hill, the small Village of Tankersley.[88]

Richardson uses the term 'Egyptian' elsewhere in her journals to describe a Diocletian window.[89] Such a window form points to a classical design for the building. It was much used by Burlington and his circle, and would have been particularly apt for a bath house: its name derives from the windows in the *thermae* (baths) of Diocletian in Rome. It is worth noting too that the form was used by Gibbs in his design for the (unexecuted) bath house at Kiveton.

[86] SA, VWM/Maps/3, Plan of a water course from Cold Bath to Wentworth Castle (July 1882). The plan marks 'hydrant' by the mansion, so this might have been for fire-fighting purposes.

[87] Old photos of Rockley Woodhouse (*c.* 1900) show this was the 'Building with two Wings' Richardson referred to (this no longer survives).

[88] John Rylands Library, University of Manchester (hereafter John Rylands), English MS 1122, Journey into Derbyshire & Nottinghamshire, fols 22–24. My thanks to Karen Lynch for these extracts from Richardson's travel journals.

[89] The window, on the south front of Boynton Hall, East Yorkshire, survives, and can be identified from Richardson's description. John Rylands, English MS 1126, fol. 187.

The 'pair of gates' mentioned by Richardson formed the entrance to the estate from the south, at Birdwell, which has been dislocated by the construction of the M1, ironically marooning the landmark Birdwell obelisk (erected in 1775 to mark the limit of the Wentworth Castle estate and its boundary with Wentworth Woodhouse) on the 'wrong' side of the motorway. Were Richardson to emerge from the park here today, she would find herself just metres from the motorway traffic.

Richardson's description of the building and its location is so detailed that we might conclude that this is the 'little summer house' over 'a very fine spring' noted by Richard Pococke on the route he took from Wentworth Castle to Wentworth Woodhouse (then known as Wentworth House) in August 1750:

> From this [Argyll Monument] there is a riding towards Wentworth House, in which there is a very fine spring and a little summer house built over it. This riding extends as far as two miles from the house, with mile stones set up, it being the road to Wentworth House, the Marquis of Rockinghams, to which I went on the 7th. After having reviewed all these fine improvements of the Earl of Strafford, I passed by Tankersley Park.[90]

Until very recently, Richardson's account provided the only indication of the appearance of this bath house; but a photo of *c.* 1900, labelled 'Park Well-house' (Figure 10),[91] which has just come to light, matches Richardson's description so well that we can now say with certainty that the bath house she saw in 1767, the building in the photo, and the feature marked as 'Old Park Well' on OS maps of 1855 (Figure 11) and 1894, are one and the same. Further information from nineteenth-century Barnsley historian Joseph Wilkinson and the Wentworth Castle archives fill out the picture.

The bath house was built on a site known locally as Constantine or Constantine's Well. Wilkinson states (1879) that 'Rockley is indebted for its present attractions' to Strafford and his son William, the latter being responsible for 'the noble drive from Wentworth Castle through the woods and avenues of Rockley [...] and from the Sheffield turnpike it formed a lovely and interesting approach to the Castle'.[92] Wilkinson continues:

> At the back of Rockley Woodhouse is Park Spring Wood, and in the heart of the wood, reached by a pleasant walk, is another of these tower-like structures, no doubt erected about the same time as Rockley Woodhouse, known as 'Park Spring', and as 'Park Well Spa', by old people who remember it as being at one time a place of great resort by the inhabitants of the villages. The water is said to possess some medicinal qualities.[93]

And in a later work, Wilkinson returns to this discussion on Park Spring, concluding: 'This would no doubt be the Constantine Well.'[94]

[90] *The Travels through England of Dr Richard Pococke ... during 1750, 1751, and Later Years*, ed. by James Joel Cartwright, 2 vols (Westminster: Camden Society, 1888), I, 63.

[91] My thanks to Patrick Eyres for sharing this discovery.

[92] Joseph Wilkinson, *Worsborough: Its Historical Associations and Rural Attractions* (London: Farrington & Co; Barnsley: Thomas Lingard, Chronicle Office, 1879), pp. 100–01.

[93] Wilkinson, *Worsborough*, p. 104.

[94] Joseph Wilkinson, *Worthies, Families, and Celebrities of Barnsley and the District* (London: Bemrose, 1883), p. 421.

Figure 10 'Park Well House' (Constantine's Well), Wentworth Castle, *c.* 1900. *Collection, Mrs G. Elmhirst*

The first Earl of Strafford's own account of his landscape improvements in this area in the 1730s and payments recorded in estate accounts from 1734 over the following decades confirm that the bath house was built over or near the water source known as Constantine's Well. In April 1738, Strafford wrote to his son William, describing a visit from Lord Malton and his party, who had come over from Wentworth Woodhouse, to see his improvements. Their route would have brought them into the Wentworth Castle estate at the Birdwell entrance. Strafford writes: 'I met them at the statue by Constantines well in my Pheaton [...] I play'd my cascade at Constantine very freely.' They continued on through the park to breakfast 'by a good fire' at Stainborough Castle. Later, they returned to Constantine's Well where Strafford says: 'I play'd my waters again caryd them into the room and showed them my new couch.'[95] This last comment is consistent with the interior furnishings of more opulent bath houses. Strafford died in November 1739, and the Rockley area continued to be developed by his son, William.

According to the 1734 accounts, payments were made for work at 'Constantine Well', at the pond and cascade at Constantine Well, and work at the 'house' at the Well

[95] British Library (BL) Add. MSS 72, 713, fols 61–62. I am indebted to Patrick Eyres for this reference.

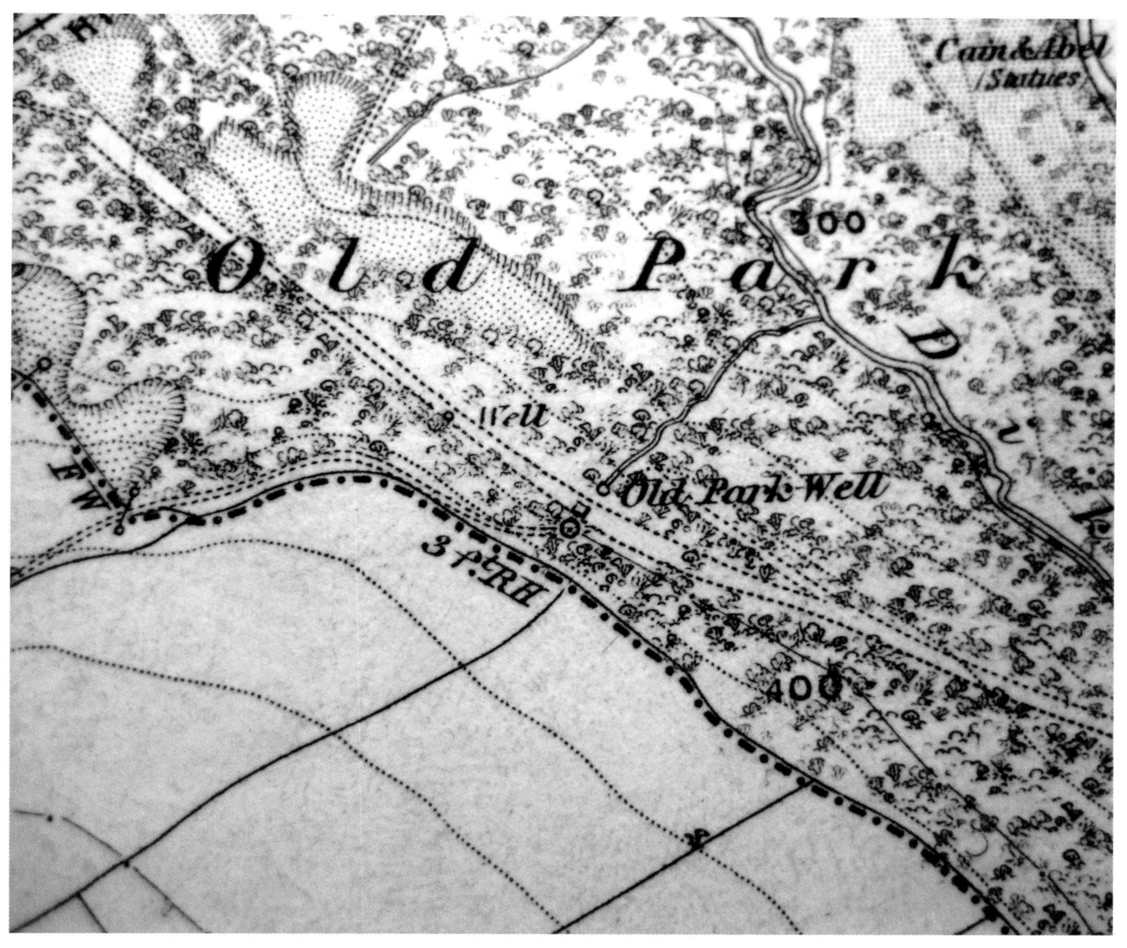

Figure 11 Old Park, Wentworth Castle, in 1850. A number of features can be seen clustered around 'Old Park Well', including the cascade. The rides, paths and cascade survive, but the M1 now passes just to the right of the statue of Cain and Abel (top right); the statue (now gone) may have been moved from an earlier position by Constantine's Well. 1855 OS map (sheet 282, surveyed 1850). *Reproduced with kind permission of The Leeds Library*

(including a fireplace in the corner of the room, and removing a door from the east to west wall). In April 1739, further payments were made to Joseph Bower Jr (mason) for work at the cascade and pond at Constantine Well. There were also payments to the painter Addinell for painting the ceiling at Constantine Well (1737), 'witening' by the plasterer (1748), and repairs or renovation work is recorded in 1754.[96] From this we might

[96] SA, A 477 VW Collection, Accounts and papers Stainborough/Wentworth Castle 1708–85, fols. 62–129 (microfilm of BL Add. 22241 Strafford papers).

conclude that the bath known as Constantine's Well was built in 1734, possibly slightly earlier.

Other payments in the Wentworth Castle accounts for work on baths are insufficiently precise to determine the building in question. In June 1731 two payments had been made to John Bower (mason) for several days' work 'Walling a tunil [–] and a Drane at the bathe by The Lack', and 'Walling the bathe by the Lack'; this suggests a bath at Law (or Low) Lake, NNE of the house, probably in woodland just behind the Temple on the large rectangular pool shown on the 1730 estate plan (see Figure 2, bottom right corner, and Figure 6, in the paper by Patrick Eyres, in this volume). Later payments were made 'for two bell glass for the Cold bath' (1764), 'for Clening ye Chimney peece at Cold Bath (1765), for 'the wall by the cold Bath' (1773), and 'Cold Bath windows' (1774) – but the bath in question is not identified.[97]

Nineteenth-century OS maps show that elements of the eighteenth-century designed landscape in Old Park survived, despite the presence of coal and ironstone pits: a network of rides and paths, the statue of Cain and Abel,[98] and a number of features and structures that could be the bath house and 'large arch', clustered at the head of what looks like the cascade. Today, paths and pits are still easily discernible, as are abundant springs and water courses, traces of a cascade, and large pieces of ashlar stone. A keystone or voussoir, and a semicircular stone basin, half-hidden in the undergrowth (Figures 12 and 13), are consistent with the classical building described by Richardson and shown in the photo – but clearly, there is much more to discover here.[99]

Planting

Contemporary illustrations, descriptions, and estate plans give some idea of planting in the immediate vicinity of a bath house. Unfortunately, such evidence is sorely lacking in Yorkshire, although we can assume that practice elsewhere in the country would also apply here, and that the same approach to planting, following prevailing fashion, would have been adopted for the bath house as for gazebos, summerhouses, temples, and similar features. In formal gardens, box hedges or topiary might have lined the approach, or yew hedges enclosed an open-air plunge pool, as is the case today at Packwood House, Warwickshire. Dark evergreens, such as yews, might be planted behind, to act as a foil, as was the case at Walton bath house;[100] and at Wardour Castle, Wiltshire, a bath house by the landscape gardener Richard Woods (1766) was set against an arc of trees on the edge of the lake, with a cascade in front.[101] The bath house might be flanked by or 'surrounded

[97] Ibid., fols 46, 152, 146, 159, 161 respectively. Bell glass may refer to a cupola or lantern, a typical top-lighting feature of bath houses. Law Lake is really the only contender for 'the bathe by The Lack' (there was no lake in Old Park), and discussions with Jane Furse (Wentworth Castle Heritage Trust) support this.

[98] It is conjectured that the 'statue by Constantines well' referred to by Strafford in 1738 is that of Cain and Abel, later moved to the position shown on the 1855 OS map (Figure 11).

[99] It is tempting but at this stage premature to speculate that the bath house in Old Park might have been to the design of James Gibbs; see Eyres on Gibbs at Wentworth Castle, in this volume).

[100] When the Walton Bath House (Warks.) was restored, the circle of original eighteenth-century yews was pruned so that they would grow again to restore the original setting: Hawkes, pp. 33–34.

[101] Wiltshire and Swindon Archives, 2667/21/12, 1773 survey of Wardour Castle by George Ingman. Information kindly supplied by Fiona Cowell.

Figure 12 Old Park, Wentworth Castle: wedge-shaped stone, possibly a keystone or voussoir, measuring approx. 75 cm in length, found near the head of the cascade. It is tempting to speculate that this might be a stone from the bath house (see the arch in Figure 10). *Photo: Dick Knight, 2009*

Figure 13 Old Park, Wentworth Castle: semicircular stone, concave beneath, diameter approx. 120 cm, possibly part of an upturned basin, found near the head of the cascade. *Photo: Dick Knight, 2009*

by flowering shrubs' as at Hafod;[102] and at Adlestrop, Warwickshire, a watercolour by Humphry Repton (*c.* 1810) shows the green and white canvas bath house (designed by John Adey Repton) set against the foliage of trees with flowering shrubs in front of it.[103] To achieve an authentic Picturesque scene, trailing plants would clothe the roof and outer walls.[104] Despite bathing being, to a large degree, a male activity, the aesthetics of the building were not, apparently, overlooked.

At Wetherby Grange, a house altered by John Carr in 1784 (to a scheme by James Wyatt), sales particulars from 1840 include 'Lot no. 4: Flower garden and bath'. It is unlikely that a private bath house would still have been used for bathing at this date (and the spa at nearby Thorp Arch would have offered more facilities), but the building might have been retained as an ornamental landscape feature, or perhaps converted for a different use, and the planting around it maintained.[105]

The setting of John King's bath house at Bungay in Suffolk seems to have been quite idyllic. As an apothecary, King was primarily concerned with cold bathing for health purposes, and his bath was clearly intended for his patients; nevertheless, he was evidently aware of the aesthetic aspects of location. In a letter to Floyer, he describes the site as being

at the Foot of a large and deep Hill, whose oblique height is not common; it's most curiously adorn'd with many Sorts of Trees standing in so handsome a Manner, as form of themselves a beautiful Landskip; the opposite Side is a fine delightful Stream encompassing a large spacious Common whose Prospect is little inferior to any.[106]

And a gentleman visitor to the bath paints this picture:

A steep and fertile Vineyard richly stor'd with the choicest Plants from *Burgundy, Champaigne, Provence*, and whatever the *East* can furnish us with. Near the Bottom of this is placed the Grotto or *Bath* itself, beautified on one side with Oziers, Groves and Meadows, on the other with Gardens, Fruits, shady Walks and all the Decorations of a rural Innocence. The Building is designedly plain and neat, because the least Attempt of artful Magnificence, would, by alluring the Eyes of Strangers, deprive them of those profuse Pleasures which Nature has already provided.[107]

[102] From a visitor's description in 1810: Caroline Kerkham and Stephen Briggs, 'A Review of the Archaeological Potential of the Hafod Landscape', in *CBA Research Report*, no. 78, ed. by A. E. Brown, 1991, p. 170.
[103] Shakespeare Birthplace Trust Record Office, DR 18/8/7/12; my thanks to Karen Lynch for this reference.
[104] A grotto by the side of Richard Payne Knight's cold bath at Downton was 'overhung with creeping plants', according to James Plumptre, when he visited in 1799: *James Plumptre's Britain: The Journals of a Tourist in the 1790s*, ed. by Ian Ousby (London: Hutchinson, 1992), p. 176.
[105] WYL 103/161, Particulars and Conditions of Sale, Beilby Grange Estate, Property of Lord Wenlock ... 28 May 1840. Wetherby Grange was earlier known as Beilby or Micklethwaite Grange. A 1793 reference to a bath situated among the 'Detached offices' of the (still unfinished) house may have been an earlier one: 'Dressing Room by Cold Bath, Pigeon House, etc. [...] These offices were meant to be removed, and others built on a uniform Plan, at a greater Distance from the House.' WYL 103/165, Particulars and Conditions of Sale ... The Manor and Hamlet of Micklethwaite Grange ... September 17th 1793.
[106] King, pp. x–xi.
[107] Ibid., pp. 171–72.

It is doubtful if Nature could have provided these same pleasures in the Yorkshire climate. We also have advice on the ideal planting for the bath house from late eighteenth-century Germany. The *Magazin für Freunde des guten Geschmacks* (Magazine for the Friends of Good Taste, 1797), which aimed at the 'elevation and refinement of taste in objects of all kinds', carried a design for a ruined Roman bath in an English park, based on the 'romantic' water area in the Villa Maecenas, Tivoli:

> This ruin was intended as a sight to be discovered, with steps leading to walkways through the structure where the wanderer would be taken by surprise at the full effect of the water feature [...] Shrubs and trees shade the ruin in a 'picturesque' fashion, and it is recommended that vegetation such as *Lycium barbarum* (wild box-thorn), *Hedera quinquefolium* (five-leaved ivy) and varieties of *Lonicera* (honeysuckle) and clematis be planted, with periwinkles and convulvulus winding themselves under the walls; on one side of the bank stand Babylonian willows, on the other, three Italian poplars [...] the classical model is reconceived in romantic form.[108]

The sepia aquatint shows a rather clean and tidy classical ruin, with the Doric columns partially submerged, and the merest suggestion of ivy.

CONCLUSION

It is strange that, with so many rich historical seams to explore (architecture, landscape gardening, science, medicine, and religion), the bath house has been so neglected; and that in garden history, so much attention has been paid to the grotto or temple, but the bath house has been almost totally overlooked.

The survival rate of these buildings is poor even by the standards of other garden structures. Changes in health and medical practices, and the growth of new spa resorts in the early 1800s, led to a decline in use. Whereas people continued to enjoy walks and take refreshment in their gardens, ensuring the future of summerhouses and temples, the cold plunge went out of fashion. Some bath houses were converted to other uses (that at Wardour became a lodge; and the room which once held the cistern is now a kitchen);[109] others were dismantled to provide material for new buildings; some were just left to fade away. The presence of water has always made their fabric vulnerable to deterioration, rendering repairs and restoration expensive. The practice of flooring over the cistern (for conversion or safety purposes) has led to the original function of these buildings becoming lost from collective memory. Widespread ignorance of the phenomenon of the cold bath means that many remain unrecognised by owners and custodians. The survival of a water tank, even drained, raises fears of legal liability, and thus access is frequently denied to visitors: access denied, existence denied, and ultimately non-existence.

[108] Sarah Richards, 'A Magazine for the Friends of Good Taste: Sensibility and Rationality in Garden Design in late Eighteenth-century Germany', *Studies in the History of Gardens and Designed Landscapes*, 20.3 (2000), 229–48 (pp. 229, 241).
[109] Information from the current owner.

ACKNOWLEDGEMENTS

Over the years, many individuals and organisations – too numerous to name here – have helped me with information on bath houses and bathing. However, I would like to thank in particular: the Leeds Philosophical and Literary Society (for a grant towards research costs in 2004); Karen Lynch, for her invaluable contributions to my database; and Dianne Barre, for sharing her research and bath-house discoveries.

‘Extraordinary convulsions of nature’: The Romantic Landscape of Plumpton Rocks

KAREN LYNCH

PLUMPTON ROCKS AND THE LASCELLES FAMILY

Plumpton, the ancient seat of the family of the same name, lay close to Knaresborough in the West Riding of Yorkshire. It had passed through many generations over seven centuries before the last of the male line, Robert Plumpton, died without issue in 1749.[1] His heirs offered the estate for sale, and the purchaser was Daniel Lascelles (1714–1784). Lascelles was the younger brother of Edwin Lascelles (1712–1795) of Gawthorp Hall, near Leeds, a medieval manor house and park that would be transformed in the following decades with the construction of Harewood House and its estate buildings.

In 1750 Daniel Lascelles was newly returned to Britain, having been abroad for ten years. In 1740 he had been ‘unwarily induced’ into a clandestine marriage and his family hastily separated him from his unsuitable wife, Elizabeth Southwick, and packed him off abroad. He spent two years in Europe and then eight in the ‘East Indies’, including some time in Bengal, before returning to England.[2] He seems initially to have given little thought to a country estate, being mainly in London, home to the family business. The Lascelles were merchants who traded in the West Indies, and in particular Barbados.[3] In 1751 Lascelles was divorced by Act of Parliament, and in 1752 he was rehabilitated into polite society, taking over from his father as one of the Members of Parliament for Northallerton.

In 1753 his father, Henry Lascelles, died, and Edwin, Daniel and the third surviving son, also Henry, inherited his vast mercantile fortune. A condition of Henry senior’s will was that each son must invest a third share of two hundred and fifty thousand pounds in property. Lascelles’s first purchase was the Plumpton estate, with the ancient Plumpton

[1] For the early history of the estate see Helen Lazenby, ‘Plumpton Rocks, Knaresborough’ (Yorkshire Gardens Trust, 1997). Plumpton is now in North Yorkshire.

[2] London, House of Lords Record Office, HL/JO/10/3/245/39, 22 November 1751; West Yorkshire Archive Service, Leeds (hereafter WYL), Newby Papers, WYL/5013/1620/32.

[3] For the family’s political and business life see Simon Smith, *Slavery, Family and Gentry Capitalism in the British Atlantic: The World of the Lascelles, 1648–1834* (Cambridge: Cambridge University Press, 2006).

Towers as its principal dwelling.[4] The purchase also included an estate at nearby Braime (or Braham) and cost him a total of £33,563 10s. 1d.[5] Lascelles, or more likely Samuel Popplewell, the Lascelles family's steward in Yorkshire, would have been aware that Plumpton would eventually come onto the market after the death of Robert Plumpton in 1749. There was to be a long wait. Legal wrangles delayed the sale, and an Act of Parliament was required before Plumpton's heirs were able to dispose of the estate.[6] Lascelles must have been poised to make a move in November 1754 when London newspapers announced that the manor of 'Plompton [...] within a mile of Knaresboro' was to be sold.[7] By the end of the year the vendors had vetted Lascelles, and deciding him 'a Gentleman of Worth & Honour' the sale was agreed and he took possession – although it would be more than eighteen months before a weary Popplewell could announce the transaction 'which compleats ye purchase of Plompton'.[8]

Lascelles was slow to reach a decision about where to live on his new estate and rented a house in nearby Knaresborough for his short visits to Yorkshire. The young architect John Carr and his stonemason father, Robert, already working for Edwin Lascelles at Harewood, were asked to draw up plans for 'necessary alterations' to the surviving portion of Plumpton Towers in April 1756.[9] Carr suggested a scheme 'to make the house habitable without any considerable additions', suggesting new fireplaces, cornices and ceilings and some new boards for the floors. His careful recycling of stone flags in the kitchen would have appealed to the frugal Lascelles.[10] No action was taken until January 1757 when Lascelles requested that the house be made 'tolerably habitable', and the plans from the previous year were hastily sought out. By summer 1758 the house was decorated and furnished.[11] Throughout the renovations Lascelles made it plain that he was not interested in ostentation and wished for 'nothing costly'.[12] Thrift became even more of an issue in 1759 when the nearby Goldsborough estate was advertised for sale and Lascelles decided to express an interest.[13] Realising that the purchase could take months, if not years, he decided to 'hold up a little' at Plumpton and keep costs to a minimum whilst pursuing Goldsborough.[14]

Documentation of what happened next is sparse and it is difficult to be certain of the sequence of events. At some stage Lascelles decided that a new house must be built and

[4] The parish is Plompton but the manor and the family name have the variant spellings of Plompton or Plumpton. The modern spelling of Plumpton is used throughout this paper.

[5] Harewood House Trust, Harewood House Archives, 'Estates bought by Dan: Lascelles Esq of his 1/3 part of £250,000', no date, uncatalogued at time of consultation.

[6] *An act for vesting one undivided fourth part of Elizabeth Knight of and in divers manors, lands, and hereditaments, in the county of York, late the estates of Robert Plumpton, Esquire, deceased, in trustees to sell the same, for the purposes therein mentioned* (London, 1753).

[7] See for example *London Evening Post* and *Whitehall Evening Post*, 21 November 1754.

[8] WYL250/SC/1/2/3; WYL250/SC/1/3/97. NB all documents with the prefix WYL250 are from the Harewood House papers.

[9] WYL250/SC/1/3/60.

[10] WYL250/SC/7/118.

[11] WYL250/SC/2/1/13.

[12] WYL250/SC/2/2/111.

[13] As early as December 1755 Popplewell had suggested Goldsborough as an estate for Daniel Lascelles's property portfolio. See WYL250/SC/1/2/185.

[14] WYL250/SC/2/3/44.

Carr drew up plans for an elegant, but compact, villa.[15] The surviving letters for the early 1760s make little specific reference to the construction of this new mansion, although there are hints of activity. John Carr was at Plumpton in June 1761 and in October the following year Lascelles complains that 'my Building has been retarded'.[16] There are also purchases of timber, iron and slate in this period. Activity must have continued into 1764, for in December of that year the mason, William Johnson, submitted a bill for work 'at the New House at Plompton' totalling close to one thousand pounds.[17]

As Lascelles procrastinated over his dwelling, work was well under way on the estate. Robert and John Carr designed and erected estate buildings including a handsome stable block surmounted by a cupola, a walled garden, a little house (a privy, or necessary) and a 'really pretty' ornamented farm.[18]

The pleasure ground was developed concurrently around a series of huge millstone grit rocks (Figure 1), or 'extraordinary convulsions of nature' as one visitor named them.[19] There does not appear to have been a plan for the garden, and few written instructions survive. Lascelles seems to have issued instructions to his staff during his visits to Plumpton, and then to have trusted them to implement the work in his absence.

From the first days of ownership Lascelles's priority had been a major programme of tree planting under the direction of the gardener, John Banks. Banks was already familiar with the site, having paid rent for 'y[e] Garden' at Plumpton since at least 1743.[20] Accounts show that he supplied trees to Harewood before Lascelles purchased the estate, so it would appear that he had been operating a nursery at Plumpton.[21] In the earliest months Banks worked on a contractual basis, but in May 1756 Lascelles proposed an annual salary. Popplewell reported that Banks had requested thirty pounds a year, but told Lascelles he was confident that he could persuade the gardener to accept twenty-six pounds, with a possible gift of a guinea if he was 'diligent'.[22] Banks was clearly the stronger negotiator and the records show that he was indeed paid thirty pounds per annum.[23]

Banks began by preparing the ground and the masons built protective walls ready for 'plumps', that is clumps, of trees. As well as nurturing his own young trees, Banks was also buying huge quantities from two eminent local nurseries – Perfect's of Pontefract and Telford's of York, both of whom were also sending cartloads of trees and shrubs to Harewood. In the spring of 1756 Banks supplied 1800 trees from his own stock, including sycamores and elms that were already ten feet high.[24] At the same time Banks was also

[15] The elevation is in the collection of Fairfax House, York.

[16] WYL250/SC/3/2/60; WYL250/SC/3/3/169.

[17] WYL250/3/286, fol. 60.

[18] WYL250/SC/3/1/104.

[19] John Henry Manners [Duke of Rutland], *Journal of a Tour to the Northern Parts of Britain* (London: printed for J. Triphook, 1813), p. 123.

[20] West Yorkshire Archives Service, Bradford, MMC/9. Banks may have worked in conjunction with the gardener Richard Simpson of Knaresborough whom he names in his will as his 'friend'. For Simpson see John Harvey, *Early Nurserymen* (London: Phillimore, 1974), pp. 95–96.

[21] WYL250/3/225.

[22] WYL250/SC/1/3/73.

[23] WYL250/3/286, fols 14, 41.

[24] WYL250/3/380.

FIGURE 1 Plumpton Rocks. *Photo: the author*

planting the deliveries that were arriving from Telford's. These too included some elms up to nine feet tall and the invoices also list larch, beech, horse chestnut, mountain ash, Spanish chestnut, poplar, walnut, lime, fir and hornbeam totalling more than 2000 trees.[25]

Lascelles was impatient for results and in February 1757 he sent seeds for Banks, instructing him to plant them 'direct' and 'let them take their chance'.[26] The following month saw Banks begin planting shrubs, with Lascelles ordering that he mix 'ye Ever Green shrubs wth ye flowering ones in ye Plantations among ye Rocks'.[27] The evergreens included laurel, box and holly, but detailed planting lists of the flowering shrubs have sadly not survived.

Concurrent with the planting was the construction of the dam that transformed a stream and medieval fishponds into a lake that surrounded some of the rocks, and lapped at the edges of others. Work began on the dam in 1755 and by May 1756 Edwin Lascelles was able to visit Plumpton and report to his brother that he approved 'very well of y^e^

[25] Ibid. More specifically, the firs are referred to as 'abies' and 'spruce firs'.
[26] WYL250/SC/2/1/23.
[27] WYL250/SC/2/1/43.

Dam head', subject to a few minor changes.[28] Little is known about the design and construction of the dam as the archives for Plumpton in this period are incomplete. The Carr scholar Brian Wragg saw a design for the dam in the 1950s at Harewood, and his sketch after the original was published in 1956 (Figure 2), a vital piece of evidence as the location of the original is currently unknown.[29] Wragg states that Carr submitted the elevation in 1755, but he does not say if the drawing was dated, or if he makes this assumption based on the known date of construction of the dam. Wragg thought the design a 'bizarre conception [that] was never built' but the dam as seen today does bear a strong resemblance to Carr's design – the arches are clearly visible, and the balls with rusticated bands remain in situ, or can be found buried in the undergrowth (Figure 3).[30] None of the eighteenth-century visitors mention the dam, and surely such a curious structure would have excited some comment. Whilst there is no evidence that the central obelisk, or pyramid, was constructed in 1755, the dam did carry a structure of some kind, of which more below.

The only other structure within the garden was the boathouse, and here again Lascelles was averse to any unnecessary spending, stressing that it was to be a 'thing of no great Expence'.[31] He appears to have designed the structure himself, giving orders to the mason in 1759 that he simply turn an arched roof across a chasm between two of the rocks to create a chamber. Once completed the roof was planted with ling turf so that it appeared 'all of a piece' with its surroundings.[32]

In 1762 Lascelles completed the protracted purchase of the Goldsborough estate and asked Carr to remodel parts of the Jacobean house there, making the property his principal seat. Lascelles lost interest in Plumpton and abandoned the partially built new mansion, leaving just 'One Wing covered in, but the Center & the other [...] only about half a yard high'.[33] Although the house is shown on the estate map of 1777, it appears to have been crossed through, presumably to represent the aborted structure.[34]

The garden became a detached pleasure ground visited from Harewood and Goldsborough for picnic parties.[35] The southern side of Carr's fine stables was converted into a banqueting house with 'two or three rooms [...] accordingly fitted up' for use by the family.[36] An inventory shows that the principal room was the ground floor Dining Room, furnished to seat twelve, and above this there was a Drawing Room with chairs, sofa and inlaid semi-circular tables. The ancillary rooms included a Kitchen, Scullery, Butler's Pantry and Servants' Hall. There were tea and coffee services as well as fine china and glassware for more elaborate meals.[37] As the fame of the new house at Harewood

[28] WYL250/SC/1/3/82.

[29] Brian Wragg, 'John Carr: Gothic Revivalist', in *Studies in Architectural History*, 2 vols (York: St Anthony's Press, 1956), II, 9–34 (p. 15).

[30] Ibid.

[31] WYL250/SC/2/3/44.

[32] WYL250/SC/2/3/74.

[33] University of Manchester, John Rylands Library, Dorothy Richardson papers, English MS 1122 (Richardson papers), fol. 220.

[34] WYL250/3/81.

[35] The drive from Goldsborough to Plumpton was particularly attractive as the family could travel via the picturesque Grimbald Crag on the River Nidd.

[36] Manners, p. 123.

[37] WYL250/3/310; the inventory is undated but appears late eighteenth-century and was probably taken after the death of Edwin Lascelles in 1795.

FIGURE 2 Proposed elevation of the Dam Head, Plumpton. Sketched by Brian Wragg after the original by John Carr. *Courtesy Mrs Mary Wragg*

spread, Plumpton became a retreat for the Lascelles family on Saturdays. This was the day when visitors were admitted to Harewood House and Lord Harewood soon found they 'unpleasantly interrupted the quiet retirement that he wished to enjoy'.[38] Somewhat ironically, it appears that the growth of Harrogate as a resort, and the popularity of excursions to Plumpton, contributed to Daniel Lascelles's decision to move to Goldsborough. One visitor, noting that the house at Plumpton had never been completed, commented that 'the reasons which prevented this grand undertaking being finish'd was its Contiguity to Harrogate'.[39] Despite owning two fine estates in the county, there is little evidence that Lascelles spent much time in Yorkshire. Business and politics kept him in London, and as well as having a town house he was also renting Upper Gatton Park, a country estate in Surrey, as a retreat from the city.[40]

Such a pleasure ground, situated some miles from the owner's principal estate, had an important precedent within Yorkshire. John Aislabie of Studley Royal, just outside Ripon, had created a formal water garden on his estate, complete with classical temples and statuary. Aislabie died in 1742 and his son, William, continued to develop the grounds at Studley, whilst also creating a very different landscape on a steep wooded site on the River Ure, near the village of Grewelthorpe, about 6 miles north of Ripon. Hackfall, as this garden became known, was as wild as Studley was manicured, and William added a sham ruin and a sham castle to add to the atmosphere. The sham ruin, Mowbray Point, was constructed in the 1760s as a banqueting house where the family could dine when they visited, and the ruins of its detached kitchen can still be seen.

Daniel Lascelles died in London on 26 May 1784. He left no legitimate issue and his estates passed to his brother, Edwin, of Harewood. Edwin had married for the second time in 1770 and his wife, Jane, known as Lady Fleming, her title from her first marriage, was a keen gardener. Lady Fleming may have been involved with her absentee brother-in-law's garden at Plumpton before his death, but she was certainly the driving force by June 1785 when Samuel Popplewell wrote to her in London to report that 'your Ladyship's Garden at Plompton looks as well as can be expected considering the dryness of the season'.[41] Her role was acknowledged in 1814, when Sir George Shiffner noted in

[38] Manners, p. 123.
[39] Manchester, Chethams Library, A.2.34, Travel Diary of Morris Moule, *c.* 1796, fol. 7.
[40] At the time of his death, Daniel Lascelles was the tenant of Upper Gatton Park in Surrey, a substantial house in a 'Capability' Brown park, *Morning Post and Daily Advertiser*, 17 July 1784.
[41] WYL250/SC/5, fol. 350.

FIGURE 3 Detail of the dam at Plumpton. *Photo: the author*

his travel journal that Plumpton was 'very pretty Rock and Water' that had been 'laid out by Mr Lascelles and L^y^ Flemming'.[42] The accounts show a flurry of activity at Plumpton in the months after Edwin Lascelles inherited, and his wife began to implement her plans for the garden. A sunk fence was constructed, the lake cleared of weeds, and more importantly, the last traces of the mansion were removed and hay seed was sown 'where the house stood'.[43]

It was perhaps Edwin Lascelles and Lady Fleming who were responsible for adding ornament to the dam. As detailed above, the only known design for the dam features a central obelisk, or pyramid, and it seems unlikely that this was built in 1755. There is, however, visual evidence for a structure on the dam from late in the eighteenth-century when J. M. W. Turner first visited Plumpton in 1797. On this visit he made preparatory studies for the two large oil paintings of the rocks completed in 1798 that hang at

42 East Sussex Record Office, SHR830B, Sir George Shiffner's Tour in 1814, no pagination.
43 WYL250/3/223.

Harewood House. One of these sketches distantly shows a small classical structure, pierced by an oculus, on the dam.[44] Turner returned to Plumpton in 1816, and his sketchbook includes a drawing of the dam from the lake; although a much looser sketch, this too shows a structure with a round window.[45] A vignette published in 1857 focuses on the dam from downstream with the rocks in the background (Figure 4).[46] The view appears to show a raised section of rustic masonry in the centre of the dam, and the oculus frames a view away from the rocks down the valley. These small engravings exercise varying degrees of artistic licence, but this image does corroborate the evidence in Turner's works.

There is a suggestion that the dam may have been considered inadequate as early as 1762; in that year John Carr had discussed a new 'head' for the lake with the civil engineer John Smeaton.[47] No further documentation survives about this meeting of the two eminent Yorkshiremen. Entries in the account books show substantial work on the dam soon after the death of Daniel Lascelles, probably as Lady Fleming began to make her own mark upon Plumpton. In August 1784, the engineer James Hudson, who also worked on the dam at Harewood, was paid the large sum of £124 10s. 0d. for 'making the Dam Head &c' and the masons were paid £64 3s. 10d. 'for the Dam Head'.[48] The structure on the dam may have been added at this date, as part of a programme of repair or renovation. It remains a mystery why this ornamented dam, whatever its date, was not discussed by any of the visitors, or mentioned in the many tourist guides.

The garden remained a favourite picnic spot in the time of Edwin's successor, his cousin Edward Lascelles, created Baron Harewood in 1796 and elevated to the peerage as the first Earl of Harewood in 1812. In fact, Plumpton was one of the first places Edward and his family visited after they arrived at their newly inherited Harewood House in April 1795.[49] In summer the households from Harewood and from Goldsborough dined at Plumpton, where they went out in the boat and showed their frequent houseguests the garden.[50] The artist Thomas Girtin dined with the family there on 2 August 1800, and watercolours and sketches of Plumpton and of nearby Grimbald Crag probably date from this visit (Figure 5).[51] Only a few days later, Humphry Repton and his son John Adey Repton drove to Plumpton with Lord and Lady Harewood.[52] It seems unlikely that the eminent landscape gardener would have been able to resist commenting on the layout of the garden, but sadly no record of his thoughts is known to survive.

[44] Tate Britain, D17202 (CXCVII L).

[45] Tate Britain, D10876 (CXLIV 4a). My thanks to Professor David Hill for dating the sketch based on his work on the Turner collection at Tate Britain in 2009.

[46] University of Leeds, Special Collections (hereafter Leeds), MS194/15/264(a).

[47] WYL250/SC/3/3/199.

[48] WYL250/3/217.

[49] University of York, Borthwick Institute, York of Hutton Wandesley papers, Diaries of Lady Mary York (York papers), uncatalogued at time of consultation.

[50] After Daniel's death, Goldsborough Hall was at various times the home of the heir, a dower house, and was also occasionally let.

[51] York papers. See for example *Grimbald Crag*, British Museum 1855.0214.33; *The Hall Stables, Plompton Park*, Whitworth Art Gallery, Manchester D.1977.15.17.

[52] York papers.

FIGURE 4 Plumpton Rocks and Terrace, Yorkshire, Rock & Co, 1857. These vignettes were popular collectables for mounting in scrapbooks.
University of Leeds Library, Special Collections

FIGURE 5 The Stables, Plumpton, by Thomas Girtin. Probably sketched when he visited with the Lascelles family in summer 1800. The sketch shows the west side of the stables, surmounted by a cupola. The south front, housing the banqueting house, is hidden by the trees on the right of the drawing.
The Whitworth Art Gallery, University of Manchester

Plumpton Rocks, as the garden became known, was rapidly established as an essential sight for genteel folk visiting the nearby spa resorts of Harrogate and Knaresborough, and happily many of these visitors recorded their impressions of the landscape. One of the earliest, John Courtney of Beverley, visited in 1759 and again in 1761 and noted that the place was 'much improved' in that two-year period.[53] No doubt he was enjoying the fruits of the gardener's early labours as the planting matured.

The surviving accounts vary from such brief but evocative phrases as a 'small, pleasing wild place'[54] to meticulous descriptions covering a number of pages. Many accounts appear interesting until one becomes aware that the text seems familiar. The Reverend John Swete, for example, left a detailed account in his travel journal in 1786 but on closer inspection it is largely lifted from Hargrove's popular guide to the area.[55] One of the most comprehensive accounts discovered to date was penned by Dorothy Richardson, who visited in late August 1771, and her journal shows how the garden had been developed by that date:

> The Gardens are uncommonly Romantic; & tho they are not large, appear so, from being laid out with great Judgement; an old Gardener betwixt Eighty & Ninety shows the Place, & is a very great Curiosity. – A Range of very large Earth fast Stones, & huge Rocks run along the Side of a Hill, among which are a great number of winding walks, with seats cut in the Rocks; which retire into abrupt Chasms, & in one place surround a beautiful Lawn; several fine Shrubberies are intermix'd; in which grow great variety of Shrubs, & Ground Plants, & being most of them in full Blow, they perfum'd the Air and made the place quite Delightful; Upon the Top of one of the Rocks is a Chinese Seat, commanding a view of Follyfoot. [...] below the Rocks, is a fine Lake, with some wild fantastic Rocks standing in it, & upon one is a little Garden; No Idea can be given of these Gardens by an description [*sic*], they are particularly pleasing, but in a different style from any I ever saw, tho I know none that exceed them, or where so great Taste has been shewn.[56]

Dorothy found the garden unique, as did Amabel Yorke who first visited in 1774.[57] She wrote in her journal that the garden was 'very singular, the Soil being full of Stony Rocks [...] which seem split and tumbled about as if by an Earth-Quake'. She was unfamiliar with gardens of this kind and concluded that the place was 'pretty & odd, & not easy to describe'.[58] Nevertheless, in a letter describing the same visit, Amabel managed an admirably succinct account of the garden: 'an odd & pretty bank of Rocks, with Walks of

[53] Susan & David Neave, *The Diary of a Yorkshire Gentleman: John Courtney of Beverley, 1759–1768* (Otley: Smith Settle, 2001), pp. 18 & 43.

[54] East Sussex Record Office, SHR 1928, Frances Bridger's Northern Tour 1768, fol. 6.

[55] Leeds, MS Trv q 4 SWE, Reverend John Swete's travel journals, IV, fol. 59; Ely Hargrove, *The History of the Castle, Town and Forest of Knaresborough, with Harrogate, and its Medicinal Waters ...*, 3rd edn (York: printed by W. Blanchard & Co. for the author, 1782), pp. 90–91.

[56] Richardson papers, fols 221–22.

[57] Amabel Yorke was the eldest daughter of the Earl of Hardwicke and was Baroness Lucas and Countess de Grey in her own right as well as Lady Polwarth via her marriage to Viscount Polwarth. She is referred to here by her maiden name to avoid confusion.

[58] WYL, Vyner Papers, WYL150/2299/IV, 2 July 1774.

Flowering Shrubs between them & Water beneath'.[59] Edward Witts, who toured the north in 1777, also noted that the pleasure ground was 'the only of its kind in England'.[60] It would seem that the garden was viewed as unique because of the marriage of the recognised components of the Picturesque – irregular trees, rocks and water – with the less conventional use of flowering shrubs in an informal setting.

It is interesting that the two female diarists note their sensual appreciation of the landscape. Both were educated women with vast libraries at their disposal, and would have had an understanding of contemporary writings on gardens such as Edmund Burke's essay *A Philosophical Enquiry into the Origin of our Ideas of the Sublime and the Beautiful*, first published in 1757.[61] Burke identified as Sublime those elements of landscape that inspired awe and a degree of horror, and both Richardson and Yorke are suitably moved by Plumpton with its 'abrupt Chasms' appearing to be caused by an 'Earth-Quake'. Both women would also have been aware of the fashionable discussion of the Picturesque, soon to be brought to a wider audience in the writings of William Gilpin.[62] Plumpton would have been recognised as a scaled-down version of such awe-inspiring landscapes as the Wye Valley in the Welsh borders or Matlock Crags in Derbyshire, both of which were firmly on the polite tourist's trail. The satirical writer Barbara Hofland had one of her heroines visit Plumpton, where 'Nature seems to display, in miniature, whatever she has performed on a wider theatre'.[63] In describing the garden as 'Romantic', Richardson records her reaction to the landscape; her emotions are stirred and her imagination fired by nature. But Richardson also detects and appreciates the hand of art in the landscape. She notes the 'great Judgement' of the design of the garden that allows a relatively small area to appear much more extensive.

At Plumpton it appears that even the gardener contributed to the atmosphere, being a 'very great curiosity' on account of his advanced age, although Richardson does not elaborate on whether he represented the Sublime or the Beautiful. This was presumably the long-serving John Banks, who died in January 1774 after more than two decades of dedication to the gardens.[64]

59 Bedfordshire & Luton Archives & Records Service, Lucas Papers, L30/24/5.

60 Extract from the Witts Papers by permission of Francis E. B. Witts.

61 Amabel Yorke's family seats included Wimpole and Wrest. Dorothy Richardson had access to the library of her grandfather and uncle, both called Richard Richardson, who were eminent physicians, naturalists and botanists. For a biographical account of Richardson see Karen Lynch, 'Taking Great Notice: Dorothy Richardson's Account of Ornamental Buildings on the Boynton Estate, East Riding of Yorkshire', *Follies Journal*, 7 (2007), 1–22.

62 William Gilpin's thoughts on the Picturesque were circulating in manuscript after his tour of the Wye and into Wales in 1770 but were not widely available until published as *Observations on the River Wye and Several Parts of South Wales etc Relative to Picturesque Beauty* in 1782. There is a slim chance that Dorothy Richardson might have seen an early copy of the manuscript if it was obtained by her uncle.

63 Anon [Barbara Hofland], *Patience and Perseverance; or, The Modern Griselda*, 4 vols (London: A. K. Newman & Co., 1813), III, p. 106.

64 Banks was buried on 20 January 1774, only 8 days after his wife, North Yorkshire Record Office (NYCRO), Knaresborough parish records. Thanks to Tony Cheal for details of Banks's will in which he is described as 'of Plompton, Gardener'.

Witts wrote that the rock garden was an 'exact resemblance to a Chinese Garden'. This is problematic as Witts had no first hand experience of the gardens of China – but he would have been aware of the contemporary passion for chinoiserie, the craze for oriental-inspired design in interior decoration and garden design. The fashion had grown as the eighteenth century progressed and was fed by a growing number of books and prints featuring the Far East and by the import of exotic goods such as silks and cottons, hand-painted wallpaper and lacquer. On a more commonplace level, Witts and his contemporaries would also have been familiar with the fashionable blue and white patterned porcelain popularly called Delft, or – by the end of the century when British manufacturers had developed a version of the design – 'willow pattern'. All of these goods, and the porcelain in particular, featured compositions of fretwork, rocks and water, and Witts would have recognised similar scenes at Plumpton.

Visitors to Plumpton in the second half of the eighteenth century would also have been familiar with the works of the architect Sir William Chambers, both published and constructed (remembering that only the educated classes of society would have been admitted to the garden in this period). Chambers was that rare being – a writer on Chinese architecture who had actually visited the country. In 1757 he published *Designs of Chinese Buildings, Furniture, Dresses, Machines, and Utensils*; an essay in the book caught the public imagination and 'Of the Art of Laying Out Gardens Among the Chinese' was quickly disseminated to a wider audience in the *Gentleman's Magazine* and the *Annual Register*, two of the most popular journals of the day.[65] Whilst current academic thinking is that Chambers may only have had very limited exposure to Chinese architecture, and that he was influenced equally by existing prints of pagodas and temples, the British public were fascinated by his descriptions of an exotic world. The Lascelles brothers were certainly familiar with Chambers, who had executed 'many' drawings (subsequently rejected) for the proposed new mansion at Harewood in 1755–56.[66]

Witts saw the whole of Plumpton as a Chinese garden, a very different entity to the landscape parks that featured an isolated structure *à la chinoise*. Chambers had described in detail the manner in which the Chinese created gardens, based on his observations in the country. Their main aim, he believed, was to imitate the irregularities of nature and, anticipating the Picturesque movement, he called the creators of gardens 'artists'.[67] These artists had identified the three 'species of scenes' called 'pleasing, horrid and enchanted' and examples of each can be found at Plumpton.[68] The enchanted scene excited surprise – the sound of the wind echoing in a cave or the introduction of curious trees and flowers. Scenes of horror were composed of gloomy caverns and narrow chasms and

[65] In 1757 and 1758 respectively.

[66] Chambers claims that he made 'many' drawings for Lascelles when discussing his re-use of one of the end pavilions of a proposed design for Harewood at the Marina Casino outside Dublin. See the enlarged 3rd edition of his *A Treatise on Civil Architecture* (London: printed for J. Smeeton, 1791).

[67] William Chambers, *Designs of Chinese Buildings, Furniture, Dresses, Machines, and Utensils* … (London: printed for the author, 1757), p. 15.

[68] Ibid.

were to be followed by pleasing scenes, as dark passages led out into bright daylight. Contrast was key – light and dark, smooth and rugged; and a variety of viewpoints was essential, so that the viewer was sometimes peering up and sometimes gazing down. It is when Chambers describes the use of rocks and water that the parallels with Plumpton can be most appreciated:

if the situation admits, they frequently lay almost the whole ground under water; leaving only some islands and rocks [...] The banks of their lakes and rivers are variegated in imitation of nature; being sometimes bare and gravelly, sometimes covered with woods quite to the water's edge. In some places flat, and adorned with flowers and shrubs; in others steep, rocky and forming caverns [...] In their lakes they intersperse islands; some of them barren, and surrounded with rocks and shoals; others enriched with every thing that art and nature can furnish most perfect.[69]

In these few sentences Chambers effectively summarises Plumpton, and echoes of his words can be found in the accounts of visitors. The travel writer William Bray described how the rocks were covered 'with greensward, shrubs and flowers' whilst the 'sides were quite bare', and the Revd Swete noted that some rocks had 'hoary tops and sides [...] fluted by the weather, whilst others are covr'd over with grass, shrubs and flowers'.[70]

Daniel Lascelles may have been particularly attracted to the Chinese style as he would have been very familiar with depictions of Chinese gardens in prints or on porcelain. We don't know if he actually visited China, but during his eight years in the east he would have seen goods from China as well as the reproductions of Chinese goods manufactured in India to meet demand in Europe, and as a merchant may have been responsible for sending such works to Europe. It seems likely that Lascelles may have sent home the hand-painted Chinese wallpaper that was an admired feature of his brother's mansion at Harewood.[71] The paper was hung in one of the principal bedrooms by Thomas Chippendale's men in 1769 (although evidence suggests it may previously have hung elsewhere) but was taken down, possibly in the Victorian era, when it was out of fashion and the house was remodelled.[72] The paper was restored and re-hung in 2008 and features scenes from everyday life against a background of rocks and water that may have inspired the introduction of chinoiserie at Plumpton (Figure 6).

It is tempting to imagine that the 'Chinese seat' seen by Richardson was a temple, or kiosk, but there is no evidence of this in the surviving accounts or in any views of the rocks. The term 'Chinese seat' was used in a number of ways in this period and could just as easily refer to a building, such as the elaborate chinoiserie pavilion at Stowe in Buckinghamshire, as to an ornate bench. The 'seat' at Plompton may have been an ephemeral building that did not survive for many years, but this seems unlikely as it receives little attention from visitors. It is most likely that the 'seat' was a bench with

[69] Ibid. pp. 16–17.

[70] William Bray, *Sketch of a Tour into Derbyshire & Yorkshire*, 2nd edn (London: printed for B. White, 1783), p. 271; Swete, IV, fol. 56.

[71] Alternatively, the paper may have been brought home by Daniel's younger brother, Henry, a Captain in the service of the East India Company.

[72] For a full account of the paper see Melissa Gallimore, *The Chinese Wallpaper: Harewood House* (Leeds: Harewood House Trust, 2008).

Figure 6 Chinese Wallpaper, East Bedroom, Harewood House, Yorkshire (detail). *Reproduced by kind permission of the Earl and Countess of Harewood and Trustees of the Harewood House Trust*

Chinese-inspired fretwork set in an alcove carved into the rock; the alcove survives and now houses a modern seat. The original chinoiserie bench disappeared many years ago, but old photos show a similar seat used elsewhere in the garden (Figure 7). Holes drilled in the rock at the back of the alcove suggest that it may once have featured a plaque or shelf for a statue. The views from the alcove are now blocked by mature trees but must once have been wide-ranging.

Contemporary with the early development of the garden at Plumpton were a number of pattern books, such as those produced by William and John Halfpenny, that featured designs for 'garden seats in the Chinese taste'.[73] Such books might have been influential, but Daniel's designs may have originated from one of two men closely involved with the Lascelles estates in Yorkshire. In 1754 Thomas Chippendale's *Gentleman and*

[73] William and John Halfpenny, *New Designs for Chinese Temples* . . . (London: printed for Robert Sayer, 1750–52).

FIGURE 7 Chinese bench at Plumpton, date unknown. *Private collection*

FIGURE 8 'Mr Carr's design of 4 different Chinese Pales or Gates' (detail). This design bears a strong similarity to the fretwork on the bench in Figure 7. West Yorkshire Archive Service, Leeds, WYL250/Acc3763/2. *Reproduced by kind permission of the Earl and Countess of Harewood and Trustees of the Harewood House Trust*

Cabinet-maker's Director had been published, and as well as furniture in the Chinese taste there were a number of designs for Chinese-style fretwork and railings. By 1771, when the Chinese seat at Plumpton is first mentioned, Chippendale was four years into working on the huge Harewood commission for Edwin Lascelles and was supplying furniture to Daniel for Goldsborough. Although very few examples of garden seats have been confidently attributed to Chippendale, he did design a pair of what were described as 'enriched garden seats' for the north front of Harewood in 1774, one of which survives today.[74] But the most likely case is that the estate joiners made the bench to the designs of John Carr. The Harewood archives contain drawings of fretwork panels, inscribed 'Mr Carr's design of 4 different Chinese Pales or Gates' (Figure 8), and one of the designs appears to have been adapted for use as the back of the bench seen in Figure 7.[75]

There is no doubt that Lascelles would have been familiar with Chinese garden features in England, and closer to home in Yorkshire. By the mid-eighteenth century garden buildings in the Chinese style were features of many of the great landscape parks of England. Stowe and Wroxton were the trendsetters in *c.* 1738 and 1740–41 respectively, but others soon appeared, including an open pavilion at Shugborough, in Staffordshire, the seat of Thomas Anson.[76] It is worth noting that this building, completed in 1747, was based on drawings made in China for Anson's brother, Admiral Anson, who stopped off in Canton during his circumnavigation of the globe.

One local garden with which Lascelles must have been familiar was Studley Royal, where disgraced Chancellor of the Exchequer John Aislabie had created a magnificent landscape featuring views of Fountains Abbey. In the 1740s the narrow valley of the River Skell with its steep and rocky sides was given arched bridges with Chinese fretwork rails, and in 1745 a Chinese temple was constructed.[77] This was originally to have been a 'Chinese house of pyramidal form, with a gallery encircling every story', presumably what we know as a pagoda, but the grandiose plan must have been too much even for Aislabie's purse and a simpler pavilion was built.[78] Brightly painted in reds and blues and with gilded Chinese dragon ornaments, the open temple was supported by seven columns.[79] Like Plumpton, this area of the park, with steep rocks, was also described as a 'Chinese landscape'.[80]

[74] Christopher Gilbert, *The Life and Works of Thomas Chippendale*, 2 vols (London: Studio Vista/Christies, 1978), I, 94, 203.

[75] WYL250/Acc/3763/2.

[76] Thanks to Michael Cousins for sharing his research into Chinese garden buildings. For the full picture see Michael Cousins, 'Chinese Architecture in England in the 18th Century and its Influence on Germany', in *Proceedings from the Symposium 'China im Schloss und Garten', Pillnitz 2008*, due for publication autumn 2009.

[77] Historical Manuscripts Commission, *Report on the Manuscripts of His Grace The Duke of Portland, K.G., Preserved at Welbeck Abbey*, VI (London: HMSO, 1901), p. 182. This account of a tour made by Lady Oxford is actually in the hand of her niece, Lady Margaret Hay. The original is in the British Library, Add. MSS 70436, Portland Papers, CCCCXXXVI, fol. 76.

[78] Yorke, p. 132.

[79] The temple does not survive. It is best delineated in a contemporary drawing and description in the Staffordshire Record Office, D260/M/F/4/21.

[80] Philip Yorke, 'A Journal of what I observed most remarkable in a tour into the North 1744' in Joyce Godber, *The Marchioness Grey of Wrest Park* (Bedfordshire Historical Record Society, 47, 1968), 125–35 (p. 132).

It is worth noting, however, that not all visitors looked at Plumpton and envisaged China. At least two were able to compare the landscape to a park a little closer to home and with which they were personally familiar. In 1790 the prolific diarist and letter writer Miss Berry visited the Forêt de Fontainebleau outside Paris and, admiring the scenery, wrote that the 'large abrupt masses of rocks scattered everywhere' put her 'in mind of Plumpton in Yorkshire'.[81] Early in the nineteenth century the Romantic poet Robert Southey visited Harrogate and made an excursion to Plumpton where he too found the 'rocks very much resemble the scenery at Fontainbleau [*sic*]'.[82] Sadly, neither writer appears to have recorded the Plumpton landscape in further detail.

THE LATER HISTORY OF PLUMPTON ROCKS

After Henry Lascelles succeeded as the 2nd Earl of Harewood in 1820, there were plans to enlarge the south front of the stables (used as the banqueting house) into a substantial dwelling. Atkinson and Sharp, the successors to Carr's York practice, submitted a number of designs, but for reasons that are now lost the project never came to fruition.[83] Most of the stable block remained in agricultural use until it was sympathetically converted into a number of residential units in the later twentieth century. The banqueting house retained its function for around two centuries – in the second half of the nineteenth century, when the Lascelles family had ceased to use the building, it became the tea-room for weary tourists.

The garden, now known as Plumpton Rocks, has continued to attract tourists since it was first created some 250 years ago. The Victorian era saw numbers increase with the arrival of the railway in Knaresborough, and the garden became the resort both of courting couples walking amongst the romantic rocks, and learned societies studying the composition of the rocks; a guidebook of 1864 jocularly noted that visitors to Plumpton were a 'strange amalgamation – geologists and lovers'.[84] By the nineteenth century the rocks had acquired names based on their shape – the Lion's Paw, the Lion's Den – or their unique properties, such as the acoustics at Echo Rock. The chasm between two rocks gained romantic fame as 'Lover's Leap', supposedly after the sad demise of a young man attempting to demonstrate his love by jumping across. The rocks continued to appeal to artists, and as the century progressed the increasingly accessible medium of photography brought amateur and professional photographers to the rocks (Figure 9), and soon numerous picture postcards of scenes at Plumpton were in circulation. As well as the lake and rocks, visitors could also admire formal gardens in the former kitchen garden by the stables, and take refreshments in the tea-rooms.[85]

[81] *Extracts of the Journals and Correspondence of Miss Berry from the Year 1783 to 1852*, ed. by Lady Theresa Lewis, 3 vols (London: Longmans, Green, and Co., 1865), I, 220.

[82] *The Life and Correspondence of Robert Southey*, ed. by Revd C. C. Southey (New York: Harper and Brothers, 1855), p. 454.

[83] WYL250/4/7.

[84] *A Guide to the Healthiest and most Beautiful Watering Places in the British Isles* (Edinburgh: Adam and Charles Black, 1864), p. 77.

[85] *Thorp's Illustrated Guide to Harrogate of 1886* (Harrogate: printed for R. Ackrill, 1886), p. 134.

FIGURE 9 An artist taking a view from the dam, May 1891. Godfrey Bingley Collection, University of Leeds Library, Special Collections

By the end of the nineteenth century the tourism industry was well developed and a story in Charles Dickens's magazine *All Year Round: A Weekly Journal* must surely have been the brainchild of one of Yorkshire's first public relations managers. The story features Uncle Fred, whose nieces are keen to join the masses touring Europe. Uncle Fred, unimpressed with the Continent, advises against joining the 'great tourist caravanserai [...] with a motley crowd of English and third-rate Americans'. One niece asks, 'with a delicate sarcasm', if he would advise they go to Margate. Rather unconvincingly, Uncle Fred is able to persuade the girls into a trip following the river Nidd and the story then becomes a thinly-disguised tourism blurb. But a highlight is of course the Plumpton Rocks that stand 'like giants'.[86]

The 7th Earl of Harewood succeeded in 1947 and was forced to sell some outlying estates to meet the death duties on his late father's estate. In 1951 'the Well Known Beauty Spot known as Plumpton Rocks' was one of the lots sold at auction.[87] The purchaser was Edward de Plumpton Hunter, a descendant of the Plumpton family who had maintained a keen interest in his former family estate. Today he and his son Robert maintain the

[86] *All Year Round: A Weekly Journal*, n.s. 42 (1888), p. 56.

[87] NYCRO, PC/FOL 10/2, Second Sale of Outlying Sections of the Harewood Estate mainly in Wharfedale and Nidderdale and including the Plompton Estate. Sale conducted by Hollis and Webb, Chartered Surveyors, Leeds, 21 June 1951.

Grade II*-listed landscape, and add to its history with their own innovations. In 2004 and 2005, for example, a collaboration with students from Ampleforth College saw contemporary benches replace the long-vanished seats provided by Daniel Lascelles. Visitors continue to be welcomed; only the media used to record their impressions have changed, with photo-sharing websites and blogs replacing the sketchbooks and journals of the early tourists.

ACKNOWLEDGMENTS

Special thanks to Catherine Thompson-McCausland and Robert de Plumpton Hunter for sharing their time and knowledge; Michael Cousins, Michael Symes and Dick Knight for their useful comments on drafts of this paper and for stimulating discussions on chinoiserie in the English garden; Bill Barber; Mary Wragg. Many thanks to the staff of the Harewood House Trust, University of Leeds Library Special Collections, University of Manchester John Rylands Library Special Collections and the West Yorkshire Archives Service, Leeds.

From Marton Lodge to Stewart Park: The Evolution of a Municipal Landscape

LINDA POLLEY

Stewart Park lies to the south of Middlesbrough, in what was once the village, now the suburb, of Marton. The site of the present-day park was originally part of a much older and larger estate and manor and, lying south of the Tees, historically located in the North Riding of Yorkshire. By the early eighteenth century the manor and the estate were in the hands of the Lowther family, and what follows charts the gradual diminution of that holding, as well as its evolution from private estate to municipal park.

MARTON LODGE 1786–1853

In 1786, Bartholomew Rudd (1726–1808) of Guisborough and Marske purchased the Marton estate from Sir John Ramsden of Byram Hall. Ramsden had inherited the land through his marriage to Margaret Norton, niece to John Lowther of Ackworth Park near Pontefract, in whose family the possession of the manor and estate had 'continued a long time'.[1]

At the time of the purchase it would appear that Rudd was a relatively well-off landowner and gentleman farmer. Diaries kept by Ralph Jackson, a close friend, indicate that by the late 1760s and early 1770s Rudd was a man of property and with enough leisure time to spend a great deal of it shooting partridges. He appears regularly in the 1768–74 volume of the diaries, and was not only Jackson's close friend but also his landlord; one of the entries, dated 11 April 1767, reads, 'Paid, Bartholomew Rudd, one year's rent for "Thistle Farm", Egton.'[2]

Both Jackson and Rudd were men of a certain type, living in a sympathetic time and place. The late eighteenth-century English countryside was reaping the benefits of an increasingly scientific approach to farming and animal husbandry. One direct result of this was a better informed interest in regional differences, more profitably based on soil types and farming practices than on dialects and shared customs. The regional dimension encouraged a focussed and systematic examination of local agricultural

[1] Revd John Graves, *The History of Cleveland* (Carlisle: Jollie, 1808; repr. Stockton on Tees: Patrick and Shotton, 1972), p. 455.

[2] Middlesbrough, Teesside Archives (TA), U/WJ, Ward Jackson Diaries, Journals of Ralph Jackson.

activity and achievement, and a growing body of agrarian literature fostered the exchange of ideas and experience, all designed 'to enable land to be put to more productive use'.[3] Rudd's activities at Marske and at Marton reflect a great deal of the current thinking and also indicate his level of participation.

A number of agricultural commentators visited the region during this period: Arthur Young in 1770, William Marshall in 1788, and John Tuke, a professional mapmaker, in 1794. They travelled widely, interviewed farmers, and then published descriptions of the farming activities they had witnessed and discussed. John Tuke mentions 'Bartholomew Rudd of Marske' in his *General View of the Agriculture of the North Riding of Yorkshire*, and reports on Rudd's experimentation with soil improvement. Rudd, Tuke tells us,

> makes composts of kelp ashes, slam from the alum works, and lime, all mixed together with earth, and finds them to answer well. Slam has not long been used; but from the experience he has had of it, he thinks it very beneficial.

He also explains in a footnote that 'slam is a refuse in the making of alum; but of the component parts of which, I am not sufficiently acquainted with chemistry to be qualified to speak'.[4] It would appear that Rudd was a practical farmer, recognised as an 'improver' prepared to try new ideas in order to increase productivity 'scientifically'. An earlier Tuke publication described his touring of the south of England, and one can see all of these investigative writers as disseminators of information as well as gatherers.

In 1803 Rudd purchased the adjacent Tollesby estate from Sir William Lowther, and the consolidated holdings were subsequently recorded in an estate plan drawn up by Joseph and William Walker in 1804 (Figure 1). The plan clearly shows the layout of the grounds and the location of Marton Lodge, which had been built in 1786.[5] Bartholomew Rudd the elder never lived at Marton, and it was probably never his intention to do so. His plan was to build upon and improve both estates for each of his two surviving sons, Bartholomew, who moved to Marton Lodge 'around the turn of the century',[6] and Thomas who settled at Tollesby.

Rudd's Marton Lodge was a relatively large and modern country mansion, built in a symmetrical Georgian classical style, located within a series of landscaped gardens and fields. Graves described it as

> a convenient mansion in the centre of [Rudd's] estate, in an open situation, on the summit of a gentle slope; from whence the sea, generally crowded with ships employed in the coal-trade, presents an interesting object on the east, with a view to the west, north, and south, which is extensive and pleasingly attractive.[7]

[3] R. A. C. Parker, *Enclosure in the Eighteenth Century* (London: Routledge and Kegan Paul, 1960), p. 3.
[4] John Tuke, *General View of the Agriculture of the North Riding of Yorkshire* (London: W Bulmer & Co., 1794), p. 52.
[5] J. Walker Ord, *The History and Antiquities of Cleveland* (London: Simpkin and Marshall; Edinburgh: Tait, 1846; repr. Stockton on Tees: Patrick and Shotton, 1972), p. 547.
[6] Beryl Bass, *The Rudds of Marton* (British Columbia: Earth-Net Communications, 2001), p. 18.
[7] Graves, pp. 462–63.

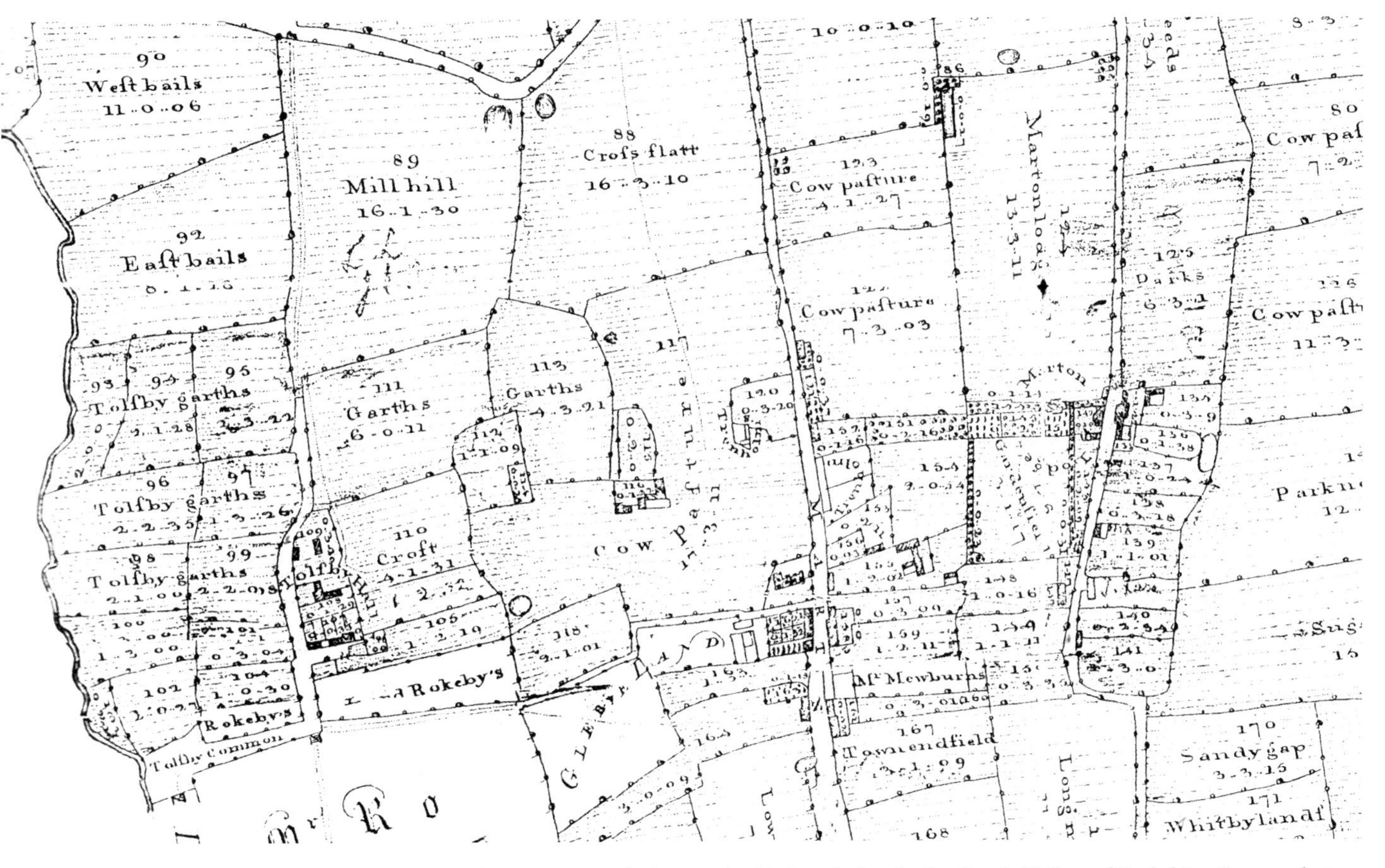

Figure 1 'Plan of Marton and Tollesby Estates Belonging to Bartholomew Rudd, Esq., Lying in the North Riding of Yorkshire, Surveyed 1804 by Jos. & Will. Walker' (detail). Marton Lodge is centre right of the plan; the Tollesby estate is far left. Teesside Archives (U/S/89)

The planted areas closest to the house (see Figure 1) can perhaps be read as orchards, walled gardens or small woodlands. Rudd did plant a good number of trees, as Graves again bears witness:

There are no plantations within the parish [of Marton] except those lately made by Mr Rudd, who has planted upwards of one hundred acres of waste grounds in different parts of his estate, chiefly with oak and larch, which are in a thriving condition; but the hedges being in general good, with a number of trees in the hedgerows, the country has a pleasing and cheerful aspect.[8]

There are also what appear to be hedges or shelterbelts planted on either side of the 'Gardenfield' to the south. This field name and the planting around the house indicate a self-conscious attempt to provide a smaller-scale, more domesticated landscape to frame the house. It might also mean that Rudd was aware of fashionable garden practices of the time such as the *ferme ornée*:

The intention of the *ferme ornée* was to take a piece of farmland and prettify it so most of it could offer at least some visual delight. Unimproved farmland was not found to be beautiful, perhaps because it was itself too new a phenomenon (enclosure of land was still unfinished by the end of the century) to be really appreciated.[9]

Bartholomew Rudd the younger (1769–1829) studied law at Cambridge, but became better known for breeding shorthorn cattle. He was appointed Deputy Lieutenant for the North Riding, and in 1804 Major of the Cleveland Corps of Voluntary Infantry. It would appear that the fashionable combination of beauty and utility, implicit in the *ferme ornée*, was well suited to his combined agricultural and social purposes. J. C. Loudon's inclusion of the *ferme ornée* in his *Encyclopaedia of Gardening* in 1822 is another indication that this style of garden and estate design had become well established by the beginning of the nineteenth century, when the Walker plan was drawn up.

Bartholomew Rudd the elder died in 1808; local history holds Rudd and the building of his son's house responsible for the demolition of Captain Cook's birthplace cottage which was on the estate. No doubt the pragmatic and unromantic Rudd considered a 'hovel' located so close to the new house an eyesore rather than an interesting landscape feature or an historical monument, and had it reduced to a pile of stones. More information regarding the planting at Marton Lodge might rescue Rudd from his philistine reputation, as he was only replicating what so many others in his position were also doing. The agrarian historian Hugh Prince tells us: 'In places distant from London landowners were pulling down dark hovels and putting up well-proportioned cottages, and were designing model farms.'[10] In her account of the Rudd family, Beryl Bass states:

While in possession of Marton Lodge, Bartholomew made many improvements to the property. He made additions to the mansion erected in Marton by his late father, finishing

[8] Graves, p. 465.

[9] David C. Stuart, *Georgian Gardens* (London: Robert Hale, 1979), p. 68.

[10] Hugh C. Prince, 'The Changing Rural Landscape, 1750–1850', Chapter 1 in *The Agrarian History of England and Wales*, ed. by G. E. Mingay (Cambridge: Cambridge University Press, 1989), p. 27.

the rooms with wainscoting, marble slabs, chimney pieces and highly polished grates. He took down several dilapidated farm buildings in order to establish a very extensive farmyard, gardens, orchards, pleasure grounds and plantations.[11]

Bartholomew the younger's breeding of short-horned cattle appears to have earned him at least a local reputation, and provides another example of the family's involvement in the region's agrarian progress:

After 1800 one breed, the shorthorn, began to oust all others. It was versatile as a producer of either milk or meat and it was also efficient as a converter of fodder crops or grass into yields of milk or gains in weight. From its place of origin in south Durham it spread along the Great North Road north to Scotland and south to the midlands. By 1850 it was the leading breed throughout England.[12]

However, this venture may not have been as successful as he and his father had hoped. In a later potted Rudd family history, the *Marton-in-Cleveland Parish Magazine* rather waspishly tells us,

The elder son, Major Bartholomew Rudd [...] lived in Marton Lodge, and occupied himself chiefly in farming, not however with great financial success, as from time to time he was compelled to sell a portion of his estate to meet the losses that arose from this or perhaps another cause.[13]

Bartholomew Rudd the younger died in 1829 and the estate passed to his eldest son, George Thomas Rudd, a clergyman and amateur entomologist, 'in whose tenure the house was burnt down' in 1832.[14] Local historian J. Walker Ord wrote about Marton Lodge in 1846 that 'the Stables and outhouses are rather extensive with excellent gardens and pleasure grounds',[15] but failed to elaborate further. If we augment that with the tithe map of Marton dated 1841,[16] and the earliest Ordnance Survey of 1853 (Figure 2), we can see evidence of both informed thought and some artistic intent. We can see both Bartholomews altering the grounds to suit their purposes, and we also have an (at this stage unproven) allegation that the holding was beginning to be whittled away. Two passing references were made to Marton Lodge, albeit to a later incarnation – an erroneous one from the *Newcastle Daily Chronicle* in 1868: 'on the south front of the lawn, is an old ruin covered with ivy; this is all that remains of the cottage in which Captain Cook was born'[17] (this 'old ruin' was the remains of the burnt out Marton Lodge); and one from *The Garden* in 1874:

[11] Bass, p. 20.
[12] Prince, p. 44.
[13] TA, U/S/461, *Marton-in-Cleveland Parish Magazine*, June 1988, p. 79.
[14] Ibid.
[15] Ord, p. 552.
[16] TA, PR/MAC 3/1.
[17] *Newcastle Daily Chronicle*, 11 August 1868, p. 3.

147

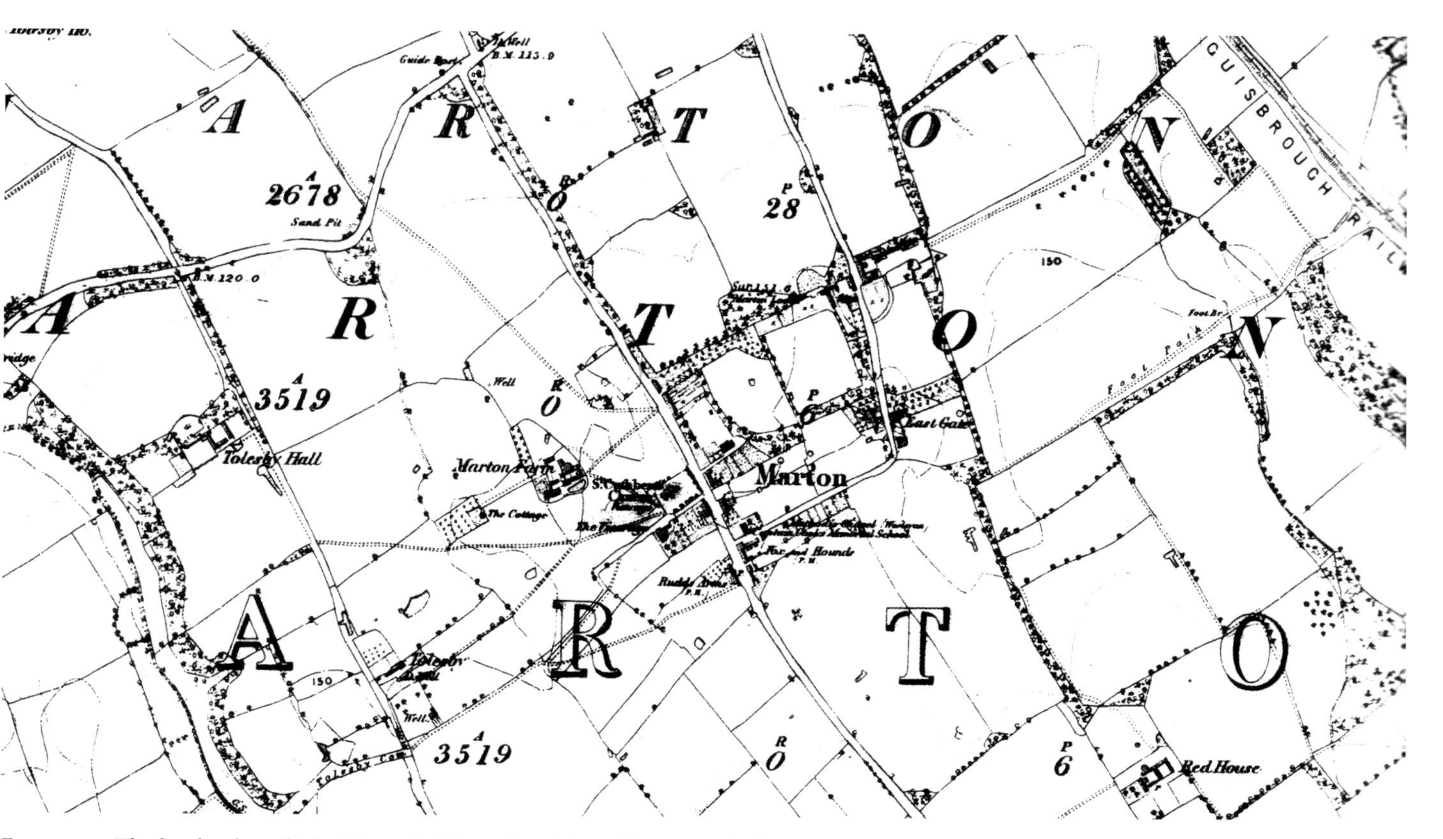

FIGURE 2 The land as bought by Henry Bolckow. Reproduced from 1853 Ordnance Survey map

In making some improvements in the ornamental portion of the grounds, several old fruit trees that stood in little gardens adjoining have been wisely spared, and the trees yield good crops of fruit, besides forming ornaments to the lawn when in blossom in the spring.[18]

After the fire, the estate remained in the possession of the Rudd family for possibly two subsequent generations, although the house was never rebuilt; the 1841 tithe map shows Marton Lodge 'in Ruins'. The holding subsequently passed into the hands of the Park family of Elwick Hall, and the Reverend James Allen Park sold the estate to H. W. F. Bolckow. It would be useful to know how long the Park family owned the Marton estate, whether they carried out any improvements, or even whether they continued to farm the land, but to date no records for this period have been found. One assumes it was ultimately surplus to their requirements.

H. W. F. BOLCKOW'S MARTON HALL, 1853–78

Henry W. F. Bolckow, who had migrated from northern Germany to Newcastle in 1827, and then to Middlesbrough in 1840, bought the Marton estate in 1852 or 1853, in many ways a propitious time in his professional and personal life. In 1850, after a lengthy period of exploration, iron ore was discovered in the Eston hills, and its extent and proximity were about to transform the scale of operations for Bolckow and his business partner John Vaughan, as well as the growth and economic success of Middlesbrough. In 1851, Bolckow married for the second time, his first wife having died in 1842 after only two years of marriage. For Bolckow, already a wealthy man from earlier business activities in Newcastle, the iron ore and its location meant wealth of an entirely different magnitude. It also dictated that his future was to be even more firmly tied to Middlesbrough and the Cleveland hills. The year 1853 further encouraged the entwined fortunes of Henry Bolckow and Middlesbrough; it was the year of the town's incorporation, and Bolckow was elected its first mayor. This was not his first public role, as he had been a JP for the North Riding for some years, although it no doubt strengthened his sense of commitment to, and position within, the community.

Within these varying contexts, it is not surprising that Henry Bolckow felt the need to mark his arrival as an established and valued member of the community he had helped to create. The rechristened Marton Hall, and its surrounding grounds, could also provide evidence for his claim to membership of what J. Mordaunt Crook has called 'a new aristocracy of money':

During the Victorian period as a whole as many as eight out of ten millionaire or half millionaire families acquired landed estates within two generations; between 1858 and 1879 the proportion is as high as 26 out of 30. At the top or magnate level – an Arkwright, a Peel, a Brassey or a Guinness; an Armstrong, a Baring, a Guest or a Rothschild – this involved, besides a London house, the acquisition of a country seat and 10,000 acres; in all perhaps a half million pound investment. Lower down, for those aiming at gentry status only – Marshall, Pease, Bolckow or Lowthian Bell – 1,000 or 2,000 acres might suffice. Lower still –

[18] J. Thompson, [no title], *The Garden*, no. 6 (5 September 1874), p. 224.

Kenrick or Cadbury, Chamberlain or Attwood – it was a villa rather than a seat; but a villa with the appurtenances of rurality.[19]

It has proven difficult to establish the extent of Bolckow's land acquisition at Marton, or an accurate chronology for the purchase of the land, the building of the Hall and the taking up of residence. The Ordnance Survey dated 1857 (but surveyed in 1853, see Figure 2) shows the Marton Hall grounds probably as purchased. The property is still labelled 'Marton Lodge' and the layout of fields and planting follows that of the earlier tithe map of 1841. In his will, Bolckow lists the components of his estate, 'my capital freehold mansion house called Marton Hall and the freehold parish lands gardens pleasure grounds plantations stables lodges messuages and appurtenances to the same belonging and all my other freehold messuages farms lands manors tithes and hereditaments whatsoever situate and being so arising in the Parish of Marton',[20] but fails to quantify acreage or the number of properties. Marton Hall was probably built between 1854 and 1856, and then added to dramatically in 1867, in preparation for Prince Arthur's stay, when he officially opened Middlesbrough's centrally located Albert Park (a gift to the town from Bolckow) in 1868.

Judging from the 1895 Ordnance Survey (Figure 3), combined with accounts by visitors, the grounds were designed as sweeping green park lands, planted with shrubs and specimen trees, with flower beds kept to a minimum, all intended to be viewed from the house. The *Newcastle Daily Chronicle*, reporting on Prince Arthur's visit, mentions the tower 'surmounted by a lantern, from which a most extensive view of the sea, the Cleveland hills, and different parts of south Durham is obtained' and the 'beautiful drawing room [that] looks onto the south lawn'.[21] Somewhat surprisingly, according to J. Thompson writing in *The Garden* in 1874, 'no flower beds are in close proximity to the residence; on the contrary, the beautiful green sward is clothed over in a very natural manner with endless variety in the shape of graceful trees and shrubs.' He mentions 'rare conifers, purple Beeches, and weeping trees of various kinds', as well as 'many fine standard Rhododendrons of the newest varieties'. The soil, he is informed by the gardener, is 'dry and light, and well adapted for the growth of Conifers'. He identifies a number of varieties of Lawson Cypress and says that 'different kinds of Japanese conifers are here in abundance'. Thompson judges the Retinosporas 'truly charming' and singles out for particular praise a Golden Juniper (*Juniperus japonica aureovariegata*) which he believes will 'become a thing of great beauty here'. He has only this to say about flowers:

The flower garden, which is small, occupies a hollow in the lawn, about fifty yards from the west end of the hall, and a broad terrace from the south front leads to it, past a small conservatory that is attached to the house.[22]

A lake or pond was excavated to the north west, and an ornamental boathouse placed for picturesque effect (Figure 4). To the south of the Hall, denser tree and shrub planting

[19] J. Mordaunt Crook, *The Rise of the Nouveaux Riches* (London: John Murray, 1999), p. 21.
[20] TA, U/S/684, Family trees and wills of the Bolckow family, 1806–1983.
[21] *Newcastle Daily Chronicle*, 11 August 1868, p. 3.
[22] Thompson, p. 224.

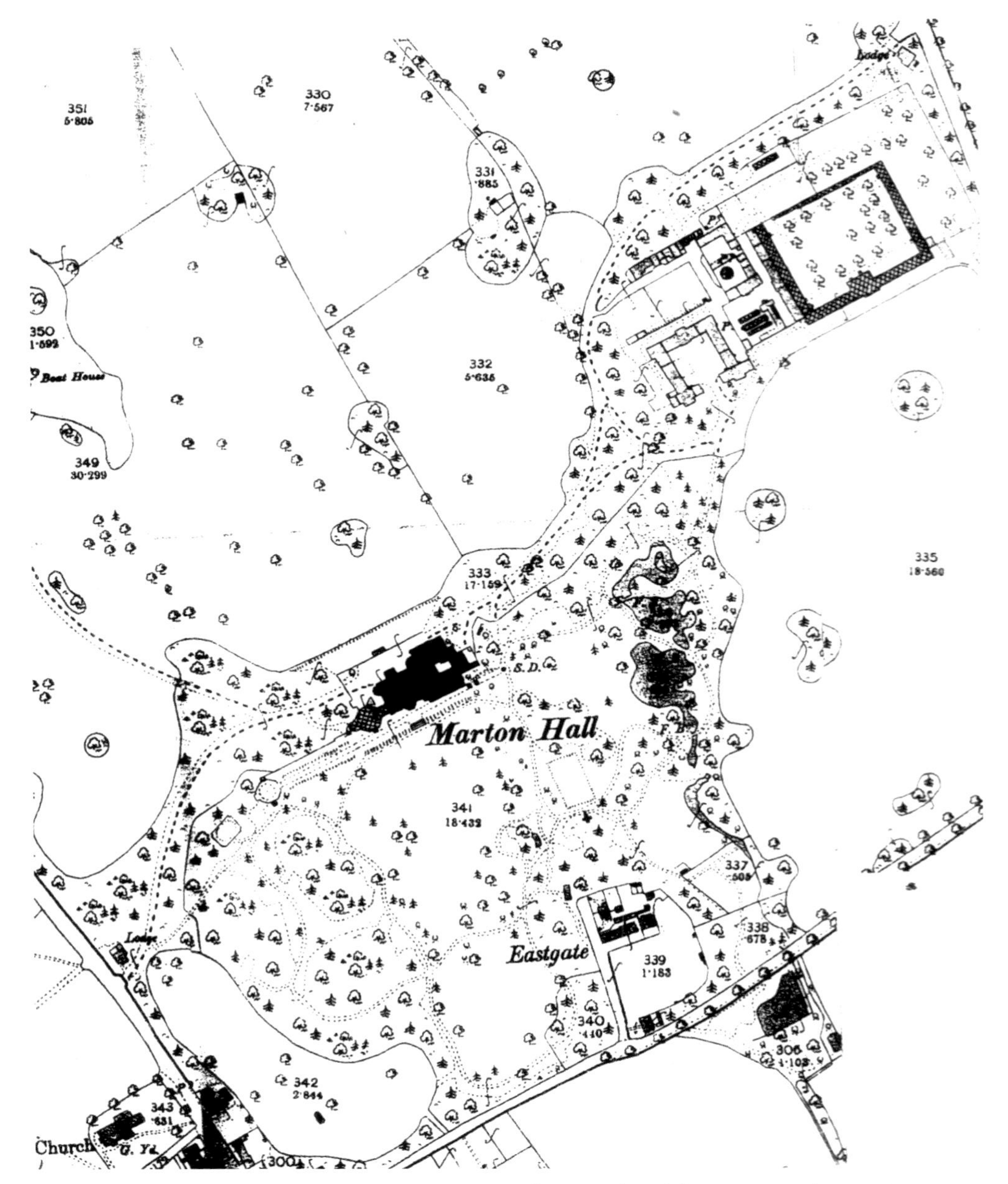

FIGURE 3 The established planting at Marton Hall. Reproduced from 1895 Ordnance Survey map

FIGURE 4 Boathouse and lake, Marton Hall, *c.* 1924, photographer unknown. Teesside Archives (CB/M/C 10/23)

created a natural, more wooded effect, with paths winding through the shrubbery; two further ponds were excavated to the west. In 1858, Bolckow installed a memorial to Captain Cook, a granite vase placed on the south front of the lawn, inscribed, 'To Mark the Site of the Cottage in Which Captain James Cook the World Circumnavigator, was Born Oct. 27, 1728'.

The lack of floral planting in the grounds was compensated by extensive and well-stocked forcing houses and orchard house erected to the north east of the Hall. Located between the equally impressive stable block and the easterly lodge cottage, the glass-houses were entered through 'a very spacious' potting shed 'finished and fitted with the latest improvements'. So wrote J. T. Burns, one of the gardeners at John Vaughan's neighbouring Gunnergate Hall, in a very informative account of Marton Hall's glasshouses for *The Gardener*. Describing their organisation and contents in a manner well suited to the journal's readership, his local knowledge and experience give the article authenticity and an air of professional admiration.[23]

[23] J. T. Burns, 'A Peep through Marton Hall, the Seat of H. W. F. Bolckow, MP for Middlesboro (Yorkshire)', *The Gardener: A Magazine of Horticulture and Floriculture* (December 1872), p. 575.

The impressive series of lean-to glasshouses was built to form a quadrangle, enclosing and sheltering a kitchen garden, and further protected to the north west and north east by a walled area, possibly orchards. The glasshouses were identified according to their specialised functions and environments, but also pressed into multiple use when the season required. The Vine House also housed camellias; the Strawberry House was filled in winter with tender stove plants such as 'Allamanda, Rondeletia, Stephanotis, Plumbago, Swansonia, Vinca, Clerodendron, Dipladenias, Bougainvillaea' [*sic*], and a few 'fruiting pines' or pineapples.[24] Most of these are relatively easy to obtain and popularly grown today, but at the time were still exotic and treasured novelties. The Orchid House held a range of these Victorian favourites, also known as 'pitcher plants', while the Cucumber House boasted Dracaeneas. Fruiting trees in the Orchard House (peaches, pears, apples, plums) were combined with pillar roses and clematis, presumably trained up the glasshouse supports. Much of what was grown under glass might have survived outside, but the intention was to create an impressive and controllable experience for visitors as well as a reliable year-round crop of fruit and potted flowering plants for the house and conservatory:

Under glass [...] there was little conflict between production and display [...] Everything was destined for the mansion but, in the meantime, the scale and out of season splendour made for a display which was as magnificent as it was fruitful. The distinction between production and display in the glasshouses was blurred still further by the fact that at many places a section of the kitchen ranges might be taken up by anything from a modest conservatory to a major collection of exotic specimens. Owners and guests would thus pass freely, and without a second thought, between houses composed expressly for their delight, and those whose primary purpose was more practical.[25]

Fruit that was 'difficult', or at least labour intensive, was extremely important, and, according to Burns, the Marton Hall glass complex included an Early Peach House, a Late Peach House and a Late Vinery. The varying widths or depths of the houses, indicated on the OS map, would suggest that the narrowest range housed the peaches, although it is not certain which route Burns took on his descriptive ramble, and therefore less possible to clearly identify the other three sides of the square. Pineapples too were very demanding of both time and money. 'Pineries' required a great deal of heat, although their cultivation in the right conditions was fairly straightforward. John Robson, head gardener at Linton Park, near Maidstone, Kent, knew how it was done:

Success in the 'whole affair was one of pocket' declared Robson bluntly, 'coupled of course with some cultural details not difficult to understand.' As possession of a coal field offered a distinct advantage, it is not surprising that [...] one of the most productive pineries was at Cyfartha Castle, the Rhondda seat of the South Wales iron master, R T Crayshay.[26]

[24] Ibid.

[25] J. Morgan and A. Richards, *A Paradise Out of a Common Field: The Pleasures and Plenty of the Victorian Garden* (London: Ebury Press, 1990), p. 191.

[26] Morgan and Richards, p. 110.

Henry Bolckow was equally able to avail himself of plentiful supplies of coal as a number of collieries had been added to his highly successful and interrelated business ventures. The impressive but practical central 'entrance' to the potting shed buildings led into the boiler house and its coal bunker, the gable possibly dictated by the need for a double height space and the wide double door facilitating the installation of a large piece of equipment. The heating technology demanded by large greenhouses gradually developed as the century progressed, but the relatively 'low tech' approach to creating heated spaces using hot water pipes meant the largest possible boiler was no doubt in place fairly early on.

As well as the boiler house, the brick garden buildings housed a large potting shed with separate pottery or pot store to the right, and a wash house to the left with another external door. Beyond the wash house there was a pantry, also with access from the yard, and beyond that, 'dwelling houses'. The provision of only one door might indicate that the end house was self-contained while the rest of the buildings were communal provision or lodging for however many young, unmarried gardeners were employed.

Without more information, it is impossible to know just how involved Bolckow and/or his wife were in the choice or the nurturing of Marton Hall's glasshouse specimens. A hard-working and knowledgeable gardener played an extremely important part in the success or failure of such an enterprise, and could be as influential as his situation and employer allowed. John Burns's article provides ample evidence of the knowledge and expertise required by (and often found at) a large-scale country house, but not the level of responsibility shouldered. It also raises interesting questions about the relationships between neighbouring local estates. The exchange of information and experience, the 'networking' that develops to support any collective endeavour, must have been in operation here.

In the auction catalogue for a sale in 1907 of what remained of the Marton Hall library,[27] there were a few specialist horticultural books, some 'how-to' instruction manuals, and a number of fairly predictable fashionable volumes. They are listed here with the date of the edition for sale:

Mrs Loudon	*Gardening for Ladies* (1841)
J. C. Loudon	*Trees and Shrubs of Great Britain* (1842)
E. J. Lowe	*Ferns British and Exotic* (1856)
(author unknown)	*The Cottage Gardeners' Dictionary* (1857)
E. J. Lowe	*Beautiful Leaved Plants and a Natural History of British Grasses* (1861–62)
(author unknown)	*Villa and Cottage Architecture* (1868)
Undated:	
C. E. Curtiss	*Estate Management, a Practical Handbook*
Frean	*Elements of Agriculture*
James Long	*The Small Farm and Its Management*
(probably J. C. Loudon)	*The Villa Gardener*

[27] TA, U/ZX 2/10.

Bound copies of journals were also for sale, including:
The Cottage Gardener and Country Gentleman's Companion (1857–70)
The Journal of Horticulture (14 volumes)
The Garden (1872–81)

The sale catalogue indicates a fairly representative selection for an estate the size of Marton Hall, rather than the library of a dedicated gardening enthusiast, but unfortunately the 'post heyday' date of the sale renders it inconclusive evidence.

Marton Hall and its grounds played an important part in Henry Bolckow's civic life and public persona. They served as the platform for a number of public events and commemorations, most notably for the entertainment of visiting dignitaries, including royalty. Marton Hall was also the favourite location for the Middlesbrough Temperance Society's annual garden party:

> [The second Mrs Bolckow] appears to have been the typical wife of a rich Victorian [who] spent her time doing a wide variety of charitable deeds. When the local Temperance Society held its garden parties at Marton Hall she would be in attendance showing the guests around the Hall which housed one of the finest art collections in the country.[28]

Both of Bolckow's marriages were childless; his nephew Carl, who had followed him to England, joined the firm, became a director and eventually his uncle's heir.

MARTON HALL AFTER BOLCKOW'S DEATH 1878–1924

Henry Bolckow died in 1878, after an illness which had kept him out of public life for about a year. Carl didn't stay at Marton Hall for the rest of *his* life, nor did he ensure it was kept in the family as his uncle had wished, no doubt finding it very expensive to maintain. He was not as successful in his speculative dealings as Henry Bolckow had been, and although on the latter's death Carl 'became Chairman of the company known as Bolckow, Vaughan & Co [...] by the middle of the 1890s he had lost control of the firm, although he remained reasonably well off'.[29] A house and estate the size of Marton Hall would certainly require an extremely large fortune or income to keep it functioning. It would also require a great deal of motivation and commitment, something that perhaps only Marton Hall's creator could be expected to sustain. The Hall had served much more than domestic purposes, and was inextricably bound up in Bolckow's relationship with Middlesbrough. Without him it may be that it lost its original function and wasn't given time to acquire another. The 1870s and '80s on Teesside were not the best of times economically, although they were not the worst either.[30] In the summer of 1892 the *Marton-in-Cleveland Parish Magazine* tells us 'Marton too has been a partaker of the general depression' and reports 'so much want existing in the district [and] so many calls on the charity of all able to give'.[31] By 1907 Carl Bolckow had moved south to Devon,

[28] Ron Gott, *Henry Bolckow, Founder of Teesside* (Middlesbrough, 1968), p. 99.
[29] Ibid.
[30] G. A. North, *Teesside's Economic Heritage* (Middlesbrough: County Council of Cleveland, 1975).
[31] TA, U/S/461, *Marton-in-Cleveland Parish Magazine*, May 1892.

perhaps for his wife's health as she died in 1908. Carl Bolckow died in 1915; his eldest son, Henry William Ferdinand, continued to live nearby in his estate villa, Brackenhoe, and the younger, Charles Frederick Henry, in the village of Nunthorpe. In 1878 Carl's uncle had left an estate of about £800,000; thirty-seven years later Carl left a relatively meagre £6071.

The death of Henry Bolckow marked the beginning of a long period of neglect and decline for Marton Hall and its grounds. The 1907 sale of books mentioned above tells us something of this 'down-sizing', as do successive census returns, but not the whole story. A few months before the book sale, the same auctioneers had, at Carl's request, disposed of the contents of the Hall, including 'about 450 plants in tubs and pots' and other bits and pieces from the garden and the conservatory, such as statuary, garden seats and tools, beehives and bees, and two lawnmowers, one pony drawn.[32] During the first decade of the twentieth century then, Marton Hall ceased to function as either a home or a country estate, and perhaps began by default to assume the mantle of a public park, if not officially, at least in the eyes of local residents.

From 1915, the house and grounds were used by the 12th Battalion Yorkshire Regiment, the land requisitioned for temporary occupation under the Defence of the Realm Act for a rental of £300 per annum.[33]

MARTON HALL BECOMES STEWART PARK: 1924 ONWARDS

Marton Hall and its surrounding grounds were 'gifted' to Middlesbrough County Council in 1924 and opened as a public park in an official ceremony on 23 May 1928. The state of their dilapidation by that time can be seen in a series of photographs believed to have been taken at the time of the acquisition (Figures 5 and 6). Like many of these historical 'givens', the process was slightly more complex than local histories allow.

It would appear that at the end of the First World War Henry W. F. Bolckow needed to raise money, and made it known that he was prepared to sell 300 acres of the Marton estate, including the Hall and Park, to Middlesbrough Council, identified as the most likely buyer. However, his price at this stage, £140,000 (300 acres of land at £300 per acre, plus 'the Hall and buildings', for £50,000) was deemed far too high, and given various other demands on civic budgets at this time, not a surprising response. In March 1921, Bolckow offered to re-enter negotiation, but again 'it was not possible for the Corporation to move further in the matter at that time'.[34] In February 1923, Bolckow dropped his price – 340 acres, including the Hall and all buildings on the estate for £75,000, and the Corporation's version of events is as follows:

After delicate and difficult negotiations in connection with the purchase, a munificent offer was made by Thos. D Stewart, Esquire, J.P., who desired to purchase the Park Land (including Marton Hall and buildings), and present it to the town as an open space forever, and it was

[32] TA, U/ZX 2/9, Marton Hall near Middlesbrough, Catalogue of Valuable Modern Cabinet Furniture, Persian and Turkey Carpets, Linen, Wines, etc., June 4, 5, 6, 7 & 11, 1907.
[33] TA, CB/M/C 11/2/19, Souvenir of the Opening of Stewart Park, Marton, Wednesday 23 May, 1928.
[34] Ibid.

FIGURE 5 The Marton Estate, *c.* 1924, photographer unknown. Teesside Archives (CB/M/C 10/23)

FIGURE 6 The Marton Estate, *c.* 1924, photographer unknown. Teesside Archives (CB/M/C 10/23)

ultimately arranged that the Corporation should purchase the whole of the farmlands (comprising about 210 acres) from Mr Bolckow for £35,000, and Mr Bolckow should sell the Marton Hall and the Park Lands attached to Mr Thos. D. Stewart, who would convey the same by way of gift to the Corporation for the perpetual use thereof by the public as an open space or Park for exercise and recreation.[35]

Dormand Stewart's letter to the Mayor, printed in the souvenir booklet, offers 'a free gift to the inhabitants of Middlesbrough' based on an altruistic wish by himself and his wife to extend the amenities offered by Albert Park to a wider audience.

Thomas Dormand Stewart (1854–1946) had lived in Middlesbrough since the late 1870s, establishing the very successful Stewart & Co (Clothiers), first in rented accommodation in 1880 and then his own premises in 1893. Eventually, branches appeared in a number of towns and cities in the north east and further afield. Dormand Stewart and his wife were active members of the local Methodist Church, and he had been one of five who together purchased land in Middlesbrough for a new Wesleyan chapel. By 1924 he was a well-known and well-respected member of the community: Councillor of Linthorpe Ward from 1911 to 1927, Mayor of Middlesbrough in 1911, and created a Freeman of the town in 1924, the timing of that accolade no doubt related to his gift of Stewart Park.

A final auction of 'The Remainder of the Collection of the Late H W F Bolckow, Esq MP' was held in May of 1924, and in the following month the deeds for a 'piece or parcel of land forming part of the Marton Hall Estate' were jointly registered in the names of Dormand Stewart and the Borough of Middlesbrough. A number of undated and contradictory plans of the Stewart Park boundaries provide an inconclusive version of events and property transactions. A plan of the land attached to the transfer does not include any of the building plots along what would eventually become The Grove, nor does it incorporate the properties at Eastgate. A further (undated) plan drawn up by the office of S. E. Burgess, the Borough Engineer, between 1909 and 1936, provides a range of 'Park Amenities' but there is no indication here how many were realised, whether this is a record or merely a suggested wish list.[36] A 1928/9 Ordnance Survey (Figure 7) charts the boundaries of Marton Hall rather than Stewart Park. This is all complicated by simultaneous extension of the borough boundary to the southern extent of the park, thereby excluding houses along both sides of what is here called Marton Lane.

Burgess's plan also indicates how the glasshouses and part of the walled gardens would be dispensed with and replaced by building plots along the eastern boundary. A very large plot north of the lodge was also outside the park (and the borough) boundary, Inwood House. The souvenir booklet marking the opening of the park (1928: see n. 33) mentions 'delicate and difficult negotiations in connection with the purchase' and one wonders whether Stewart was repeating Bolckow's earlier astute 'betterment' of the Albert Park's surrounding land's value by its retention and development for housing. An undated redrawing of the 1928/9 Ordnance Survey map, with pencilled additions, shows

[35] Ibid.

[36] TA, CB/M/C(2) 9/218.

FIGURE 7 Land allocated for Stewart Park. Reproduced from 1929 Ordnance Survey map

that quite large houses on leafy garden sites were intended to occupy this strip, and this would probably benefit from further investigation.

In September 1924, the local Park Curator, Samuel Rymer, was dispatched to London to look at the best examples the capital had to offer. He visited Hyde Park, St James's Park, Battersea Park, Victoria Park, Finsbury Park, Regent's Park Zoological Gardens, Green Park, Greenwich, Hampton Court, Kew and Kensington Gardens. In his report, Hampton Court and Kew were singled out as the best kept, but no doubt they all provided inspiration and examples of good practice. In February of 1928, the year of the official opening, notice was given at a Parks Committee meeting of a Royal Horticultural Society *International Exhibition of Garden Design and Conference of Garden Planning*, to be held in November. Committee members were not interested in attending, perhaps feeling that by November they would have achieved what little 'design' or 'planning' was required.[37] Also in February, the Committee received the Park Curator's estimated expenditure for the opening of the Park. Samuel Rymer submitted two alternative schemes of varying price: £1096 and £784. Scheme 1, the most expensive, called for three gardeners, one labourer and one working attendant, whereas Scheme 2 only allowed for two gardeners and one working attendant. As well as differences in the workforce, the most expensive scheme also allowed for a motor mowing machine, weed killer, manure, and £35 worth of new tools rather than £25. Rymer argued that the most expensive scheme would allow as much work as possible to be done before the admittance of the general public, including improvement as well as tidying, 'otherwise the place will have such a dilapidated appearance, I am afraid many people would not respect it as they should.'[38] After a site visit by the Committee, it was ordered that Stewart Park should be opened 'as soon as possible', and that the cheaper Scheme 2 be implemented, although at a cost of £1000. The additional funds were 'considered essential for the proper supervision and maintenance of the Park when opened to the public'. So no money to invest in preparation, but for 'working attendants' who presumably cost less than gardeners. At this stage, the Hall itself was not opened to the public, but the Parks Committee asked for a Borough Engineers report 'as to which portions of the hall could be used with safety [...] and as to the estimated cost of making such available for public use'.[39]

The year 1928 was also the bicentennial of Captain Cook's birth. The Bicentennial Celebrations were recorded in words and photographs for the *Stockton & Teesside Herald* on Saturday, 15 September, 1928. After the unveiling of a plaque on Great Ayton's High Green, Cook's old school room was opened as a museum, followed by a procession to the Parish Church for a service and a visit to the Cook family grave. The celebrations continued at Marton Hall/Stewart Park with the unveiling of an engraved marble plinth and close inspection of Bolckow's own 1865 memorial urn. The newspaper photographs certainly show the sad state of the Hall and the overgrown condition of the conservatory, but they also indicate the Park's suitability for, and reaffirmation as, a place of public gathering, municipal history and outdoor recreation (Figure 8).

[37] TA, CB/M/C2/267, Minutes of the Park Committee, 21 February 1928, p. 16.
[38] TA, CB/M/C2/267, Minutes of the Park Committee (Special), 29 February 1928, p. 610.
[39] Ibid., p. 612.

FIGURE 8 Bicentennial of Captain Cook's birth, September 1928; after leaving Great Ayton, celebrations continue at Stewart Park. Teesside Archive (CB/M/C 19/5–23)

Stewart Park very quickly became an important recreational facility for Middlesbrough residents. Its mature parkland in an out-of-town, almost rural location, combined with its historic provenance, provided an irresistible attraction. The Park Committee Minutes detail responses to demands from a range of interest groups and individuals, as well as the day-to-day running of this large green civic space. The park soon became the regular platform for any number of organised civic activities: school children's outings, bowls tournaments, band concerts, tennis matches, rose society meetings, as well as for individual relaxation and recreation such as fishing and ice-skating on the lakes, and walking, having picnics or taking tea.

The Park Curator's Reports outline the seasonal activities undertaken by himself and his team of Park Attendants, either 'potting plants, planting flower beds, cutting grass, hoeing and cleaning borders, trimming verges, cleaning walks' during the summer, or 'propagating and transplanting herbaceous borders and laying turf' in November. By July 1928 the one full-time working attendant and his family were 'installed in one of the cottages' (at Eastgate) and all attendants plus the Curator had been made Special

Constables, which indicates the other side to their working day, that of policing this public space.[40] As early as September 1928,

The Town Clerk reported that the Chairman of the Public Libraries and Museums Committee at the Meeting on the 17th September, had stated that there were many interesting objects at the Dorman Museum which they were unable to exhibit owing to lack of space, and Alderman Kedward had suggested that if this Committee were inclined to consider favourably the question of the provision of a Museum at Marton Hall, a fine collection of exhibits could be transferred there from the Dorman Museum.[41]

With hindsight, one wonders whether a stronger commitment to making this work on a much larger scale might have proven one means of saving the Hall from its ignominious fate. A small collection was eventually housed there before World War II, but any serious strategic planning of a more permanent exhibition space or building never materialised during the interwar period. The timing was certainly not right. Given the dilapidated state of the building, the investment required was always going to be a stumbling block; inevitably the longer this project was 'considered', the more expensive it became.

By the outbreak of the Second World War, Stewart Park had become well established as a popular and much used urban recreational facility, although the Hall itself continued to deteriorate. In February of 1940, Samuel Rymer reported

that the severe climatic conditions, caused quite a lot of damage in the roof of the above building and it is very essential that this be given some attention as early as possible. The thaw last week revealed this, when it was found that water was teaming [*sic*] from broken lead work and some timbers, and dropping on to the marble stairway below, causing much flooding.[42]

This seriously destructive incursion of water was allowed to continue unabated – on 23 January 1942, the Town Clerk reported to the Parks Committee 'that after lengthy negotiations with the Ministry of Home Security, the proposal to construct a new roof on Marton Hall had been abandoned owing to the difficulty of coming to satisfactory financial arrangements with the Ministry'.[43]

In June of 1941 the Town Clerk had reported to the Committee that Stewart Park would again be used for 'War Emergency purposes'. This time it was mainly for the activities of Local Defence Volunteers, or the Home Guard. The Hall's lantern made the ideal fire-watcher's 'look-out point' over all of Middlesbrough, and there were plenty of buildings large and functional enough to be pressed into service as garages; these were added to by the Auxiliary Fire Service during their stay. An adjacent nineteen-acre field near Ormesby Station was identified by the County War Agricultural Executive as ideal for the 'further production of food', and was subsequently cleared of tenants' livestock and ploughed up for the duration. Some thirty-eight and a half acres of the Park itself was let out for grazing, perhaps to compensate for this.

[40] TA, CB/M/C2/267, Minutes of the Park Committee, 10 July 1928, p. 1295.
[41] TA, CB/M/C 2/267, Minutes of the Park Committee, 18 September 1928, p. 1487.
[42] TA, CB/M/C 2/269, Minutes of the Park Committee, 16 February 1940, p. 753.
[43] TA, CB/M/C 2/269, Minutes of the Park Committee, 23 January 1942, p. 337.

In July 1941, the Committee considered the role Middlesbrough's parks might play in the national 'War-time Holidays at Home Scheme', designed to discourage unnecessary travel and to present one negative social impact of the war in a positive way. These Holidays at Home provided an easily accessible alternative to the heavily fortified seaside resorts, out of bounds for the duration of the war. A number of morale-boosting activities were mounted under this rubric in Albert Park, as well as at Claireville Road Recreation Ground and at the Gilkes Street Central Baths. Stewart Park did not appear to play such an important role here, and one wonders how much its more important military role precluded this. Stewart Park appears to drop out of the public domain until 1944, when the Parks Committee minutes record a gradual reclamation and replanting of the parkland.[44] The war-time entertainment programme in the parks had obviously been a popular success, as it continued in the immediate aftermath as the 'Pleasure in Parkland' scheme. Stewart Park was used almost exclusively for firework displays in this respect, and the extent of public access was curtailed for a number of years after the war as well.

POST-WAR STEWART PARK

The post-war period brought with it a different mood, inevitably reflected in the tone and priorities of all Council activities and records. Initially we see a slow but steady attempt to return to some sort of normality, and then a new set of attitudes to civic roles and amenities emerge.

The Town and Country Planning Act of 1944 called for local authorities to take responsibility for modernising and improving their cities and towns, and to produce development plans indicating how they might do this. The Middlesbrough Survey and Plan, 'directed' by town planner Max Lock and published by the Corporation in 1947, argued that 'because its central built-up areas are seriously deficient in green spaces, the planning of open space is of great importance to the plan' and identified Stewart Park as 'Middlesbrough's chief link with the country'. However, in keeping with the planning team's focus on 'the legacy of interwar muddle and blight' and 'the redevelopment of town environment',[45] recommendations tended to discount existing green space and in this case proposed a number of smaller 'green wedges' projecting into 'the heart of each neighbourhood, acting as buffers as well as green links between the housing groups'.[46] So rather than large 'green lungs' serving the entire population of a town, with implications of distance and transport, every neighbourhood would benefit from green open space on its doorstep. This prioritising of a different *type* of municipal green space no doubt helped change local government attitudes to existing parkland; in many instances it also provided the impetus for reduced park staffing and maintenance in the face of constrained budgets and local government reorganisation.

[44] TA, CB/M/C 2/270, Minutes of the Parks Committee, 1944–47, passim.
[45] Max Lock, *The County Borough of Middlesbrough Survey and Plan* (Middlesbrough: Middlesbrough Corporation, 1947), p. 10.
[46] Lock, p. 251.

The gradual dereliction, and in 1960 the demolition, of Bolckow's Marton Hall, following destruction by fire, reflects a low level of historic appreciation at that time, particularly for the 'frightful architectural exuberance' of the Victorians, as one Middlesbrough Council employee noted.[47] On the other hand, in 1978 the Captain Cook Birthplace Museum opened in the Park, located in award-winning purpose-built accommodation. A tropical conservatory was erected on the site of the Hall in 1960 and proved a popular attraction for thirty years, whilst the walled garden became the site of herb gardens and an aviary. A number of local historical 'threads' are therefore woven into the story of this landscape, and the public green space does retain its popularity and its accumulative meaning among Middlesbrough citizens. The first stage of a combined BIG Lottery and Heritage Lottery Fund bid has been successful, providing the means to realise detailed restoration and interpretation plans. Should the application be successful at Stage 2, then work to restore the historical buildings and parkland will be completed by 2012. Middlesbrough Council's ambitious restoration project will mark the beginning of the next phase of this historically layered parcel of land, and further encourage increased awareness of its local and regional importance.

POST SCRIPTUM

In October 2009 it was announced that Stewart Park has been awarded a grant of just under £4.4 million pounds and, after a long wait, Phase 2 of its refurbishment and development plans can now begin.

[47] Middlesbrough, Dorman Museum, Archive Box 16.

The Cemetery Reality: Two Case Studies from Sheffield

FIONA STIRLING

The introduction of the cemetery in the nineteenth century is credited with having revolutionised the place of burial from the overcrowded and insanitary churchyard and burial grounds in town centres to large landscaped grounds on the outskirts of towns and cities. This paper considers the establishment and development of two cemetery landscapes in Sheffield: Burngreave and Crookes. Documentary analysis of the minutes and annual reports relating to the cemeteries' establishment and management, and grave-by-grave mapping, have revealed a detailed understanding of the use of the landscape for burial and a wider appreciation of the historic development of the two cemeteries.

CONTEXT

Prior to the nineteenth century, burials took place in the parish churchyard with the same ground being re-used for burial over a period of time. The parish church was obliged by law to provide a place of interment for all except those who had not been baptised or those who had committed suicide.[1] In return, all parishioners, regardless of their denomination, were obliged to pay towards the upkeep of the church and churchyard through a tax known as the church rate. The re-use of graves was a commonly accepted practice that provided a sustainable solution to burial provision for centuries.

Like many towns, Sheffield experienced major population growth and urban expansion during the industrial revolution. This dramatic rise meant that there was a growing number of dead to be interred in the town's churchyards and burial grounds. By the early nineteenth century there were still only three parish churchyards in Sheffield – the Cathedral, St Paul's and St James's – and a number of small Nonconformist burial grounds that provided for limited numbers of interments outwith the control of the Church of England. This provision was soon struggling to cope. Burial facilities were expanded by way of several new churchyards established between 1825 and 1840: St

[1] Jim Morgan, 'The Burial Question in Leeds in the Eighteenth and Nineteenth Centuries', in *Death, Ritual, and Bereavement*, ed. by Ralph Houlbrooke (London: Routledge, 1989), pp. 95–104.

George's, St Philip's, St Mary's, and St John's. This additional provision soon proved inadequate for the ever-expanding population, however.

A group of Nonconformists formed the first private cemetery company in Manchester in 1820.[2] They established Rusholme Road Cemetery as the best means of ensuring adequate burial provision outwith the control of the established church. Further cemeteries were established through private enterprise during the 1820s, '30s and '40s, including the Sheffield General Cemetery opened in 1836. Nationally, pressure was growing for burial to be reformed. These private cemeteries set a precedent for a new burial landscape.

A series of burial acts were introduced during the 1850s to deal with the problem of providing adequate burial. The Burial Act of 1853 empowered parishes to establish local burial board cemeteries and during the second half of the nineteenth century the municipal cemetery became the main place of burial in many urban centres. The cemeteries offered a range of burial options, from interment in an unpurchased plot to the purchase of a grave in perpetuity. The sale of graves with perpetual rights created a fundamental change: the cemetery would be forced to continually expand in order to provide new graves. A further burial act introduced in 1857 also required that once buried, human remains could no longer be disturbed unless a special licence was obtained from government. Previously, grave re-use had enabled the churchyards to serve communities for unlimited generations. Re-use only became a problem with the rapid expansion of the population in the early 1800s, when burial provision did not grow correspondingly. The new cemeteries provided far larger landscapes and grave re-use should have been possible with acceptable time intervals. From the beginning there was no clear strategy about how cemeteries would be financed after they had run out of burial space. The system of burial in perpetuity results ultimately in the cemetery becoming a wasting resource, despite the often considerable investment that went into its establishment and infrastructure.

THE ESTABLISHMENT OF BURNGREAVE AND CROOKES

Burngreave and Crookes cemeteries represent different eras of establishment and reflect different trends in design and layout, but both are typical of their period. Burngreave, which opened to burial in 1861, was the first large-scale burial board cemetery to be established in Sheffield following the passing of the 1853 Burial Act. The cemetery's design was carefully considered and the site became an important local landmark and one of the largest cemeteries in the city. Crookes Cemetery opened to burial in 1909 and was the first City Council-established site.

[2] J. Rugg, 'A New Burial Form and its Meanings: Cemetery Establishment in the First Half of the Nineteenth Century', in *Grave Concerns: Death and Burial in England 1700–1850*, ed. by Margaret Cox (York: Council for British Archaeology, CBA Research Report 113, 1998), pp. 44–53 (p. 46).

BURNGREAVE CEMETERY

The ratepayers of Brightside Bierlow first raised the need for a parish cemetery in 1855.[3] The majority of the large-scale steelworks built in Sheffield in the 1850s and '60s were located in the parish and the population had increased dramatically. A three-quarter-acre churchyard had been opened at Christ Church in 1850 but this provision proved inadequate with the rapid population explosion in the parish. This local pressure resulted in the formation of a committee to consider local needs, but it did not immediately result in the formation of a burial board.[4] It was not until April 1858 that the Vestry finally elected a burial board and it would be another three years before the parish cemetery finally opened to burials.[5] Burngreave Cemetery opened in 1861 and was Sheffield's first large-scale, designed burial board cemetery. It covered approximately 27 acres, had space for over 70,000 interments, and proved immediately popular as a place for interment.

The cemetery was established on land belonging in part to the Duke of Norfolk and in part to Earl Fitzwilliam. The area as portrayed by the first edition OS map (1854–55) is a semi-rural landscape. The site consisted of part of Burn Greave Wood, and several adjacent fields, with scattered areas of small-scale quarrying, mining and gravel pits. Authorisation was given for work to begin on the buildings and on the laying out of the cemetery landscape in March 1859. It was to include two chapels, a superintendent's house, boardroom, office and a house for the grave digger, as well as roads, planting, draining and fencing of the land, and an approach road from Burn Greave Road.[6] In total £8050 was earmarked for the cemetery. The Mayor of Sheffield convened the meeting to discuss the laying out of the cemetery, suggesting that the new cemetery was of significance to the whole city and not just the parish.[7]

At the time of purchase, it is clear that the Burial Board already had definite ideas about the cemetery's layout. Indeed, the plan relating to the sale of the land indicates a faint access road between Burn Greave Road and the land for the new cemetery.[8] The same route is later used to provide an access road into the new cemetery off Burn Greave Road. The deed plan indicates a second potential access route from the southeast, but this is not adopted. The plan also identifies two pieces of land within the area earmarked for the cemetery that are 'to be left solid': one located at the proposed entrance, the other situated just beyond. The first of these areas later becomes the entrance to the cemetery, complete with two lodge houses, and the second becomes the location of the cemetery chapels. A local firm of architects was appointed to design the cemetery chapels: William Flockton & Son.[9] Flockton already had a strong reputation in Sheffield for his

[3] Sheffield Archives (hereafter SA), Brightside Bierlow Vestry Minutes (hereafter BBVM), 1801–1857, CA 16 (6), 26 May 1855.
[4] BBVM, CA 16 (6), 11 June 1855.
[5] BBVM, 1858–1899, CA 16 (1), 8 April 1858.
[6] Ibid., 19 March 1859.
[7] Ibid., 8 April 1859.
[8] SA, Land Sale Deed Plan, Deed Conveying Land to Brightside Burial Board 1859, ACD SD 693.
[9] BBVM, CA 16 (1), 25 June 1862.

ecclesiastical and cemetery architecture, including the design of the parish church itself in 1850, and the Anglican chapel for the General Cemetery extension in 1848.[10]

The final layout for the new cemetery used the site's topography to best advantage (Figure 1). The main avenue runs through the lowest part of the site, the ground rising up on either side, creating the atmosphere of a small valley. There is a slight incline to the avenue, which gradually rises up towards the horizon. The atmosphere is peaceful and uplifting. Beyond the chapels, the cemetery is more formal and rectilinear, working with the existing topography and ensuring economical layout for burial. The planting also added to the grandeur and tranquillity of the cemetery. Avenue planting was used extensively, to control and frame views within the site and also to create more formality. Some of the original avenue trees remain today and can be appreciated at their most dramatic (Figure 2). This formal design was typical of burial board cemeteries established around this time, but in Sheffield, Burngreave was the first cemetery to adopt this grand and formal layout.[11]

Several features within the final design seem to relate to its pre-cemetery layout. The main avenue appears to follow the route of several of the earlier field boundaries that ran through the centre of the land. A number of walks lead off from this main avenue to the right and left, providing access to the different burial sections. One uses an existing lane which passed between Pitsmoor Abbey and Pitsmoor Colliery. Two thirds of the cemetery was consecrated for use by members of the Church of England and one third was left unconsecrated.[12]

One of the most successful aspects of the cemetery is the chapels, particularly their setting just beyond the cemetery entrance (Figure 3). At a slightly elevated position, they provide a dramatic focal point on the uphill approach from Burngreave Road. From the entrance, a curved carriageway leads further uphill towards the chapels. The design is not untypical of the period: the chapels appear as a single symmetrical building, the Anglican chapel on the left, with the Nonconformist on the right, linked by a covered carriage entrance with a tall and imposing spire. For the cortege, this prospect created an atmosphere of solemnity and grandeur. The rest of the cemetery is only revealed on arrival at the covered carriageway, which frames a view up the cemetery's main axial avenue. By contrast, on leaving the cemetery, mourners are met with a city panorama, denoting their return to the land of the living.

The cemetery was an important local development. There were no other publicly accessible parks in the area at the time and the site had received careful consideration in its design, architecture and planting. The atmosphere within the cemetery would have been in complete contrast to the thick pollution that characterised the rapidly expanding industrial corridor to the south.

[10] SA, Sheffield General Cemetery Company Minutes 1846–1913, CA 697/1/3, 1 March 1847; 14 April 1847.

[11] C. Brooks et al., *Mortal Remains: The History and Present State of the Victorian and Edwardian Cemetery* (Exeter: Wheaton/Victorian Society, 1989), p. 58.

[12] J. Hunter, *Hallamshire: The History and Topography of the Parish of Sheffield in the County of York* (Sheffield: Pawson and Brailsford, 1869), p. 304.

Figure 1 Extract of the 1892–93 OS plan showing the formal layout of Burngreave Cemetery. The cemetery was heavily planted with avenue trees and also some specimens. © *Crown Copyright/database right 2009. An Ordnance Survey/ EDINA supplied service*

Figure 2 (above)
Top path on the consecrated side of Burngreave Cemetery.
Photo: the author

Figure 3 (right)
Burngreave chapels from the cemetery entrance.
Courtesy Sheffield Local Studies Library

The establishment of, and financial investment in Crookes Cemetery was, like Burngreave, an important development for the local area and the whole city. Crookes was the first cemetery to be established by the Sheffield Corporation, now the City Council. The need for a new cemetery for Crookes and Walkley was first raised with the Sheffield Corporation in 1900.[13] The area's population had risen dramatically during the second half of the nineteenth century as urban development had spread out from the city centre. By 1900 local burial provision was limited. By 1904, Upper Hallam was also running short of burial space and approached the Corporation with a similar request.[14] A few months later, an area of land in Crookes was offered to the Corporation, for the purpose of creating a public cemetery.[15] The site consisted of 30 acres of agricultural land, with commanding views out over the Peak District. It was noted by the Burial Grounds Subcommittee that the local population was increasing rapidly, that local provision was becoming scarce, and that little suitable land was available.[16] The Corporation purchased the land in May 1905.[17]

Much of the land was initially set out as allotment gardens. The Corporation's intention was to establish this land as additional burial space when required.[18] The City Surveyor prepared a scheme for the layout of internal roads and pathways, which was approved by the Burials Subcommittee in October 1905.[19] During the winter of 1905–06, unemployed workers undertook the construction of the main carriageway, which extended from the proposed entrance at Lydgate Lane to a secondary entrance at Mulehouse Road.[20] A wall was also constructed along the north-eastern boundary of the land, which was a condition of the sale of the land.[21] Only later were local architects, C. & C. Hadfield, commissioned to design the cemetery buildings. By this stage, the Subcommittee had clear ideas about its requirements.[22] The Headland Road approach was to form the main entrance, with a house and office for the cemetery superintendent. A further lodge was to be located at Mulehouse Road. The cemetery size justified two chapels, the second to be erected when interment numbers made it necessary. A waiting room and shelter and dwarf boundary wall topped with iron railings were also to be provided. The architect's original design was more ambitious, including two chapels, a gatehouse and offices complete with a tower, at Headland Road.[23] Following a review by the City Council, it was decided the plans should be simplified and that there should be

[13] Sheffield Local Studies Library (hereafter Sheffield LSL), Minutes of the City of Sheffield: General Purposes and Parks Committee, Burial Grounds Sub-Committee Minutes, 1900–1919 (hereafter City of Sheffield 1900–1919), SQ 352.042, 11 October 1900.

[14] Ibid., 4 March 1904.

[15] Ibid., 6 June 1904.

[16] Ibid., 8 July 1904.

[17] Ibid., 5 May 1905.

[18] Ibid., 10 April 1906; 1 May 1906; 7 August 1908.

[19] Ibid., 2, 13 October 1905.

[20] Ibid., 7 November 1905.

[21] Ibid. 5 October 1906.

[22] Ibid., 18 December 1906.

[23] 'Crookes Cemetery', *The Builder*, 8 October 1910, p. 396.

only one chapel.[24] Construction work began in September 1908 with the Lord Mayor laying the foundation stone.[25]

The final scheme incorporated one chapel, with mortuary aisle and an office to the rear, an entrance lodge at Mulehouse Road and conveniences at the main entrance.[26] The sweeping carriageway linked the principal and secondary entrances, with the chapel located off to the west (Figure 4). A low stone wall with iron railings defined the southern edge of the cemetery. A main avenue on axis with the chapel and a secondary rectilinear network of paths divided the land into different burial sections. The main avenue also divided the unconsecrated area to the south,[27] from the area to the north, which was consecrated by the Lord Bishop of Sheffield on 29 July 1909.[28] The cemetery was declared officially open to the public and open to orders for interment on 6 November 1909.[29] It was considered a great success for its picturesque setting and impressive architecture and featured in *The Builder* magazine in 1910.[30]

Soon after opening the Council erected a greenhouse and cold frames[31] and employed a gardener to ensure that the cemetery was well-planted and high horticultural standards maintained.[32] Only limited tree planting appears to have been undertaken at Crookes, in contrast to Burngreave. Trees planted in pairs flank either side of the main avenue, framing the view leading down towards the chapel. Similar planting can be found on some of the subsidiary walks and there appears to have been some tree planting in the area around the chapel. This limited planting was probably deliberate, ensuring that the far-reaching views across the surrounding landscape and Peak District would remain open in years to come.

Like Burngreave, Crookes Cemetery provided an important and necessary local amenity, but its design was enhanced visually by its architecture, location, and horticultural treatment. By the time that Crookes was established, the contemporary image of the ideal cemetery had changed and both cemeteries were influenced by these new trends.[33] Throughout the last decades of the nineteenth century the use of coloured flowerbeds became increasingly fashionable and cemetery layouts also became less formal. Crookes Cemetery appears to have followed some of these new ideas with its sweeping carriageway and extensive use of annual bedding. At Burngreave the Burial Board had also introduced formal bedding schemes throughout the cemetery in the mid-1880s.[34] The commitment to high standards above ground was evident at both cemeteries. Yet, it is the cemeteries' use for burial that ultimately determines their development and the levels of maintenance achieved.

[24] City of Sheffield 1900–1919, 6 September 1907.
[25] Ibid., 4 September 1908.
[26] Ibid., 6 December 1907.
[27] Ibid., 12 February 1909.
[28] Ibid., 6 August 1909.
[29] Ibid., 6 November 1909.
[30] 'Crookes Cemetery', *The Builder*, 8 October 1910, p. 396.
[31] City of Sheffield 1900–1919, 4 August 1910.
[32] Ibid., 4 June 1909.
[33] Brooks et al., pp. 58–60.
[34] BBVM, CA 16 (1), Report Year Ending 25 March 1884.

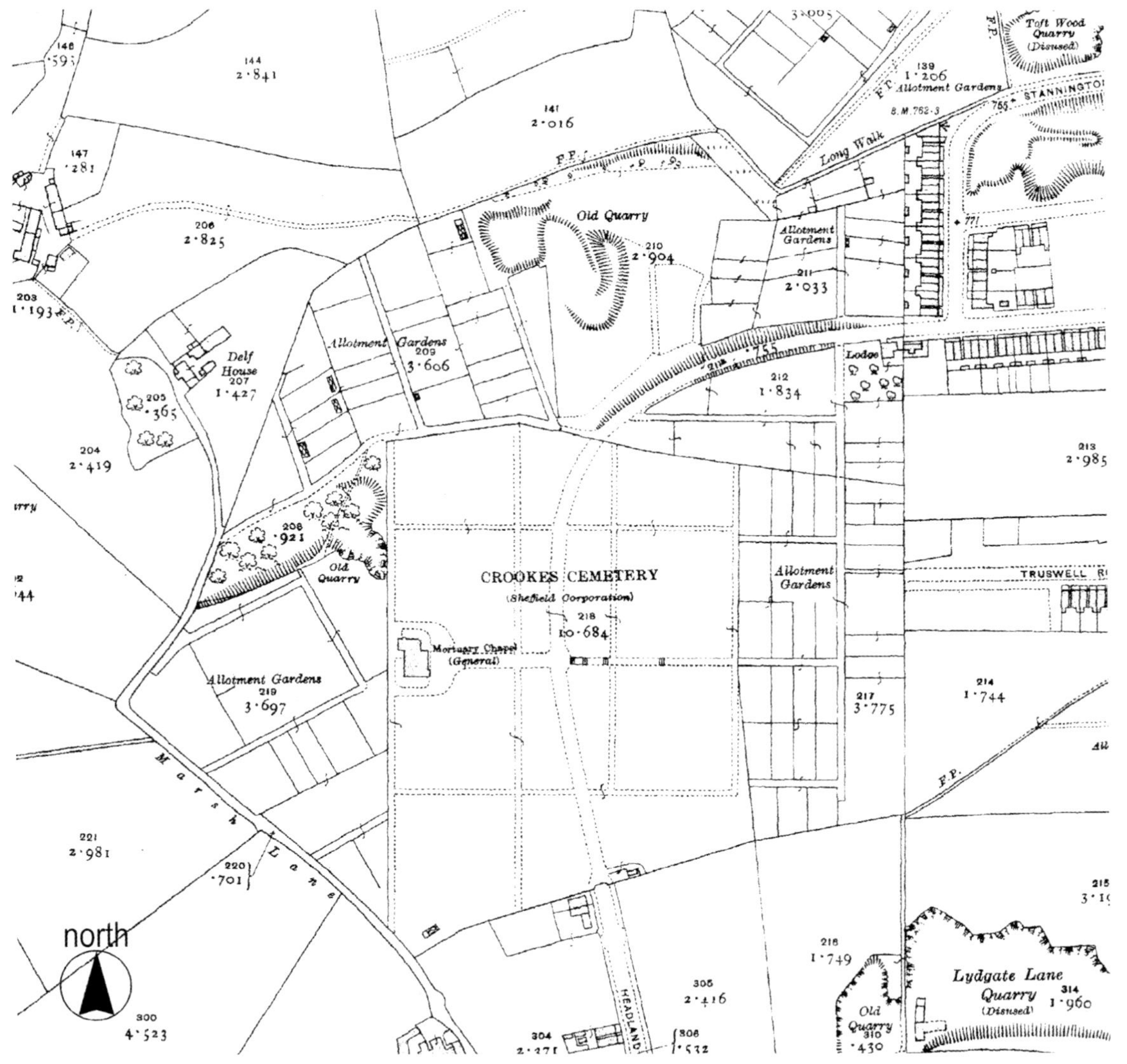

Figure 4 Extract of the 1923 OS plan showing the layout of the land purchased for Crookes Cemetery. The areas to the north, east and west were let out as allotment land, the intention being to incorporate them as further burial land was required. *© Crown Copyright/database right 2009. An Ordnance Survey/ EDINA supplied service*

USE FOR BURIAL

Like their predecessors the parish churchyards, both cemeteries were located near to the community they served, providing important local amenity and ensuring local attachment. The new cemeteries were civic rather than ecclesiastical, however. They were also far larger in scale and more impressively landscaped. Both cemeteries had a wide range

Figure 5 Plan of Burngreave Cemetery indicating the year of the first interment in each grave within the original part of the cemetery from the year of the first burial in 1860. *Base OS plan: © Crown Copyright/database right 2009. An Ordnance Survey/ EDINA supplied service. Aerial photograph: Cities Revealed ® copyright by the GeoInformation ® Group, 2002 and Crown Copyright © All rights reserved*

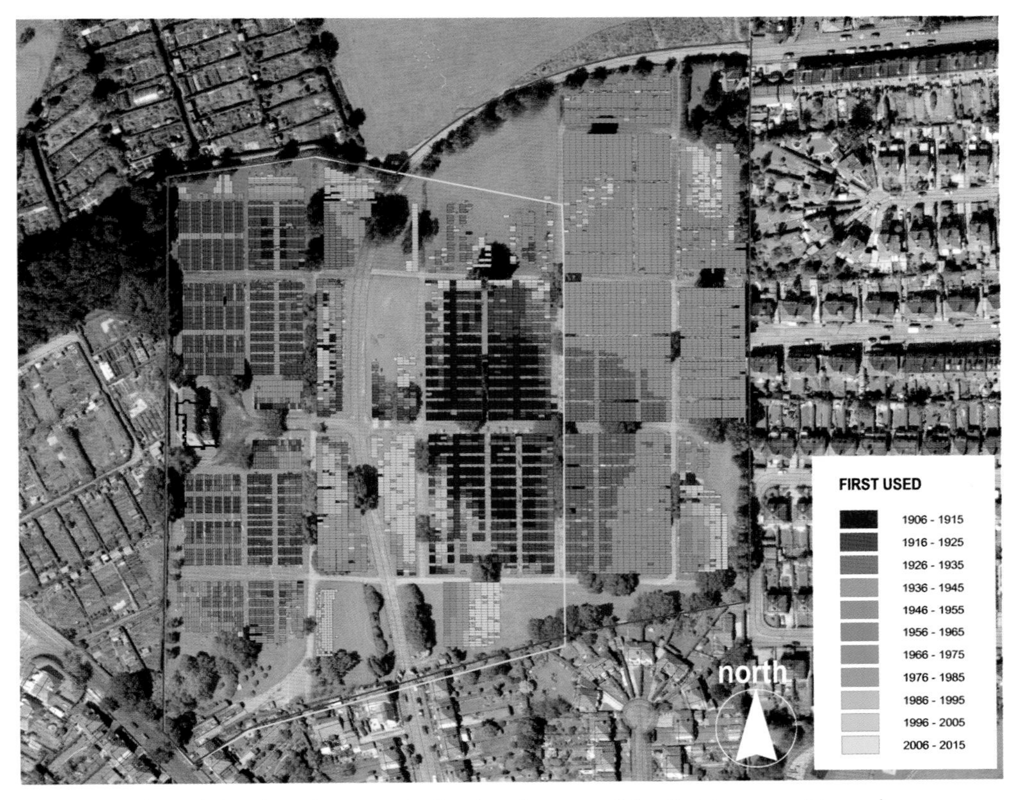

Figure 6 Plan of Crookes Cemetery indicating the year of the first interment in each grave from the date of the first burial in 1906: that of Councillor John Maxfield who was buried before the cemetry officially opened. The sections to the north of the main avenue on axis with the chapels are consecrated; those to the south remain unconsecrated. *Base OS plan: © Crown Copyright/database right 2009. An Ordnance Survey/ EDINA supplied service. Aerial photograph: Cities Revealed ® copyright by the GeoInformation ® Group, 2002 and Crown Copyright © All rights reserved*

of burial options and different pricing structures, which influenced grave selection, burial practice, and development of the landscape.

At Burngreave the 1861 pricing structure shows the different options available, depending on whether the deceased was a parishioner or not[35] and whether the grave was purchased as a private plot, or remained unpurchased.[36] With burial in an ordinary or common grave, a fee was paid for the interment only – the exclusive rights of burial were retained by the Burial Board. For an additional fee, the situation of the grave could be selected. The price of a private family plot depended on whether the grave was earthen, brick or vault. The most expensive option was purchase of a double vault. Subsequent

[35] BBVM, CA 16 (1), 3 March 1873. Initially non-parishioners paid one third more, but in 1873 this was increased to two thirds more.
[36] Ibid., 11 March 1861.

interments in the grave cost less. At Burngreave all graves appear to have been available for burial from initial opening of the cemetery. The cemetery core was used initially for interments and as space filled, later burial was pushed towards the perimeter (Figure 5). Areas of steep ground in the unconsecrated part of the cemetery were avoided, at least initially, in favour of flatter areas, even though these were located further towards the perimeter. The graves fronting the main avenue, at the junctions of the cemetery walks and near to the chapel, were the first to be used for burial, probably due to their prominent location. Vistas were also important, either towards the grave, where the memorial became a focal point, or from the grave, where the grave site allowed good views towards the chapel or across the city.

Unusually, a prominent consecrated area fronting the east side of the main avenue remained unpopular amongst those purchasing private graves. This area is one of very few consecrated sections on this side of the main avenue. The graves are orientated along the traditional east–west axis. This meant that the headstones back on to the main avenue, with the inscriptions facing the cemetery walk to the east – a less impressive prospect. Consequently, much of this area was used to accommodate common graves.

At Crookes, pricing arrangements were more complex and hierarchical than at Burngreave. Graves could be purchased with exclusive rights of burial in perpetuity, or with exclusive rights lasting for a set period – 14 years – within which time the grave could be purchased in perpetuity upon payment of a further fee.[37] Prices also varied between burial sections and rows within sections. So, the first row was always more expensive than the second, which was always more expensive than the third. Grave selection was heavily influenced by pricing, with people making choices based on price, location and prospect. Two particular sections situated within the core of the cemetery were most popular for early burials – a reflection of their good value (Figure 6). They offer views down towards the chapel and across the cemetery. Sections located towards the boundary were more affordable but their location was less ideal. Graves fronting onto the main avenue leading up to the chapel and in the sections on the main carriageway were the most prestigious and were also used for early burials, particularly for private family vaults.

COMMON GRAVES

Common burials took place at both cemeteries: a fee was paid for burial only and the right of burial was retained by the burial authority. Unlike a private family grave, burials in common graves were typically of unrelated individuals. Where a family could not afford the burial fee, the cost was met by the local authority. At Burngreave many of the early burials took place in common or ordinary graves, as they were later referred to.[38] Fir Vale Workhouse was located nearby and the poor from this institution probably

[37] City of Sheffield, *Crookes Cemetery: Rules and Regulations, Tables of Burial Fees and Ministers' Fees; Particulars of Extra and Optional Fees, and Plan of the Cemetery* (Sheffield: Independent Press, 1910), Sheffield LSL, Local Bye Laws, vol. 4, no. 7, 352.042S.

[38] BBVM, CA 16 (1), 5 January 1874.

contributed to the number of such interments. Unusually, these common graves were located in prestigious positions, along the edges of the main avenue and the cemetery walks, within specific sections of either one or two rows of graves. No headstones were permitted on common graves and so the impression on the ground was of wide grass verges. These areas also provided space for the planting of the avenue trees (Figure 2). Other common graves, located on either side of the main avenue near the chapels, were also planting areas. The location of common graves ensured that the site was used economically for burial below ground, but above ground they gave the impression of space and so the cemetery remained uncluttered.

At Burngreave careful management of early common or ordinary graves provided access rows to adjacent private graves, allowing ease of excavation and a route for the funeral cortege. At Crookes, a similar policy was adopted, with every fourth row apparently laid out as a common row. Most of the common graves at Burngreave have been used for burial, but at Crookes many remain unused – a reflection perhaps of the increasing affordability of a private family grave during the twentieth century.

At Burngreave, the sale of grave space was also heavily influenced by factors outside the Burial Board's control. The Burial Board minutes from 1877 report that income was being badly affected by a trade recession,[39] which continued for a number of years. During this time, fewer private graves were being purchased and more burials were taking place in the lower classes of grave: common or ordinary, or in selected ordinary.[40] The common row plots already set out would have had sufficient space remaining to accommodate the increased number of common or ordinary interments. The Burial Board highlighted the economic downturn, drawing attention to the problem of rate collection in the parish.[41] The loss of revenue was of obvious concern, affecting both the Burial Board's ability to pay back loans, but also maintenance costs.

In 1881, the Burial Board introduced a further option of deferred purchase on 'selected ordinary graves' on payment of an extra fee of 2s. 6d within a three-year period of the first interment.[42] In addition, selected ordinary graves which had reverted to the Burial Board, having not been purchased within the three-year period, could be used for common or ordinary interment at a reduced rate, thus offering a further option for the poor to secure a private grave at a reduced cost.

THE CEMETERIES EXTENDED

By 1892 the Burial Board was pursuing a scheme to extend Burngreave Cemetery by approximately ten acres to the north east.[43] By this time approximately 17,000 of the original 27,371 graves had already been appropriated for burial. The surrounding area was also becoming increasingly urban. The Board was keen to expand while there was still land available. In 1893, the Board received formal approval to purchase nine acres

[39] Ibid., 9 April 1877.
[40] Ibid., 9 April 1877; 25 March 1878; 7 April 1879.
[41] Ibid., 25 March 1878.
[42] Ibid., 17 April 1881.
[43] Ibid., Report Year Ending 25 March 1892.

and three roods of land from the Duke of Norfolk, using funds borrowed against the poor rates of the township.[44] The following year, conditions of sale were settled[45] and in June the land was purchased at a cost of £4290.[46] Work started on the extension in 1899, with the contract for building the boundary wall, lodge, and draining and laying out the ground being awarded to a local firm.[47]

Members of the Burial Board seem to have determined the layout of the new extension rather than a professional architect or designer. Their initial ideas were quite innovative, including a proposal for a crematorium,[48] though this was not executed in the final more restrained scheme. The central avenue was continued through the extension up to a new entrance.[49] A circular drive marked the connection between the existing part of the cemetery and the new, with a shelter located in the centre surrounded by lawn and flowerbeds (see Figure 7). The Board thought that the shelter would look attractive and provide an important amenity.

Closer inspection of the 1923 OS plan shows that the circular drive and shelter served another purpose. It had not been possible to align perfectly the extended part of the main axial avenue with the existing avenue. The shelter and circular drive overcame this problem, but also provided a focal feature from the new entrance off Scott Road and from the chapels. To accommodate the new drive, modifications were necessary to the existing burial plan, with a number of graves being removed. Three used graves were incorporated into the central lawn area.

The extension also enabled a supply of running water to be connected. A water supply had been provided previously via a pond, but this had not been acceptable to HM Inspector of Burial Grounds.[50] The pond was drained and filled and a town supply was laid through the cemetery extension.

The extension provided important additional burial space, but the creation of the second entrance also changed the way that the cemetery was used by the local community. The cemetery developed as an important thoroughfare. As the surrounding area increasingly built up, the cemetery's role in providing urban green space became more significant.

The Burial Board was not able to oversee the completion of the extension. In 1900, Sheffield City Council was established and it took over the control and management of the burial board cemeteries in the city, including Burngreave. The cemeteries came under the newly formed Burials Subcommittee, which was part of the General Purposes and Parks Committee. By early 1901 it was reported that new ornamental flower beds had been created in the extension and that these had been filled with trees and plants propagated in the cemetery.[51] By September work had begun to level the ground and

[44] Ibid., 24 January 1893.
[45] Ibid., Report Year Ending 25 March 1894.
[46] Ibid., Report Year Ending 25 March 1895.
[47] BBVM, 1898–1912, CA 16 (2), Report Year Ending 25 March 1899.
[48] BBVM, CA 16 (1), 12 April 1897.
[49] BBVM, CA 16 (2), Report Year Ending 25 March 1900.
[50] Ibid.
[51] City of Sheffield 1900–1919, 8 January 1901.

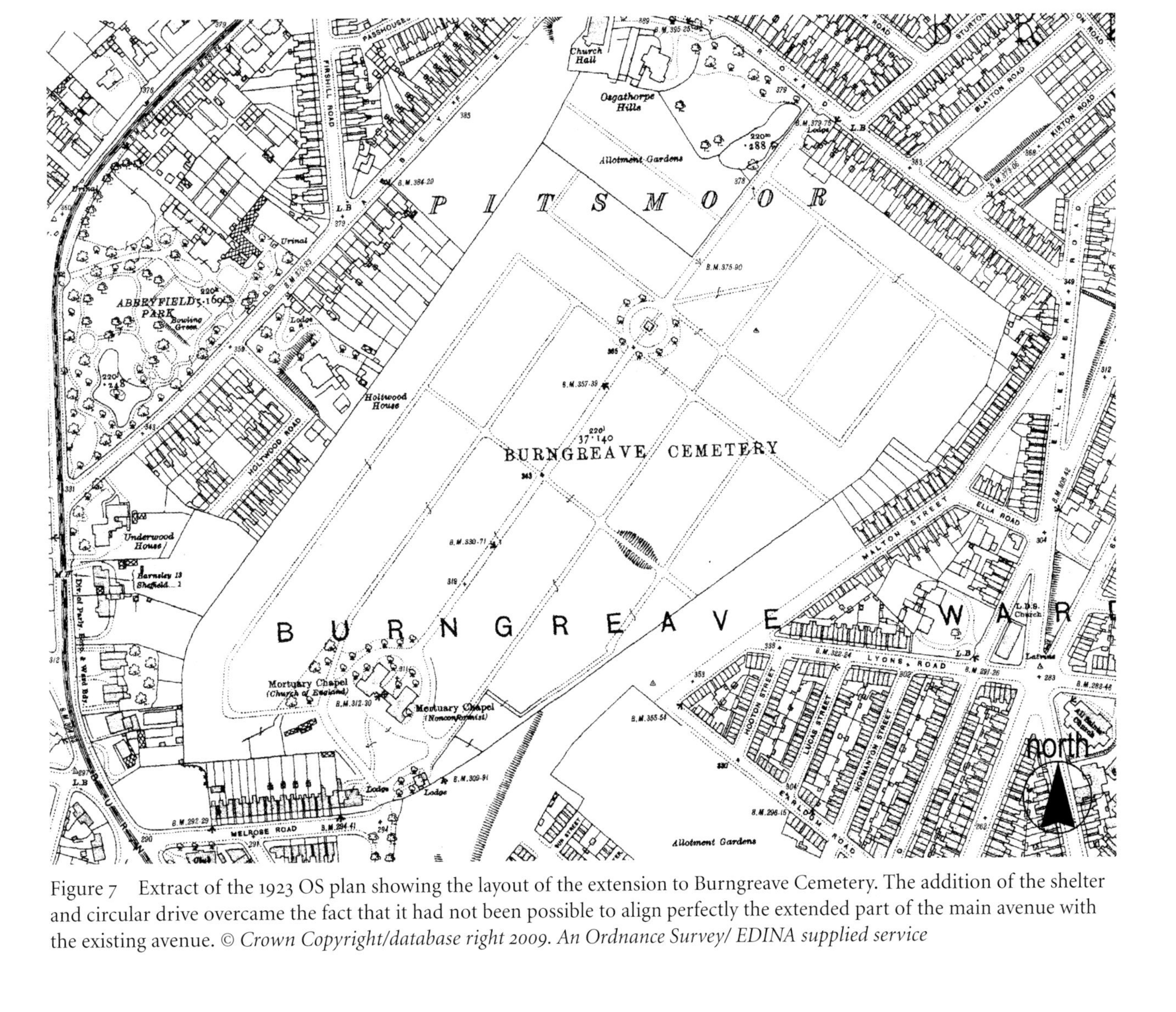

Figure 7 Extract of the 1923 OS plan showing the layout of the extension to Burngreave Cemetery. The addition of the shelter and circular drive overcame the fact that it had not been possible to align perfectly the extended part of the main avenue with the existing avenue. © *Crown Copyright/database right 2009. An Ordnance Survey/ EDINA supplied service*

50 young oak trees were sent from Tinsley Park Cemetery to Burngreave.[52] By early 1902 the shrub and tree planting had been completed and the ground had been levelled ready for use.[53]

The transfer of administration to the City Council meant that a new pricing structure was adopted in the Burngreave extension. The structure was similar to that implemented at the newly opened Crookes Cemetery and was more hierarchical than that applied by the Burial Board. The graves in the cemetery extension were not available for burial until 1912,[54] by which time few new graves remained in the original cemetery.

Despite the substantial number of new graves provided by the extension, it seems that there were immediate attempts to maximise the available land at Burngreave, suggesting a growing awareness that virgin space would eventually run out. The area around the new shelter was not intended for burials, but by 1911 a fourth grave had been used in this area, with further graves being used in subsequent years. Graves were also accommodated on a strip of land that ran along the edge of the original cemetery.[55]

Unlike Burngreave, plans for a cemetery extension at Crookes had existed from the outset and were to be implemented as additional burial space was required. The decision to rent out much of the land initially as allotments was both pragmatic and financially sensible: it generated an income and reduced the maintenance burden. By 1919, the Burials Subcommittee had decided that an extension was required into the area of allotments to the east of the original cemetery.[56] The first burials were taking place within the new extension by the closing months of 1930 (Figure 6).

At Crookes, the City Council appears to have adopted a different management policy to that at Burngreave. The Burngreave extension, completed in 1902, was not opened until 1912: the policy had been to use all available burial space within the original cemetery before interments were permitted in the extension. At Crookes however, all of the original sections had unused grave spaces. The sections fronting the main carriage-way had remained unpopular, in part due to the relatively high price of the graves. The sections made available in the new extension ensured the continued supply of more affordable graves. The pattern of grave use in the Crookes extension, unsurprisingly, follows the development of the paths. Again, a clear preference is shown for graves in more prominent situations, with the first burials located close to the avenue on axis with the chapel. The pattern of grave use also appears to be more controlled and regulated than previously.

[52] Ibid., 27 September 1901.

[53] Ibid., 8 April 1902.

[54] City of Sheffield, *Burngreave Cemetery Added Portion: Tables of Burial Fees and Ministers' Fees and Particulars of Extra and Optional Fees, and Plan* (Sheffield: Independent Press, 1912), Sheffield LSL, Local Bye Laws, vol. 4, no. 10, 352.042S.

[55] Sheffield LSL, Minutes of the City of Sheffield: Parks, Cemeteries and Allotments Department, Burial Grounds Sub-Committee Minutes, 1919–1968 (hereafter City of Sheffield 1919–1968), SQ 352.042, 18 March 1924.

[56] City of Sheffield 1919–1968, 28 May 1919. The burial rate at Crookes and Burngreave Cemeteries shows an increase for both World Wars; for 1914–18, this might in part be accounted for by the 1918 flu epidemic, and Sheffield having two war hospitals.

MAINTAINING THE CEMETERY

The cemeteries required significant labour to maintain them. Both were already far larger than any parish churchyard. The extent of memorialisation meant that the grass had to be cut by scythe, the planting had to be tended and the infrastructure maintained. Where graves had sunk, they required topping up. The primary commitment to bury the dead also had to be met. This involved grave digging and backfilling by hand after the interment. As more graves were memorialised the cemetery became increasingly cluttered.

Private graves were often fully kerbed with headstone and footstone. At Burngreave and Crookes, where a full-size memorial could not be afforded, a footstone could be used as a headstone. Even where there were no kerbstones or memorial, it was common to create a permanent earth mound to indicate use.[57] All of this ruled out the use of a mower. A further level of complexity resulted from the custom of planting within the kerbs or on the earth mound and in common with today's conventions, decorating with mementoes. Some of this memorialisation might have extended to common graves, though the cemetery authorities are unlikely to have approved of the practice, given that no memorialisation was permitted on these graves.

At Burngreave, the Burial Board's minutes indicate the commitment to achieve high standards of maintenance, but also acknowledge the difficulties. As early as the 1880s, Brightside Bierlow's Vestry was raising concerns about the condition of the cemetery. In 1881 the Burial Board declared its intention to improve the appearance of the cemetery grounds.[58] Sheffield Burial Board's cemetery at City Road had recently opened and perhaps the improvement work at Burngreave allowed Brightside Bierlow to compete for business. By 1884 many of these works appear to have been completed. Greater attention was paid to the formation of the ordinary graves, the rough ground was levelled and additional trees and ornamental shrubs were planted.[59] A greenhouse was also purchased and erected within the cemetery at this time to propagate flowers and shrubs for use in the cemetery grounds, the cost of which the Burial Board believed could be recouped. The commitment to maintain high standards of maintenance at Burngreave remained after the cemetery's administration was transferred to the City Council in 1900, with one of the Subcommittee's first tasks being an inspection of each cemetery.[60]

The Council minutes indicate a commitment to achieving high standards of horticulture in all its cemeteries. All the city's cemeteries employed trained gardeners and all the large cemeteries – City Road, Tinsley Park, Burngreave and Crookes – had their own greenhouses and propagating frames.[61] As was typical in many cemeteries, grave owners could pay an annual fee for various extra services, including maintenance, planting with a mixture of herbaceous plants and annuals, and plant maintenance and watering.[62]

[57] J. Rugg, 'Lawn Cemeteries: The Emergence of a New Landscape of Death', *Urban History*, 33.2 (2006), 213–233.

[58] BBVM, CA 16 (1), 17 April 1881.

[59] Ibid., Report Year Ending 25 March 1884.

[60] City of Sheffield 1900–1919, 25 March 1900.

[61] City of Sheffield 1900–1919. Reference to the purchase of a greenhouse for City Road 16 March 1906 and the purchase of a new boiler for an existing greenhouse at Tinsley Park 16 February 1920.

[62] City of Sheffield, 1910.

There was also a horticultural policy for fresh graves, which were turfed, planted with shrubs or other suitable vegetation, or prepared and sown with seeds, unless a monument or tombstone was to be erected.[63]

The Subcommittee was realistic in its approach to maintenance, which allowed resources to be concentrated on achieving high standards in the cemetery core. Unlike today, some areas of grass were allowed to grow and sold as hay: local farmers cut and collected it under the supervision of the superintendent.[64] This was an accepted practice which not only saved on maintenance costs, but also generated a small income. At Crookes a small income was also generated from ganister which was sometimes excavated when opening a grave.[65] Ganister, a type of stone, was in demand locally to create bricks to line the steel manufacturers' furnaces. Selling the ganister made it easier to backfill the grave and to reopen it for subsequent burials.

The Council also had firm rules in place to direct visitor behaviour and to influence opinion about the cemeteries: clearly defined opening times; the non-admittance of children under ten years unless under the care of a responsible person; no touching of flowers or shrubs; no venturing off thoroughfares; no smoking, and no dogs.[66] The lodge houses at Burngreave and Crookes and the cemetery offices provided an important point of contact for the local community seeking advice and wishing to purchase grave space, and the dedicated cemetery staff ensured site security and management. As today, misdemeanours were not uncommon, but staff would have scrutinised visitors' conduct and inappropriate behaviour would have been dealt with seriously. For instance, in 1904, a woman was caught and charged with stealing flowers from graves in Burngreave and ordered to pay eight shillings.[67]

The City Council therefore combined strict regulations and a pragmatic approach to the management and resourcing of the cemeteries. Its ability to maintain these high standards of service and maintenance was severely tested by the World Wars, however. Of constant concern during the First World War was the loss of staff to the armed forces whilst at the same time meeting the demand for graves. By 1917, the cemeteries superintendent was requesting that staff be exempt from war service stating that any further loss of staff would be viewed with 'alarm'.[68] An exemption was secured on condition that staff remained employed in the cemeteries.

Few photographs exist to track maintenance and horticultural standards in Sheffield's cemeteries, as strict regulations applied to photography: no photographs of funerals were permitted, and photographs of graves had to be authorised by the superintendent and grave owner.[69] A photograph of Burngreave Cemetery, dating to the late 1920s or early

[63] City of Sheffield, 1910; City of Sheffield, 1912.

[64] City of Sheffield 1900–1919. Reference to the sale of grass at Burngreave in January 1902, Crookes in May 1910, and May 1915.

[65] City of Sheffield 1919–1968, 15 April 1924; 8 June 1926.

[66] City of Sheffield, 1910; City of Sheffield, 1912.

[67] City of Sheffield 1900–1919, 18 July 1904.

[68] Ibid., 5 October 1917.

[69] City of Sheffield, *Cemeteries and Crematorium Rules and Regulations: Table of Burial Fees, Crematorium Fees and Ministers' Fees; Particulars of Extra and Optional Fees* (City of Sheffield, 1937), Sheffield LSL, Local Pamphlets, vol. 299, no. 4, 042S.

Figure 8 Burngreave Cemetery *c.* 1930: the cemetery is heavily planted and many of the graves appear to be memorialised. *Courtesy Sheffield Local Studies Library*

1930s, illustrates the extent of memorialisation and planting at the cemetery (Figure 8). Despite the complex nature of the landscape, the cemetery appears well maintained, suggesting that the Council was able to return to high standards of upkeep after the First World War and into the 1930s.

Information relating to the management of the city's cemeteries during the Second World War is also limited, but it is clear that there would have been similar pressures to those experienced in the First World War. The war brought an increased death rate, a shortage of resources and labour, and the threat of bomb damage. In addition there were far more Council cemeteries to be maintained by this time.

SIMPLIFICATION OF THE CEMETERY LANDSCAPE

From the outset the size of the cemeteries meant that maintenance was a significant task. The landscape was not designed for ease of upkeep and increasing use for burial meant ever greater resources were required to maintain them. The full extent of the maintenance challenge was brought into sharp relief by the lack of staff during the World Wars. By the 1940s, it was becoming clear that it would be necessary to simplify the landscape, a process that would continue throughout the twentieth century.

In 1943, work began at Burngreave to level the earth mounds and kerbs which typified many of the graves in the original part.[70] Simplification of the landscape had probably been part of general but unrecorded site management for some time. A letter to a local newspaper in 1947 reveals that problems remained, with descriptions of 'wild disorder' and 'dense undergrowth' in the 'once neat burial ground'.[71] A response, possibly from a cemetery employee, indicates the difficulties of maintaining such a large and busy cemetery and the implications of limited resources.[72] Prior to the war seventeen men had been employed to maintain the 37-acre cemetery, now there were just ten staff. By comparison, in 1900, eleven members of staff had been employed to maintain the original 27 acres.[73]

The large extent of the city's cemeteries and the complicated nature of the cemetery landscape meant that maintenance costs continued to increase and that burial required more and more subsidy. The Council recognised that the current system was not sustainable and by the late 1940s ways of improving cemetery standards were being considered. At the same time there was a growing interest in cremation, which appeared modern and straightforward in contrast to burial and the demands of cemetery maintenance.[74]

By the 1950s the City Council, like many local authorities, was pursuing a new cemetery aesthetic: the lawn cemetery. The Council believed the lawn plots improved the appearance of the cemeteries, whilst also making the maintenance task easier, with regulations and restrictions on the size of headstone and a ban on the use of kerbs.[75] Victorian cemeteries like Burngreave were now seen as outdated and the lawn cemetery was regarded as the model for the future.[76]

At Burngreave, the last burial in a new grave took place in the 1950s and so the lawn aesthetic could not be applied. With no further extension land purchased, the cemetery's role as a place of burial declined markedly. The maintenance of the older section continued to be a problem throughout the 1960s and into the 1970s, prompting further phases of memorial clearance to simplify the landscape and ease upkeep. The landscape deteriorated further in the early 1970s due to the effects of Dutch elm disease, which were particularly devastating with the loss of almost all avenue trees in the Nonconformist part of the original cemetery and some in the cemetery extension.[77] Additional plantings of flowering and ornamental trees in the older parts of the cemetery took place at this time.[78]

[70] Parks, Cemeteries and Allotments Department, Plan of Burngreave Cemetery: Areas Where Mounds and Kerbs Levelled (City of Sheffield, July 1943), Sheffield City Council Bereavement Services.

[71] M. Ellis, 'Letter of Complaint as to the Neglect of Burngreave Cemetery', *Sheffield Star*, 17 September 1947.

[72] C. H. Stevenson, 'Letter: Untidy Cemetery', *Sheffield Star*, 20 September 1947.

[73] City of Sheffield 1900–1919, 26 March 1900.

[74] Rugg, 'Lawn Cemeteries …', p. 217.

[75] City of Sheffield, *Ten Years: A Brief Account of the Work of the Parks, Cemeteries and Burial Grounds Committee from 1952 to 1962* (City of Sheffield, 1962), Sheffield LSL, Local Pamphlets, vol. 20, no. 7, 042S.

[76] '4,000 Cremated Each Year at City Road', *Sheffield Star*, 31 August 1960.

[77] The extent of the original avenue planting is clear on the 1953 National Grid 1:2500 plan of the area.

[78] A. L. Winning, 'Burial and Cremation Services in the City of Sheffield: Past, Present and Future', in *37th Joint Annual Conference of Members and Officers of Burial and Cremation Authorities* (Sheffield: IBCA and FBCA, 1978), pp. 31–36 (p. 35).

Resource constraints meant that maintenance across the city's cemeteries was simplified further. In the 1970s, the practice of carrying out twice-yearly planting of graves was abandoned and one permanent planting of bulbs, roses and heathers was undertaken, reducing the need for annual bedding.[79] This approach allowed the City Council to fulfil its obligation of planting a grave in perpetuity – a purchase option available into the early 1950s, which the Council was finding increasingly burdensome.[80] The annual flowerbeds throughout the cemeteries were also replaced with more permanent planting schemes and drifts of bulbs.

STATUS OF THE CEMETERIES TODAY: THE CEMETERY REALITY

Burngreave has continued to provide for burial, albeit to a very limited extent. There are now approximately five or six burials per annum within existing family graves where space permits. The landscape appears on first sight almost unaltered, but the regular phases of memorial clearance, the impact of Dutch elm disease, and the gradual reduction in resourcing and labour mean that the cemetery has already changed significantly. It is no longer the heavily memorialised and planted landscape of the early twentieth century, portrayed in Figure 8. The avenue trees planted by the Burial Board remain in some parts and can now be appreciated fully. Recent tree planting has been undertaken to reinstate the main avenue and some of the subsidiary walks, as well as some individual planting of specimen trees in several locations throughout the cemetery.

Like Burngreave, the existing planting at Crookes is restricted mainly to trees. The cemetery continues to provide burial space, but it has not been developed to cover the whole area originally purchased. By the 1960s the continued provision of a local cemetery seemed unnecessary as cremation appeared to represent the choice of the future.[81] At Crookes, the allotments to the north and west have not been incorporated and the stone wall constructed on purchase of the land has not become the boundary wall. In 1963, the area of allotments to the north was released by the Allotments Department for tipping purposes, after which it was transferred to the Education Committee for use as school playing fields.[82] The land to the north still provides amenity green space and its use for tipping now makes it unsuitable for burial. There are no plans to incorporate the allotments to the west. Thus Crookes has not developed as originally intended. The chapel would have become the central focal point, but instead it remains set off to the west.

At Crookes, many of the graves on the lawn sections are heavily memorialised and so the expectation that this aesthetic would ease cemetery maintenance has not been fulfilled. There is still a desire to mark out and define the grave, practices permitted for the traditional grave, either through the addition of kerbs or planting. Both types of memorialisation contravene the lawn cemetery regulations, presenting obstacles to grass cutting and making it difficult to reopen adjacent plots for burial.

[79] Ibid.

[80] No longer listed as an option in perpetuity by 1953. City of Sheffield, *Rules for the Management of the Cemeteries and Crematorium* (City of Sheffield, 1953), Sheffield LSL, Local Pamphlets, vol. 225, no. 10, 042S.

[81] Winning, p. 35.

[82] Sheffield LSL, Minutes of the City of Sheffield: Allotments Sub-Committee, SQ 352.042, 10 October 1963, 11 April 1968.

Figure 9 Crookes Cemetery. Maintenance can be particularly problematic within the older sections of the cemetery where the graves have become increasingly neglected with the passing of time. *Photo: the author*

Dilapidated memorials continue to present a problem at both cemeteries. Memorial safety has become an increasing concern for local authorities in recent years, after the national Health and Safety Executive issued a directive, following several instances of injury and even death resulting from unstable memorials. This has resulted in a number of stones being laid flat within the grave space at both cemeteries. These maintenance difficulties are typical of many UK cemeteries (Figure 9).

At Burngreave, the cemetery's avenue trees, monuments and formal grandeur all add to its historic character and make it distinctive from other green spaces in the area. Under the current system of burial however, and despite its Grade II English Heritage registration, the cemetery has become a wasting asset that is no longer able to provide for burial but continues to make heavy demands on resources. The cemetery chapels have also lost their purpose and have deteriorated, despite their Grade II listed status. The availability of new graves at Crookes means that the cemetery can continue to provide for the local community and that the site is still viewed primarily as a place of burial. Eventually space will run out here too and difficult decisions will have to be made regarding the future of Crookes.

The circumstances pertaining to Burngreave and Crookes are typical of the situation across the UK. Demand remains for burial provision, but the establishment of new cemeteries is not straightforward and places a further burden on limited resources. In any case new provision will present the same challenges for long-term sustainability.

Meanwhile, cemetery conservation has become a real issue of concern. Existing cemeteries are significant landscapes of potential cultural, historical, ecological and recreational importance,[83] which have to be maintained and for which a viable future should be found.

GRAVE RE-USE: AN OPPORTUNITY TO RETHINK THE CEMETERY MODEL

In 2001, a House of Commons Environment Transport and Regional Affairs Select Committee published its findings into the lack of burial space and the poor state of many UK cemeteries. One of the conclusions was that there was no alternative to grave re-use.[84] In June 2007, the Government announced its intention to take forward the proposal to re-use graves and a committee was formed to look at a pilot project.[85]

Grave re-use is seen by many as fundamental to the development of sustainable cemeteries. Re-use would involve graves being re-excavated, where the last burial was at least one hundred years ago and where there was no remaining family interest. Any remains would be carefully gathered together and re-interred at a greater depth, allowing the space above to be sold as new grave space.

In mainland Europe, regulated systems of grave re-use have been in place since cemeteries were first established. This approach ensures that existing cemeteries can continue to serve communities for unlimited generations, and problems of neglect are minimised. The practice of grave re-use guarantees the economic viability of a cemetery, by ensuring an income from the sale of established grave space, which can then be invested in the management and maintenance of the site.

It is clear that any UK strategy for the introduction of grave re-use would have to consider the wider role of the cemetery landscape: its historic, cultural and ecological value, and its use by the bereaved and local community. Significantly, the practice of re-use would offer the potential for existing cemetries like Crookes and Burngreave to continue as vibrant resources at the heart of their local community.

[83] English Heritage, *Paradise Preserved: An Introduction to the Assessment, Evaluation, Conservation, and Management of Historic Cemeteries* (2007) <http://www.english-heritage.org.uk/upload/pdf/Paradise-Preserved_20081010174134.pdf> [accessed 5 March 2008], pp. 19–22.

[84] Environment, Transport and Regional Affairs Committee, *Eighth Report on Cemeteries: Volume I* (London: HMSO, 2001), p. lii.

[85] Ministry of Justice, *Burial Law and Policy in the 21st Century: The Way Forward* (London: HMSO, 2007), p. 15.